E
ABC
4 -

Olov Skötkonung   c 1000 - 1022

Anund Jakob   1022 — 1056

        Emund
(last of line descended from Odin

 (Jarl) Stenkil   — 1066
   rivalry of 2 Eriks

  Hallsten (son of Stenkil)
  Anund (from Russia)
— Håkon the Red — ruled for 13 yrs
  Inge (son of Stenkil) - stoned & driven out
  Blot - Sven = ruled for 3 years

THE ENGLISH MISSIONARIES
IN   SWEDEN   AND   FINLAND

THE
ENGLISH MISSIONARIES
IN
SWEDEN AND FINLAND

BY

C. J. A. OPPERMANN, M.A., Ph.D.

Published for the Church Historical Society

LONDON

SOCIETY FOR PROMOTING
CHRISTIAN KNOWLEDGE

NORTHUMBERLAND   AVENUE,   W.C. 2

NEW   YORK: THE   MACMILLAN   COMPANY

1937

*This book is published with the help of
a grant from the University of London
Publication Fund.*

Made in Great Britain

TO
THE MEMORY OF
MY PARENTS

CONTENTS

PREFACE

ONE of the chief characteristics of the Anglo-Saxon Church was its zeal for the evangelization of the heathen, and the conversion to Christianity of Teutonic Europe was very largely due to the labours of its missionaries. But while the names of some of those who played their part in this achievement are still familiar to us in England to-day, other names have become well-nigh forgotten, and their mention awakens no memory of the wonderful work which they accomplished in bringing about the overthrow of heathenism, and the establishment of the Christian Church, in the lands that were the scene of their toils. The personalities of Wilfrid, Boniface and Willibrord still stand out prominently in the annals of missionary enterprise: those of Sigfrid, Eskil, David, Henry of Uppsala and Thomas of Finland, with the possible exception of the first-named, are unknown to the overwhelming majority of English churchmen.

In the following pages an attempt has been made to describe the part taken by English missionaries in the conversion of Sweden and Finland; and in addition to relate the important services rendered by certain of their fellow-countrymen—not missionaries in the strictest sense of the word—in the subsequent organization and development of the Church in those lands. But in attempting this task there is one great difficulty to encounter—the scantiness of reliable sources of information. It is true that there are in existence lives of the more prominent of the missionaries—St. Sigfrid, St. Eskil, St. David and St. Henry—but, like other medieval lives of the saints, they were written for the purpose of edification rather than of giving biographical detail, while they suffer from the further disadvantage of having been compiled long after the events they purport to record, so that there was ample time for the original traditions to acquire numerous legendary accretions. Unsatisfactory as these lives are as primary sources, they are nevertheless indispensable for the purpose of this work, and fortunately in the case of St. Sigfrid and St. Eskil their narratives can be supplemented by reference to other authorities, for the former is referred to several times in the Icelandic Sagas and is also mentioned in the Chronicle of Adam of Bremen, while the latter's martyrdom is related in the life of St. Knud written by the English priest Ailnoth about forty years after the event. In Adam, too, mention is made of Gotebald, Woldred, and certain other Englishmen who worked in Sweden as missionaries, but in some cases the record is so brief that practically nothing is known of them beyond their names.

The result of this paucity of source-material is that in no case is a really satisfactory biographical sketch possible; and although certain episodes in the lives of one and another of the missionaries stand out clearly enough, yet taken as a whole they are but shadowy personages. We do know, however, that Sweden was overwhelmingly heathen when they began their labours there; that a most striking change had been brought about in this state of affairs a hundred years later; and that they had been the chief instruments in effecting this change. Even if little is definitely known of the manner of its accomplishment, from that little much more may be conjectured. In any case it seems worth while recalling the deeds of her sons that made the English Church mainly responsible for the successful establishment of Christianity in Sweden, and helped so largely to build up the Church there into an organized body similar in structure and belief to the other National Churches of Western Christendom.

Before actually describing the work of the English missionaries in Sweden and Finland, I have given a brief account of the lands and of their heathen religious systems, as well as an outline of the missionary enterprise that preceded their appearance in the reign of Olov Skötkonung. A knowledge of the particular difficulties to be overcome in carrying out their task of evangelization, and also of the previous progress that had been made in that task by the labours of Anskar and his successors, is necessary for a

who helped to defeat O. Tryggvason
c AD 1000

complete realization of the true measure of their achievements
in this portion of the European mission-field. Those achievements were such as to make the indebtedness of the Swedish
to the English Church almost, if not equally, as great as that
of the Church of Norway; the chief difference was that the
latter could claim to be the actual daughter of the Church
of England, while in the case of Sweden the German mission,
prior in time to the English, though comparatively insignificant
as regards results, prevents any such claim from being made.

I have given elsewhere a list of the works I have consulted,
but some explanation seems necessary in regard to the use of a
few of them. Unfortunately there is no modern history of
the Church of Sweden, with the exception of that of the
former Bishop of Salisbury (Dr. Wordsworth) which, although
in many ways a remarkable work, contains a number of minor
errors, and gives a very inadequate account of certain persons
and events, a defect which is perhaps due to the fact that it is
an expansion of a series of lectures. Archbishop Reuterdahl's
massive work, " Svenska Kyrkans Historia," can hardly be said
to be completely out of date, as it is based almost entirely on
original sources; but the great progress made in historical and
archæological research since his time not only causes it to need
much supplementing, but also calls for a revision of some of
the judgments expressed in it. Recently an attempt has been
made by Henning Wijkmark to supply this want of a com-
prehensive Church History, incorporating the results of
modern historical research, but so far only Parts 1 and 2 of
Volume I have appeared and the narrative has not yet
reached the period that includes the work of the English
missionaries. A very useful work dealing with these early
times is Westman's " Den svenska kyrkans utveckling från
St. Bernhards tidevarv till Innocentius IIIs," but, as the title
shows, it only covers a period of about seventy years. Schmid's
" Sveriges kristnande," a study of the introduction of Christianity into Sweden and the early development of the Church
there, is very interestingly written, but is at times decidedly
provocative.

I have occasionally referred to the works of Von Dalin,

Lagerbring, and other of the older historians, as although they are now out-of-date for general purposes, they are sometimes useful for giving opinions on certain points that are still a matter of dispute. It is well, perhaps, to mention here that the present century has witnessed a moderate reaction from the extremely critical views that were so widely prevalent among Swedish historians in the last decades of the nineteenth century. It is, for example, now possible for a writer to maintain, without incurring the charge of being a hopeless obscurantist, that the battle of Bråvalla belongs to the realm of fact and not to that of fiction; that Sigfrid was an Englishman, not a German; and that, intermingled with much legendary matter, there is a considerable amount of genuine history recorded in the Ynglingasaga.

I have, in certain chapters, made considerable use of the Thesis "Sweden and the Papacy, 822—1248," for which I was awarded the Ph.D. degree of London University. In regard to the spelling of the Swedish, Norwegian, Danish and Icelandic proper names I have made it a rule to use the national forms, save in a few cases—such as Henry, Edward, Odin, Thor—where the English forms are in too common use to make the employment of others advisable. I have also used the nominative form of old Icelandic names in every case, but I am afraid that I may not always have been consistent in my spelling. I have noticed, however, that among modern Swedish authors there is some lack of consistency in the spelling of proper names; e.g., the name of the country appears in three forms—Sverige, Sverge, Svärge. It must be remembered in this connection that the reformed spelling, which came into use in 1906, was not at first universally adopted.

Finally, I wish to express my grateful thanks for their kindly and helpful criticisms to Prof. F. M. Stenton, F.B.A., Litt.D., the Rev. A. J. Macdonald, D.D., the Rev. W. K. Lowther Clarke, D.D., and the Rev. C. B. Moss, M.A., B.D.

C. J. A. OPPERMANN

Grimsby

LIST OF AUTHORITIES USED

A.

COLLECTIONS OF DOCUMENTS, CHRONICLES, &C.

"Acta Sanctorum," II., V., X., XI., XXIII., XXV., XXXI. Freiburg, Paris, and Rome, n.d., 1864–8.

"Adam af Bremen om Menigheden i Norden." Oversat af P.W. Christensen. Copenhagen, 1862.

Adamus Bremensis, "Gesta Pontificum Hammaburgensis Ecclesiæ." Excerpta relating to Sweden are given in "Scriptores Rerum Svecicarum," III., i. (Adam Br.)

Alford, M., "Fides Regia Anglicana," III. Liége, 1663.

"Ágrip af Nóregs Konunga Sǫgum." Ed. F. Jónsson. Halle, 1929. (Ágrip.)

"Anglo-Saxon Chronicle." Tr. J. Ingram. London, 1912. (A.-S. Chron.)

"Annales Rerum Danicarum Esromenses." Included in "Scriptores Rerum Danicarum," I. (Annales Esromenses.)

"Ares Isländerbuch." Ed. W. Golther. Halle, 1923. (Ari.)

Baring-Gould, S., "Lives of the Saints." London, 1872–98.

Beckman, N., "Ur vår äldsta bok." Stockholm, 1912. (U.Ä.B.)

Bede, "The Ecclesiastical History of the English Nation." London, 1910. (Bede, H. E.)

"Book of Saints, The." Compiled by the Benedictine Monks of St. Augustine's Abbey, Ramsgate. London, 1921.

"Bremisches Urkundenbuch." Ed. D. R. Ehmck. Bremen, 1880.

"Breviarium Arosiense." Basel, 1513.

"Breviarium Coloniense." Cologne, 1718.

"Breviarium Sacrarum Virginum Ordinis S.S. Salvatoris." Landshut, 1697.

Butler, A., "Lives of the Saints." London and Dublin, 1833.

"Cæsarius Heisterbacensis, Dialogus Miraculorum," II. Ed. J. Strange. Cologne, Bonn and Brussels, 1851.

"Catholic Encyclopædia, The." Ed. C. G. Herberman and others. London and New York, 1907–12. (Cath. Enc.)

Celse, M. von, "Apparatus ad historiam Sveo-Gothicam Sectio prima, Bullarii Romano-Sveo-Gothici recensionem sistens." Stockholm, 1782. (Celse: "Bullarium.")

"Christne Saga." Tr. in Origines Islandicæ, I.

"Corpus Poeticum Boreale." Ed. and tr. G. Vigfusson and F. York Powell. Oxford, 1883. (C.P.B.)

Curschmann, F., "Die älteren Papsturkunden des Erzbistums Hamburg." Hamburg and Leipzig, 1909. (Curschmann.)

"Diarium Wazstenense." Included in "Scriptores Rerum Svecicarum," I., i. Also translated into Swedish as "Vadstena Klosters Minnesbok." Stockholm, 1918.

"Dictionary of English Church History." Ed. S. L. Ollard and G. Crosse. London and Milwaukee, 1912.

xiii.

"Dictionary of National Biography." Ed. L. Stephen and S. Lee, London, 1885–1903. (D.N.B.)
"Diplomatarium Arna-Magneaneum," I., II. Ed. G. J. Thorkelin. Copenhagen, 1786.
"Diplomatarium Norvegicum," I., II., III., VI., VIII. Ed. C. C. A. Lange, C. R. Unger and H. J. Huitfeldt. Christiania, 1849–74. (Dip. Norv.)
"Diplomatarium Suecanum," I.–VI. Ed. J. G. Liljegren, B. E. Hildebrand and E. Hildebrand. Stockholm, 1829–78. (Sv. Dip.)
"Edda, The Older." Tr. H. A. Bellows. Oxford, 1923.
"Eddan, Den äldre." Tolkad av A. Åkerblom. Uppsala, 1920. (Cited as separate poems; e.g. Vǫluspǫ.)
"Edda, The Prose." Tr. I. A. Blackwell. London, 1847.
"Edda, The Prose." Tr. A. G. Brodeur. New York and London, 1916. (Pr. E.)
Eddius Stephanus, "Life of Bishop Wilfrid." Tr. B. Colgrave. Cambridge, 1927.
"Egil's Saga." Tr. E. R. Addison. Cambridge, 1930.
Einhard, "Vita Caroli." Ed. H. W. Garrod and R. B. Mowat. Oxford, 1915.
"Encyclopedia of Religion and Ethics," V., VI., VII., XII. Ed. J. Hastings. Edinburgh, 1913–21. (E.R.E.)
"Ericus Olai, Chronica." Included in "Scriptores Rerum Svecicarum," II., i.
"Eyrbyggia Saga, The." Tr. in "Origines Islandicæ," II.
"Fagrskinna." Ed. P. A. Munch and C. R. Unger. Christiania, 1847.
"Finnlands Medeltidsurkunder." Ed. R. Hausen. Helsingfors, 1910. (F.M.U.)
"Flateyjarbok." Christiania, 1860–68.
"Florence of Worcester, Chronicle." Tr. T. Forester. London, 1854.
Gale, T., "Historiæ Britannicæ, Saxonicæ, Anglo-Danicæ, Scriptores XV." Oxford, 1691.
Gams, P. P. B., "Series Episcoporum Ecclesiæ Catholicæ." Ratisbon, 1873.
Geete, R., "Helige Mäns Lefverne, jämte Legender och Järtecken." Stockholm, 1902.
Gummerus, J., "Synodalstatuter." Stockholm, 1922.
"Gunnlaugs Saga Ormstungu." Ed. J. Thorkelsson. Reykjavik, 1880.
"Hamburgisches Urkundenbuch." Ed. J. M. Lappenberg. Hamburg, 1842. (Hamb. U.B.)
Hampson, R. T., "Medii Aevi Kalendarium." London, 1841.
"Handlingar rörande Skandinaviens Historia," VI. Stockholm, 1818. (H.S.H.)
Henry of Huntingdon, "History of the English." Tr. T. Forester. London, 1853.
"Hervarar Saga." Ed. O. Verelius. Uppsala, 1642.
"Historia Sancti Davidis Abbatis et Confessoris." Included in "Scriptores Rerum Svecicarum," II., i.
"Historia Sancti Sigfridi Episcopi et Confessoris." Included in "Scriptores Rerum Svecicarum," II., i. (Hist. S.S.)
"Hrafnkels Saga." Tr. in "Origines Islandicæ," II.; also in Coles, "Summer Travelling in Iceland." London, 1882.
"Islandske Annaler." Ed. G. Storm. Christiania, 1888.
Janauschek, P. L., "Origines Cisterciensium," Vienna, 1877.
Johannes Magni, "Gothorum Sveonumque Historia." Rome, 1554.

Johannes Magni, "Historia Pontificum Metropolitanæ Ecclesiæ Upsalensis." Included in "Scriptores Rerum Svecicarum," III., ii. (Johannes Magni, Hist. Met.)

"Jomsviking Saga." Oversat af A. Joleik. Oslo, 1910.

Juusten, P., "Chronicon Episcoporum Finlandensium, Annotationibus H. G. Porthan." Helsingfors, 1859. (Porthan, Juusten-Chronicon.)

"Kalendarium Svecicum." Ed. R. Geete. Stockholm, 1919.

"Kalendarium Vallentunense." Ed. O. Janse. Stockholm, 1907.

"Kalevala." Tr. J. M. Crawford. New York, 1888.

"Kalevala." Tr. W. F. Kirby. London, 1914.

Krantzius, A., "Rerum Germanicarum historici clariss. Regnorum Aquilonarium, Daniæ, Sueciæ, Norvagiæ, Chronica." Frankfort-on-Main, 1575. (Krantzius.)

"Landnámabók." Ed. F. Jónsson. Copenhagen, 1900.

"Latinska källskrifter till Sveriges äldsta historia." Ed. J. Bergman. Stockholm, 1918. (Bergman, Latinska källskrifter.)

"Laxdæla Saga." Tr. T. Veblen. New York, 1925.

"Laxdæla Saga." Tr. in "Origines Islandicæ," II.

"Legenda Sancti Eskilli Episcopi et Martyris." Included in "Scriptores Rerum Svecicarum," II., i.

"Liber Censuum de l'Église Romaine, Le." Ed. P. Fabre. Paris, 1889–1905.

"Liber Pontificalis, Le." Ed. L. Duchesne. Paris, 1892.

"Liv-, Esth- und Curländisches Urkundenbuch," I. Ed. F. G. von Bunge. Reval, 1853. (Liv. U.B.)

Mansi, J. D., "Sacrorum Conciliorum Nova et Amplissima Collectio," XXI., XXII., XXIII. Venice, 1776–8. (Mansi.)

"Martyrologium Usuardi Monachi." Ed. J. B. Sollerius. Venice, 1745.

"Matthew of Westminster," "Flores Historiarum," I. Tr. C. D. Yonge. London, 1853. (Matthew of Westminster, Chronicle.)

"Medeltidens Statsskick." Ed. H. Hjärne. Uppsala, 1895.

Messenius, J., "Chronicon Episcoporum per Sveciam, Gothiam, et Finlandium." Leipzig, 1685. (Messenius, Chronicon.)

"Minsta Svenska Rimchrönikan." Included in "Scriptores Rerum Svecicarum," I., i.

"Missæ Propriæ Sanctorum Regni Sveciæ Patronorum, Ad normam Missalis Romani accommodatæ." Cracow, 1675.

"Missale pro usu totius regni Norvegie." Copenhagen, 1519.

"Missale Upsalense." Basel, 1513.

"Monumenta Germanica," II. Ed. G. H. Pertz. Hanover, 1829.

"Monumenta Germanica, Scriptores," I.-III. Hanover, 1885. (M.G.H.SS.)

"Monumenta Historica Norvegiæ." Ed. G. Storm. Christiania, 1880. (M.H.N.)

"Monumentorum veterum Ecclesiæ Sveogothicæ Prolegomena." Ed. E. Benzelius. Uppsala, 1709. (Benzelius, Mon. Vet.)

"Necrologium Lundense." Included in "Scriptores Rerum Danicarum," III.

"Nestorskrönikan." Översattning av A. Norrback. Stockholm, 1919.

"Nestors Russiske Krönike." Oversat af C. W. Smith. Copenhagen, 1869.

"Njal's Saga." Tr. G. W. Dasent. London, 1911.

"Novgorod Chronicle, The." Tr. R. Michell and N. Forbes. London, 1914.

"Oddr Snorresøn, Saga Olafs Konungs Tryggvasunar." Ed. P. A. Munch. Christiania, 1853. (Oddr, O.T.S.)

"Officia Propria Sanctorum Patronorum Regni Poloniæ et Sveciæ." Kempten, 1842. (Officia Propria S.P.)

Ogg, F. A., "A Source Book of Mediæval History." New York, 1908.
Olaus Magni, "Historia de Gentibus Septentrionalibus." Rome, 1555.
Olaus Petri, "Svenska Chrönika." Included in "Scriptores Rerum
 Svecicarum," I., ii.
"Origines Islandicæ." Ed. and tr. G. Vigfusson and F. York Powell.
 Oxford, 1905.
"Passio et Miracula Beati Olavi." Ed. F. Metcalfe. Oxford, 1881.
"Patrologiæ Cursus Completus CXXIX.—CCXVI." Ed. J. P. Migne.
 Paris, 1853–5. (P.L. ; E. and P. = Epistolæ et Privilegia.)
"Regesta Honorii Papæ III." Ed. P. Pressutti. Rome, 1888–95. (Reg.
 Honorius III.)
"Regesta Norvegica." Ed. G. Storm. Christiania, 1898.
"Regesta Pontificum Romanorum." Ed. P. Jaffé. Berlin, 1851. (This
 edition gives the Literæ Spuriæ separately at the end.)
"Regesta Pontificum Romanorum." Ed. P. Jaffé and G. Wattenbach.
 Leipzig, 1885–8. (Jaffé.)
"Regesta Pontifica Romanorum, 1198—1304." Ed. A. Potthast. Berlin,
 1873–5. (Potthast.)
"Registres de Gregoire IX., Les." Ed. L. Auvray. Paris, 1896—1907.
 (Reg. Gregory IX.)
"Registres d'Innocent IV., Les." Ed. E. Berger. Paris, 1884—1919.
 (Reg. Innocent IV.)
"Registrum Ecclesiæ Aboensis eller Åbo Domkyrkas Svartbok." Ed.
 R. Hausen. Helsingfors, 1890. (Åbo D.S.)
"Rerum Italicarum Scriptores III." Ed. L. Muratori. Milan, 1723.
 (S.R.I.)
Rhyzelius, A. O., "Episcoposcopia Sviogothica, eller en Swea-Gothisk
 Sticht och Biskopschrönica." Linköping, 1752. (Rhyzelius, Epis.)
Rhyzelius, A. O., "Monasteriologia Sviogothica." Linköping, 1740.
 (Rhyzelius, Mon. Sv.)
"Roman Martyrology, The." English Translation. London, 1923.
"Saga of Ragnar Lodbrok, The." Tr. M. Schlauch. London, 1930.
"Saxo Grammaticus, Gesta Danorum." Ed. A. Holder. Strassburg,
 1886. Excerpta relating to Sweden in "Scriptores Rerum Sveci-
 carum," III., i. Also a Danish Translation—"Sakses Danesaga"—
 by J. Olrik. Copenhagen, 1925. (Saxo.)
Schlyter, C. J., "Corpus Juris Sveo-Gotorum Antiqui III. : Uplands-
 Lagen." Stockholm, 1834.
"Scriptores Rerum Danicarum Medii Ævi I.—VIII." Ed. J. Langebek,
 P. Suhm, L. Engelstoft and E. C. Werlauff. Copenhagen, 1772—
 1834. (S.R.D.)
"Scriptores Rerum Svecicarum Medii Ævi I.—III." Ed. E. M. Fant,
 E. G. Geijer, J. H. Schröder and C. Annerstedt. Uppsala, 1818–76.
 (S.R.S.)
Searle, W. G., "Onomasticon Anglo-Saxonicum." Cambridge, 1897.
Searle, W. G., "Anglo-Saxon Bishops, Kings and Nobles." Cambridge,
 1899.
"Simeon of Durham." Tr. J. Stevenson (Rolls Series). London, 1855.
"Skriftelige Bewis hörande til Swenska Kyrckio-Historien." Ed.
 E. Spegel. Uppsala, 1716. (Spegel, Skriftelig Bewis.)
"Skrifter och Handlingar til Uplysning i Svenska Kyrko-och Reforma-
 tions Historien." Ed. U. von Troil. Uppsala, 1790–1. (Von
 Troil.)
"Snorri Sturluson, Heimskringla." Tr. W. Morris and E. Magnusson.
 London, 1893.
"Snorri Sturluson, Heimskringla." Tr. S. Laing. London, 1915, 1930.
 (Olaf Trygvessön's Saga—Heimskringla : O.T.S. ; St. Olaf's Saga—
 S.O.S. ; other Sagas under their respective names.)

"Song of Beowulf, The." Tr. R. K. Gordon. London, n.d.
Staphorst, N., "Historia Ecclesiæ Hammaburgensis Diplomatica," I. Hamburg, 1723.
"Stora Rimchrönikan." Included in "Scriptores Rerum Svecicarum," I., ii.
Stubbs, W., "Registrum Sacrum Anglicanum." Oxford, 1897.
"Supplementum ad Breviarium et Missale Romanum adjectis Officiis Sanctorum Angliæ." Ed. J. Lingard. London, 1823.
"Svenskt Diplomatorium," I.—IV. Ed. C. Silfverstolpe and K. H. Karlsson. Stockholm, 1875–92. (Sv. Dip., II.)
"Sverges traktater med främmande magter," I. Ed. O. S. Rydberg. Stockholm, 1877. (Sv. Tr.)
"Sverris Saga." Tr. J. Sephton. London, 1899.
"Syon Martyrologium." Ed. F. Proctor and E. S. Dewick. London, 1893.
Tacitus, "Germania." Tr. M. Hutton. London, 1914.
"Tale of Beowulf, The." Tr. W. Morris and A. J. Wyatt. London, 1898.
Todd, J. H., "War of the Gædhill with the Gaill." London, 1867.
Vastovius, J., "Vitis Aquilonia." Ed. E. Benzelius. Uppsala, 1708.
"Vetera Monumenta Poloniæ et Lithuaniæ," I. Ed. A. Theiner. Rome, 1860. (Vet. Mon. Pol.)
"Vetus Chronicon Sveciæ Prosaicum." Included in "Scriptores Rerum Svecicarum," I., i. (Chron. Pros.)
"Vita et Miracula S. Erici Regis." Included in "Scriptores Rerum Svecicarum," II., i.
"Vita Sancti Anscharii" per S. Rembertum. Included in "Scriptores Rerum Svecicarum," II., i. (Rimbert, V.A.)
"Vita Sancti Botvidi Martyris." Included in "Scriptores Rerum Svecicarum," II., i.
"Vita Sancti Eskilli." Included in "Scriptores Rerum Svecicarum," II., i.
"Vita S. Rimberti." Included in "Monumenta Germanica," II.
"Vita Sancti Sigfridi Episcopi et Confessoris." Included in "Scriptores Rerum Svecicarum," II., i.
William of Malmesbury, "Chronicle." Tr. J. A. Giles. London, 1847.
Wilson, J., "The English Martyrologe." St. Omer, 1672.
"Äldre Västgötalagen, översatt av N. Beckman." Uppsala, 1924.
Örnhjälm, C., "Historia Sveonum Gothorumque Ecclesiastica." Stockholm, 1689. (Örnhjälm, H.E.)

B.

OTHER WORKS.

Abercromby, J., "The Pre- and Protohistoric Finns." London, 1898.
Almedingen, E. M., "The English Pope." London, 1925.
Almgren, O., "Svenska folkets äldsta öden." Uppsala, 1920.
Anjou, L. A., "Svenska kyrkoreformationens historia." Uppsala, 1851.
Arne, T. J., "Sveriges förbindelser med Östern under Vikingatid." Stockholm, 1911.
Arne, T. J., "Det stora Svitjod." Stockholm, 1917.
Arup, E., "Danmarks Historie," I. Copenhagen, 1925.
Baaz, J., "Inventarium Ecclesiæ Sveogothorum." Linköping, 1642.
Bang, A. C., "Udsigt over den norske kirkes historie under katholicismen." Christiania, 1887. (Bang, Udsigt.)

B

Barry, W., " The Papal Monarchy." London, 1902.
Beazley, R., " Russia." Oxford, 1918.
Bell, K., " Mediæval Europe, 1095—1254." Oxford, 1911.
Belloc, H., " Europe and the Faith." London, 1924.
Bergroth, E., " Den finska kyrkans historia." Helsingfors, 1892.
Binns, L. E., " Innocent III." London, 1931.
Björkander, A., " Visby stads äldsta historia." Uppsala, 1898.
Bolin, S., " Om Nordens äldsta historieforskning." Lund, 1931.
Boyesen, H., " History of Norway." London, 1900.
Bozius, T., " De Signis Ecclesiæ Dei." Rome, 1591.
Bradley, H., " The Goths." London, 1888.
Breyer, R., " Die Legation des Kardinalbischofs Nikolaus v. Albano in Skandinavien." Halle, 1893.
Bright, W., " Early English Church History." Oxford, 1897.
Brilioth, Y., " Den påfliga beskattningen af Sverige intill den stora schismen." Uppsala, 1915.
Brilioth, Y., " Svenska kyrka, kungadöme och påvemakt 1363—1414." Uppsala, 1925.
Brooke, Z. N., " The English Church and the Papacy." Cambridge, 1931.
Browne, G. F., " Boniface of Crediton." London, 1910.
Brulin, H., " Några feldaterade påfvebref i svenskt diplomatarium." Uppsala, 1902.
Bryce, J., " The Holy Roman Empire." London, 1904.
Bugge, A., " Vikingerne." Copenhagen and Christiania, 1904, 1906.
Bugge, A., " Norges Historie," I., II. Christiania, 1910–16. (Bugge, N.H.)
Bull, E., " Folk og Kirke i Middelalderen." Christiania and Copenhagen, 1912.
Bumpus, T. F., " The Cathedrals of Sweden, Norway and Denmark." London, n.d.
Bååth, L. M., " Bidrag till den kanoniska rättens historia i. Sverige." Stockholm, 1905.
Bååth, L. M., " Vilhelms af Sabina svenska legation." Uppsala, 1902.
Calverley, W. S., " Notes on the Early Sculptured Crosses, Shrines and Monuments in the Present Diocese of Carlisle." Kendal, 1899.
" Cambridge Medieval History," II., III., V. Cambridge, 1913–26.
Castrén, M. A., " Finsk Mytologi." Helsingfors, 1853.
Chaillu, P. B. du, " The Viking Age." London, 1889. (Du Chaillu.)
Chalandon, F., " Histoire de la Domination normande en Italie et en Sicile," I. Paris, 1907.
Chambers, R. W., " Beowulf : An Introduction." Cambridge, 1932.
Coles, J., " Summer Travelling in Iceland." London, 1882.
Comparetti, D., " The Traditional Poetry of the Finns." Tr. I. M. Anderton. London, 1898.
Cornelius, C. A., " Handbok i Svenska Kyrkans Historia." Uppsala, 1875.
Cornell, H., " Sigtuna och Gamla Uppsala." Stockholm, 1920.
Coulton, G. G., " Life in the Middle Ages," I. Cambridge, 1928.
Craigie, W. A., " The Religion of Ancient Scandinavia." London, 1906.
Craigie, W. A., " The Icelandic Sagas." Cambridge, 1913.
Cronquist, M., " Ansgar." Uppsala, 1930.
Cruttwell, C. T., " The Saxon Church and the Norman Conquest." London, 1909.
Dalin, O. von, " Svea Rikes Historia," I., II. Stockholm, 1747, 1750.
Davis, H. W. C., " Charlemagne." London, 1900.
Dawson, C., " The Age of the Gods." London, 1928.
Dawson, C., " The Making of Europe." London, 1932.

Deansley, M., " A History of the Medieval Church." London, 1925.
Dehio, G., " Geschichte des Erzbistums Hamburg-Bremen," I. Berlin, 1877.
Donner, G. A., " Kardinal Vilhelm von Sabina." Helsingfors, 1929.
Duben, G. von, " Om Lappland och Lapparne." Stockholm, 1873.
Edgren, R., " Innocentius III. och Sverges inbördes strider." Uppsala, 1902.
Falk, A., " Gregorius IX. och Sverge." Uppsala, 1902.
Fisher, H. A. L., " The Medieval Empire." London, 1898.
Fisher, H. A. L., " History of Europe," I. London, 1935.
Fletcher, C. L. R., " The Making of Western Europe." London, 1912, 1914.
Fliche, A., " La Réforme Grégorienne." Louvain and Paris, 1924, 1925.
Flick, A. C., " The Rise of the Mediæval Church." New York, 1909.
Fortescue, A., " The Orthodox Eastern Church." London, 1907.
Friesen, O. von, " Upplands runstenar." Uppsala, 1913.
Fryxell, A., " Berättelser ur Svenska Historien." Stockholm, 1866.
Fryxell, K. A., " Om svenska biskopsval under Medeltiden." Uppsala, 1900.
Ganander, C., " Mythologia Fennica." Åbo, 1789.
Gathorne-Hardy, G. M., " The Norse Discoverers of America." Oxford, 1921.
Geijer, E. G., " Svenska folkets historia." English translation by J. H. Turner. London, 1842. (Geijer, E. T.)
Gjerset, K., " History of Iceland." London, 1924.
Gjerset, K., " History of the Norwegian People," I. New York, 1915.
Grandinson, K. G., " Studier i hanseatisk-svensk historia." Stockholm, 1884.
Green, A. S., " History of the Irish State to 1014." London, 1925.
Gregorovius, F., " History of the City of Rome in the Middle Ages," III., IV. Tr. A. Hamilton. London, 1903.
Grimberg, C., " Svenska folkets underbara öden," I. Stockholm, 1916.
Götlind, J., " Saga, sägen och folkliv i Västergötland." Uppsala, 1926.
Haliday, C., " The Scandinavian Kingdom of Dublin." London and Dublin, 1884.
Hall, F., " Bidrag till kännedomen om Cistercienserorden i Sverige." Gefle, 1899.
Hallendorf, C., and Schück, A., " History of Sweden." London, 1929.
Hauck, A., " Kirchengeschichte Deutschlands," I.—IV. Leipzig, 1904–13. (Hauck, K. D.)
Helsingius, G. F., " Finlands Kyrkohistoria." Tavastehus, 1855.
Helveg, L. N., " Den Danske Kirkes Historie til Reformationen," I. Copenhagen, 1862.
Hildebrand, H., " Sveriges Historia," II. Stockholm, 1903. (Hildebrand, S.H., II.)
Hildebrand, H., " Sveriges medeltid," III. Stockholm, 1903. (Hildebrand, S.M.)
Hildebrand, H., " Skara domkyrka." Stockholm, 1894.
Hodgkin, T., " Charles the Great." London, 1897.
Hodgkin, T., " History of England from the Earliest Times to the Norman Conquest." London, 1906.
Holmberg, U., " Finno-Ugric and Siberian Mythology." London, 1927.
Hunt, W., " The English Church from its Foundation to the Norman Conquest." London, 1901. (Hunt.)
Janse, O. R., " Le travail de l'or en Suède à l'époque mérovingienne." Orleans, 1922.
Jennings, A. C., " The Mediæval Church and the Papacy." London, 1909.

Jörgensen, A. D., "Den nordiske Kirkes Grundlæggelse." Copenhagen, 1874–6. (Jörgensen.)
Jörgensen, E., "Helgendyrkelse i Danmark." Copenhagen, 1909.
Kauffmann, F., "Northern Mythology." London, 1903.
Keary, C. F., "The Vikings in Western Christendom." London, 1891.
Kendrick, T. D., "A History of the Vikings." London, 1930.
Keyser, R., "Den norske Kirkes Historie under Katholicismen." Christiania, 1856–8. (Keyser.)
Kjellberg, C. M., "Den äldsta svenska konungatiteln." Uppsala, 1902.
Kjellen, R., "Om Eriksgatan." Uppsala, 1889.
Koht, H., "The Old Norse Sagas." London, 1931.
Koskinen, Y., "Finlands historia," I. Stockholm, 1874.
Krohn, J., "Finska litteraturens historia I., Kalevala." Helsingfors, 1891.
Lagerbring, S., "Swea Rikes Historia," I., II. Stockholm, 1769, 1773. (Lagerbring, S.R.H.)
Lavisse, E., "Histoire de France," II. Paris, 1903.
Lavisse, E. et Rambaud, A., "Histoire Générale," I., II. Paris, 1893.
Leinberg, K. G., "De finska klostrens historia." Helsingfors, 1890.
Leinberg, K. G., "Det odelade finska biskopsstiftets herdaminne." Jyväskylä, 1895.
Lencqvist, C. E., "De Superstitione Veterum Fennorum." Included in Porthan: Opera Selecta, IV.
Lindberg, G., "Die schwedischen Missalien des Mittelalters." Uppsala, 1923.
Lindqvist, S., "Den helig Eskils biskopsdöme." Stockholm, 1917.
Lindqvist, S., "Vendelkulturens ålder och ursprung." Stockholm, 1926.
Lindskog, P. E., "Försök till en korrt beskrifning om Skara stift," I. Skara, 1812.
Lundqvist, K. V., "Bidrag till kännedom om de svenska domkapitlen under medeltiden." Stockholm, 1897.
Lundström, H., "Fynd ock forskningar," I., II. Uppsala and Stockholm, 1912, 1914.
Macdonald, A. J., "Hildebrand." London, 1932.
Mackie, J. D., "Pope Adrian IV." Oxford, 1907.
Maclear, G. F., "The Apostles of Medieval Europe." London, 1888.
Malin, A., "Die Heiligenkalender Finnlands." Helsingfors, 1925.
Mann, H. K., "Nicholas Breakspear." London, 1914.
Mann, H. K., "The Lives of the Popes in the Early Middle Ages," II.—IX. London, 1906–14. (Mann, P.M.A.)
Martin, J., "Gustav Vasa et la Réforme en Suède." Paris, 1906.
Maurer, K., "Die Bekehrung des Norwegischen Stammes zum Christenthume." Munich, 1855, 1856.
Mawer, A., "The Vikings." Cambridge, 1913.
Mawer, A., "Problems of Place-Name Study." Cambridge, 1929.
Messenius, J., "Scondia Illustrata." Ed. J. Peringskiold. Stockholm, 1700–5. (Messenius, Sc. Ill.)
Moeller, W., "History of the Christian Church in the Middle Ages." Tr. A. Rutherford. London, 1893,
Montelius, O., "Sveriges Historia," I. Stockholm, 1919. (Montelius, S.H.)
Montelius, O., "The Civilization of Sweden in Heathen Times." Tr. F. H. Woods. London, 1888.
Nerman, B., "Det svenska rikets uppkomst." Stockholm, 1925. (Nerman, S.R.U.)
Nerman, B., "Svärges älsta konungalängder." Uppsala, 1914.
Neumann, J., "De Fatis Primatus Lundensis." Copenhagen, 1799.

Nordenstreng, R., "Vikingafärderna." Stockholm, 1915.
Olrik, A., "Viking Civilization." Tr. J. W. Hartmann and H. A. Larsen. London, 1930.
Oman, C., "The Dark Ages." London, 1928.
Oman, C., "England before the Norman Conquest." London, 1909.
Overton, J. H., "The Church in England," I. London, 1897.
Phillpotts, B., "Germanic Heathenism," in "Cambridge Medieval History," II.
Phillpotts, B., "Edda and Saga." London, 1931.
Pinnow, H., "History of Germany." Tr. M. R. Brailsford. London, 1933.
Porthan, H. G., "Opera Selecta," I., II., IV., V. Helsingfors, 1859–73.
Previté-Orton, C. W., "Outlines of Medieval History." Cambridge, 1924.
Rameen, D., "Dissertatio Academica de S. Davide, Primo Apostolo Westmanniæ." Uppsala, 1723.
Rein, G., "Biskop Thomas och Finnland i hans Tid." Helsingfors, 1839.
Reuterdahl, H., "Swenska kyrkans historia." Lund, 1838–66. (Reuterdahl, S.K.H.)
Rothery, A., "Sweden, The Land and the People." London, 1934.
Rydberg, S., "Svearnas och Gothernas Strid om Konungavalet." Lund, 1830.
"Saga-Book of the Viking Club," VI., X. London, 1908–29.
Samuelsson, S., "Datering af påfvebrefven om Nicolaus' af Albano legation." Uppsala, 1902.
Saxén, R., "Finsk guda-och hjältetro." Helsingfors, 1916.
"Scandia," IV., V. Lund, 1931, 1932.
Schlauch, M., "Romance in Iceland." 1934.
Schmeidler, B., "Hamburg-Bremen und Nordost-Europa." Leipzig, 1918.
Schmid, T., "Den helige Sigfrid." Lund, 1931.
Schmid, T., "Sveriges kristnande." Stockholm, 1934.
Schück, A., and Hallendorff, C., "History of Sweden." London, 1929.
Schück, H., "Svenska folkets historia," I. Lund, 1914. (Schück, S.F.H.)
Schück, H., "Studier i nordisk litteratur- och religions historia," II. Stockholm, 1904.
Schück, H., "Birka." Uppsala, 1910.
Schück, H., "Den äldsta kristna konungalängden i Sverige." Uppsala, 1914.
Schütte, G., "Our Forefathers, the Gothonic Nations," II. Cambridge, 1933.
Schybergson, M. G., "Finlands historia," I. Helsingfors, 1887.
Smith, A. L., "Church and State in the Middle Ages." Oxford, 1913.
Smith, C. M., "The Northmen of Adventure." London, 1932.
Steenstrup, J., "Normannerne." Copenhagen, 1876–82.
Steenstrup, J., "Danmarks Riges Historie," I. Copenhagen, 1897. (Steenstrup, D.R.H.)
Stefansson, J., "Denmark and Sweden." London, 1916.
Stephens, W. R. W., "Hildebrand and his Times." London, 1888.
Stephens, W. R. W., "History of the English Church," II. London, 1904.
Stjerna, K., "Erik den helige." Lund, 1898.
Stomberg, A. A., "History of Sweden." London, 1932. (Stomberg, H.S.)
Strinnholm, A. M., "Svenska folkets historia." Stockholm, 1834–54. (Strinnholm, S.F.H.)

Stubbs, W., " Germany in the Early Middle Ages." London, 1908.
Svanström, R., and Palmstierna, C. F., " Short History of Sweden."
  Oxford, 1934.
Söderblom, N., " Arkebiskop Stefans invigning." Uppsala and Stock-
  holm, 1914.
Taranger, A., " Den angelsaksiske kirkes indflydelse paa den norske."
  Christiania, 1890. (Taranger.)
Thatcher, O. J., and Schwill, F., " Europe in the Middle Ages."
  London, 1897.
Toll, H., " Kring Sigrid Storråda." Stockholm, 1926.
Tout, T. F., " The Empire and the Papacy." London, 1924.
Tunberg, S., " Sveriges historia. Äldre medeltiden." Stockholm, 1925.
Tunberg, S., " Studier rörande-Skandinaviens äldsta politiska indelning."
  Uppsala, 1911.
Voigt, H. G., " Brun von Querfurt." Stuttgart, 1907.
Wadstein, E., " Norden och Väst-Europa i Gammal Tid." Stockholm,
  1925. (Wadstein.)
Wahlström, J., " Om Olof Skökonungs dop." Uppsala, 1846.
Walsh, A., " Scandinavian Relations with Ireland during the Viking
  Period." Dublin, 1922.
Weibull, C., " Sverige och dess nordiska grannmakter under den tidigare
  medeltiden." Lund, 1921.
Weibull, L., " Studier i Lunds domkyrkas historia." Lund, 1906.
Weibull, L., " Kritiska undersökningar i Nordens historia omkring år
  1000." Copenhagen, 1911. (Weibull, K.U.)
Wessen, E., " Studier till Sveriges hedna mytologi och fornhistoria."
  Uppsala, 1924. (Wessen, Studier.)
Wessen, E., " De nordiska folkstammarna i Beowulf." Stockholm, 1927.
Westman, K. B., " Den svenska kyrkans utveckling från St. Bernhards
  tidevarv till Innocentius IIIs." Stockholm, 1915. (Westman.)
Whitney, J. P., " Hildebrandine Essays." Cambridge, 1932.
Wijkmark, H., " Svenska kyrkohistoria," I., i. ; I., ii. Stockholm, 1928,
  1931.
Wiklund, K. B., " När kommo svenskarna till Finnland? " Uppsala,
  1901.
Williams, M. W., " Social Scandinavia in the Viking Age." New York,
  1920.
Willson, T. B., " History of the Church and State in Norway." London,
  1903.
Wordsworth, J., " The National Church of Sweden." London and
  Milwaukee, 1911. (Wordsworth, N.C.S.)
Worsaae, J. J. A., " An Account of the Danes and Norwegians in
  England, Scotland and Ireland." London, 1852.
Zeller, J., " Histoire Résumée de l'Allemagne." Paris, 1889.

CHAPTER I

THE MISSION FIELD : SWEDEN

SWEDEN differs from most of the lands of Western Europe in that " in historic time the country has never been subjected to foreign invasion, and its population . . . has therefore not materially altered during the last ten centuries."[1] As to which of its two principal peoples—the Swedes and the Goths—was the first to make its home there, historians are not agreed,[2] and later writers usually make no attempt at deciding the question, while it has even been suggested that originally they were but one,[3] only becoming differentiated after long settlement in the land.

The Sveas or Swedes, however, under the name of Suiones,[4] are the first to be mentioned in any historical work that has come down to us. Tacitus, the Roman historian, who wrote his " Germania " almost at the end of the first century, describes them as living in the middle of the ocean,[5] and possessing in plenty both warriors and ships. The latter were of somewhat curious form, tapering both towards bow and stern, so that they could be rowed equally well in either direction ; they had no sails and the oars were free instead of being fastened to the sides. The Suiones had great respect for wealth, and it would seem, from his statement that one man had supreme

---

[1] Schück and Hallendorf : " History of Sweden," p. 4.
[2] E.g. Wordsworth : " N.C.S.," p. 19. " The balance of evidence seems to me to tell strongly in favour of the priority of the Sveas." Geijer, E.T. p. 10. " In our judgment the Goths . . . are the elder people in Scandinavia." Ericus Olai, Sweden's first historian, in his " Chronica " (S.R.S., II. i., p. 13) divides the land in early times into five kingdoms, and says : " Quartum erat regnum Gothorum, cæteris antiquius et nomen sibi retinens generale, continens in se, Ostgothiam et Westgothiam atque Verendiam, Ölandiam et Smalendiam, latas quidem et amplissimas regiones."
[3] Montelius : " Sveriges Historia," I., p. 266.
[4] For a discussion of the name Suiones see Nerman : " S.R.U.," pp. 15, 16.
[5] Germania, c. 44. " Svionum civitates, ipso in Oceano." The Baltic was thought to be an inlet of the Ocean, and Scandinavia an island lying in it. Schütte : " The Gothonic Nations," p. 403, thinks that Tacitus got his knowledge of the Swedes from the knight sent by Nero to establish an amber trade on the Baltic.

authority and an unchallenged right to obedience, that they were governed by powerful kings. [6] They differed from other Germanic tribes in the considerable restrictions placed on the wearing of arms, due no doubt to the desire to avoid internal dissensions, and to the fact that they were so well protected by the sea, or by mountains or great tracts of forest land, from sudden attacks of their enemies. Their home was in what is now central Sweden, including both the lands round the shores of Lake Mälar, and those to the north and north-west of them.

Tacitus also mentions the Fenni [7]—under which name there is little doubt that the Lapps are meant—and lays much stress on their "astonishing barbarism" and utter poverty. They had neither arms, horses, nor fixed homes; herbs were their food and skins their clothing; bone-tipped arrows formed their sole wealth, enabling them to gain their livelihood by hunting; and their only shelter against wild beasts and the inclemency of the weather was afforded by "tents" made of a few intertwined branches. Yet in spite of its hardships their nomadic life seemed to please them better than one in which field labour and house service were necessary, and they had nothing even to ask for. [8]

The Goths are first mentioned about the middle of the second century by the Greek geographer Ptolemy, who calls them Goutoi, [9] and it is possible, though hardly probable, that they had migrated to Sweden from the lands south of the Baltic only a short time previously. [10] They lived on the

[6] "Eoque unus imperitat, nullis jam exceptionibus, non precario jure parendi." Nerman: "S.R.U.," p. 267, points out that if the kingdom of Sweden had its origin in the one described by Tacitus it is the oldest European state. He also thinks (p. 7) that the finds in the mound at Håga may imply that there was a Svea king as early as 1000 B.C.

[7] Germania, c. 46.

[8] "Securi adversus homines, securi adversus deos rem difficillimam adsecuti sunt, ut illis ne voto quidem opus esset."

[9] Bradley: "The Goths," p. 8, considers that these people are not identical with the Goths, but this is improbable. Cp. Nerman: "S.R.U.," p. 25 ; Schütte: "The Gothonic Nations," I., p. 382.

[10] This is the opinion of Bishop Wordsworth. For his reasons for holding it see "N.C.S.," pp. 19–23. There is the further possibility that the Goths in early times migrated from southern Sweden and then in part returned there later.

southern plains, their lands being separated from those of the Swedes by far-stretching tracts of forest land. It would seem, too, that the Heruli, who were driven from the Baltic islands about A.D. 250 by the Danes, after wanderings in Central Europe, where they formed a kingdom bordering on that of the Gepidæ, returned in part to the north, and formed a settlement in those parts of Sweden now known as Blekinge and Skåne.[11]

What the relations were between the Swedes and Goths in early times we do not know, though it would seem that with both nations a powerful centralized state had gradually been built up by the union of numerous petty kingdoms, in the case of the Swedes at least as early as the time at which Tacitus wrote; but in the period known as that of the Folk-Wanderings (A.D. 400—800), the Goths, who seem to have been on the whole considerably more civilized than their Swedish neighbours,[12] though they were less powerful, largely owing to continuous migrations from their lands, were

---

[11] For the Heruli in the North see Schütte: "The Gothonic Nations," I., pp. 346–53; Wessen: "De nordiska folkstammarna i Beowulf," pp. 5–12. The latter thinks that the Scyldings of Beowulf are the northern Heruli. Procopius: "De Bello Goth.," II., cc. 14, 15, relates how the southern Heruli having killed their king, Okon, sent to Scandinavia for a prince of their royal blood.

[12] There were, for instance, excellent goldsmiths amongst them, and considerable quantities of the metal were imported from the south. For illustrations of their work see Janse: "Le travail de l'or en Suède à l'époque mérovingienne"; also Montelius: "S.H.," I., pp. 244, 245; Du Chaillu, II., cc. 18, 19; Almgren: "Svenska folkets äldsta öden," Figs. 20, 22. Janse, however, seems to take too extreme a view of the state of their civilization as compared with that of the Swedes, when he says (p. 9) "Les Gœtars et leurs consanguins . . . possédaient une civilisation developpée et de grandes richesses. Les Svéars . . . étaient demeurés barbares." Metal ornaments, etc. of excellent workmanship have been found in Uppland, Hälsingland and other Swedish territories proper, though it is, of course, possible that some of these were imported from Götaland or elsewhere. For examples, see Almgren, Figs. 23, 24; Nerman: "S.R.U.," Plates 5, 6; Lindqvist: "Vendelkulturens Ålder och Ursprung," Figs. 15, 21–5, 47; and compare what is said about Swedish goldsmiths by Stomberg: "H.S.," p. 66. It is, however, to be noted that the importation of gold seems to have ceased after the Swedish Conquest. One reason for undertaking this may have been that the Swedes coveted the treasure of the Goths. See Nerman: "The Foundation of the Swedish Kingdom," in the "Saga Book of the Viking Club," X., p. 124.

attacked and conquered after a long struggle by the latter.[13]
The first success of the Swedes was probably the conquest of
Öland about the year 500. The island of Gottland shared
the same fate about fifty years later, and Västergötland was
also acquired by the Uppsala king; and though the Goths
were apparently helped by their kinsmen on the continent in
the long struggle that ensued, they were unable to prevent the
final triumph of the Swedes, and after the famous battle of
Bråvalla in Östergötland,[14] fought possibly at some time in
the eighth century,[15] the two nations passed under one rule—
that of the Swedish king who reigned at Uppsala.

The Goths, though conquered, were allowed to keep their
lands, laws and customs, but the king was elected by the
inhabitants of Uppland, the most important of the provinces

[13] The general opinion of historians inclines to the idea of conquest,
though it has also been suggested that some kind of alliance was made
between the two peoples. Wessen: " De nordiska folkstammarna i
Beowulf," p. 56, thinks it improbable that an alliance for purposes of
warfare took place during the period of the Folk-wandering. Certainly
from the Anglo-Saxon poem, " Beowulf," we get the idea of bitter, if
intermittent, warfare between the Scylfings (Swedes) and the Geats
(Goths), though some think that the latter were not the Goths of
southern Sweden, but the Jutes of northern Denmark. Chambers:
" Beowulf," p. 409, says " The question of the nationality of the Geatas
of Beowulf cannot be regarded as finally settled." He discusses the Jute
theory on pp. 8–10, 333–45, 401–9, 417, 418. See also for Beowulf
and the Northern peoples, Wessen: " Studier," pp. 81–119; Nerman:
" S.R.U.," pp. 57–136; Wadstein, pp. 10–32. King Ongentheow of the
poem has been identified with the Egil of the Ynglingasaga (c. 30),
Ohthere with Ottar (c. 31), Onela with Ale (c. 33), and Eadgils with
Adils (cc. 32, 33). The expedition of Hygelac, king of the Geats, against
the Frankish tribe of the Attoarii, in which he was killed in battle against
Theodebert, son of Theoderic, is certainly historical, for it is referred to
by Gregory of Tours (" Historia Francorum," III., c. 3) and other
chroniclers.

[14] The actuality of this battle has been denied; e.g. Montelius:
" S.H.," I., (second ed.), pp. 211, 212; Steenstrup: " D.R.H.," I.,
p. 159. But though an exact date cannot be assigned to it, there seems
little doubt that it took place and had far-reaching results. It is referred
to in several of the Sagas, but it is not clear who were the combatants,
and various suggestions in regard to this have been made by historians.
The most probable is that the Swedes and West Goths under their king
Sigurd Ring defeated the East Goths, who were aided by Harald
Hildetand, King of Denmark, and that as a result Östergötland was
incorporated with the Swedish territories. K. Weibull: " Sverige och
dess nordiska grannmakter," pp. 25ff., maintains that there is no trace of
a definite Swedish suzerainty over Götaland till the eleventh century.

[15] See Nerman: " S.R.U.," pp. 246f.

that constituted his Swedish dominions. Common worship at the great temple at Uppsala, where the king himself officiated at certain of the sacrifices, as well as the benefits of the union, such as it was, no doubt did much to bring about a more friendly state of feeling between the two peoples that lasted until after the introduction of Christianity, when the more obstinate clinging of the Swedes to the old beliefs probably tended to revive the old racial jealousy, which was presently to be strengthened and perpetuated for many generations by the advent of two rival royal families—the Gothic Sverkers and the Swedish Eriks. It is possible, however, that the ill-will between the two peoples at this time has been exaggerated and that the bloodthirsty feuds so characteristic of the period were due mainly to the rivalry of certain great families.

The conversion of both Swedes and Goths was very largely due to the work of English missionaries, but in order to understand properly what they accomplished it is necessary to have in the first place some knowledge of the character of the people whom they were instrumental in winning over to Christianity, and of the religious beliefs current among them; and in the second place, since they were not the first to work in the Swedish mission-field, to note what progress the Gospel had already made in the land, when, at the close of the tenth century of the Christian era, they entered upon their labours there.

The age of the Folk-Wanderings had given place to that of the Vikings shortly before the first Christian missionaries came to Sweden, for in referring to Anskar and his companion as the first to preach the Gospel there the old legend can safely be ignored which assigns that honour to the apostle St. Philip, who is even credited with driving away into the wilderness a dragon which he found at the temple at Uppsala. It would seem that at this time the country, or rather, the cultivated part of it, was over-populated, and consequently many of the inhabitants were driven to earn their living by piracy or foreign trade or to seek fresh homes in other lands. Certainly much more of the land was capable of being brought under cultivation; but this meant strenuous toil in the way of cutting down forests, draining marshlands and such-like undertakings, and work of this kind made but a small appeal to many in comparison with the fame and wealth that might be quickly gained by participation in a Viking raid; and though, of course, the chances of a speedy and violent death were by no means small, this would act as no deterrent to men who believed that their fate was irrevocably settled for them by the Norns, and who rather than die a " straw death " from sickness or old age, would seek to end their lives in some new fight or " gash themselves to Odin." [16] It is also possible that political affairs, or even a long succession of bad harvests, may have caused many to take up a Viking career.

It must not be thought, however, that all the Viking expeditions were for the purpose of obtaining plunder or of gaining fresh lands in which to settle ; in the case of the Swedes particularly they were often undertaken for mercantile objects, for Sweden was an important trading country, exporting horses, furs, hides, salt and amber, and importing such articles as spices, silks, rugs and jewels. [17] There was a colony of foreign merchants at Birka, the great trading port on an island in Lake Mälar, [18] while Swedish merchants visited Russia and

---

[16] Bugge: " Vikingerne," I., p. 109; " Norges Historie," I., i., p. 205.

[17] Stomberg: " H.S.," c. 4. For the famous Swedish trade route, the Austvegr, see Nordenstreng: " Vikingafärderna," pp. 150–91, and for an account of Viking ships, Nordenstreng, pp. 20–8; and " Saga Book of Viking Club," X., pp. 1–11.

[18] Adam of Bremen has a description of this place in Book I., c. 62. Its importance as a port is indicated by his statement: "Ad quam stationem, quia tutissima est in maritimis Suevoniæ regionibus, solent omnes Danorum vel Nortmannorum, itemque Slavorum ac Semborum naves, aliique Scithiæ populi pro diversis commerciorum necessitatibus sollempniter convenire." There was some doubt as to the site of Birka, though it is now generally agreed that it was situated on the island of Björkö. Reuterdahl: " S.K.H.," I., pp. 201–3, identifies it with Sigtuna, and so does Willson: " History of Church and State in Norway," p. 20. Such identification, however, does not harmonize with a statement of Adam in Book IV., c. 28, where he mentions them as distinct places. Also in III., c. 70, Schol. 94, Archbishop Adalbert of Bremen is mentioned as consecrating bishops for both Sigtuna and the isles of the sea, and reference to Book IV., c. 20, shows that the latter bishop was John the Monk, appointed to Birka. Olaus Petri: " Chrönika, S.R.S.," I., ii., p. 233, also distinguishes them. He says: " Men the städer som något kunde räknas före Kiöpstäder, voro tre Byrcköo, Sigtuna och Skara, och synes Byrcköo hafva varit äldst." Cp. " Chron. Pros., S.R.S.," I., i., p. 242. Montelius (" S.H.," I., p. 425), Hildebrand

Birka

the lands of south-eastern Europe, and possibly also the lands of Western Asia that bordered on the Mediterranean, following the trade routes along the Oder and Vistula. Many Swedes also took service with the Eastern Emperors in the famous Varangian guard.

From records preserved on the rune-stones, as well as from the large number of Anglo-Saxon coins found in Sweden, we learn that many Swedes must have joined with their Danish and Norwegian neighbours in the plundering expeditions against the coasts of Britain,[19] though we know of no purely Swedish expedition, for those of Ragnar Lodbrok and his sons cannot rightly be reckoned as such, since even if he was a Swede, which is extremely doubtful, he seems to have made his home in Denmark or Frisia.[20] But the Swedes for the most

("S.M.," III., pp. 28, 29), Jörgensen (p. 103), Grimberg (I., p. 322), Stomberg ("H.S.," p. 115) and Kendrick ("H.V.," p. 96) all agree that Birka was situated on Björkö. The town is usually supposed to have been destroyed about the year 1000, possibly by Styrbjörn before the battle of Fyrisval, possibly by St. Olav of Norway when he invaded Sweden. The latter is the opinion of Von Dalin (I., xx., 6). Montelius: "The Civilization of Sweden in Heathen Times," p. 148, says that nothing has been found in graves at Birka which can be referred with certainty to a date after 1000; but it is strange that a bishop should be appointed to it in the time of Adam of Bremen if it had been utterly destroyed, and his other references to it seem to imply that it was still in existence. Schol. 138, however, says ". . . Bircam, quæ nunc in solitudinem redacta est, ita ut vestigia civitatis vix appareant." It therefore seems possible that its destruction took place about 1075 or shortly afterwards.

[19] Such stones have been found in Gästrikland, Uppland, Västmanland, Södermanland, Östergötland and Småland. In Montelius: "S.H.," p. 325, there is an illustration of a stone in Orkesta parish, raised in memory of a certain Ulv, who had three times received Danegeld in England. For the Swedes in England see further, Schück: "S.F.H.," I., pp. 220, 221; Stomberg: "H.S.," pp. 90–3.

[20] Although Ragnar Lodbrok is certainly an historical character the accounts of him are confusing and conflicting, and Koht: "The Old Norse Sagas," p. 123, well says: "In all probability the viking hero of the sagas, Ragnar Lodbrok, has absorbed the lives and exploits of several men." According to one account he was the son of the Swedish king, Sigurd Ring; Saxo IX., c. 896, makes him the son of a Sigvard Ring, King of Zealand and Skåne, and assigns a later date for him; the English annalists call him a Dane of royal blood; Halliday: "The Scandinavian Kingdom of Dublin," pp. 31–3, identifies him with the chief Thorgils who was captured in 843 by King Malachy and drowned in Loch Uair (Lough Owel in West Meath). Dr. Todd in the "War of the Gædhill with the Gaill," p. 15, gives 845 instead of 843 for this event, but this change of date still makes it impossible for Thorgils to be the Ragnar Lodbrok who was the leader of the Viking host that besieged Paris in that year; nor could he either have been the Ragnar Lodbrok

part concentrated their energies on the lands bordering on the
Baltic and its inlets, and unlike their Norwegian and Danish
neighbours, made no settlements, save as individuals, in the
countries whose shores are washed by the Atlantic, while their
greatest accomplishment was the founding of the Russian
state by Rurik in 862,[21] which was in after times to
become Sweden's bitterest enemy.

It has been thought that the desire to establish the religion
of Odin and Thor on the ruins of English Christianity, to
found a great pagan empire in Western Europe with its
centre in England, was the main motive for the repeated
expeditions to the shores of Britain.[22] Certain it is that of all
the rich conventual establishments that studded the kingdom
of Northumbria not one escaped destruction; certain, too,
that a period of settlement followed that of mere plunder;
and if the main Viking aim were indeed the establishment of
a great heathen empire, this may account to some extent for
the comparatively minor part played by the Swedes in these
expeditions, for persecution for the sake of religion appears on

who was captured by Ella of Northumberland and caused to perish in a
pit of serpents (Ragnar Lodbrok's Saga, c. 15). His saga is largely
legendary, but his death song, though in its present form it probably
belongs to a much later date, is interesting as showing the spirit that
animated the Vikings. Matthew of Westminster's "Chronicle," sub
anno 870, gives a very different story of his death. For Ragnar, see
further Steenstrup: "Normannerne," I., pp. 81–106; Keary: "Vikings
in Western Christendom," pp. 255–62; Mawer, in "Saga Book of
Viking Club," VI., pp. 68–89.

[21] Nestors Krönikan, c. 15. Rurik has been identified with the Frisian
Viking Rorik; see Belaiew: "Rorik of Jutland and Rurik of the
Russian Chronicles" in the "Saga Book of the Viking Club," Vol. X., ii.
This identification seems less improbable than that which makes Rorik
the same person as Horik I. of Jutland.

[22] Spence: "The Church of England," I., p. 347. "The Viking
leaders . . . dreamed of a pagan empire, to be built up on the ruins of
the Christian domination, in England and on the continent of Europe."
Cp. also what he says on pp. 339, 349. That the Vikings contemplated
the establishment of a great empire, though not primarily from anti-
Christian motives, is not unlikely. Cp. Smith: "The Northmen of
Adventure," p. 118. "It is the fashion to think of the Vikings as pagans
hammering at the gates of Christendom, ignorant robbers, inconsequent
marauders of settled states: it would be more accurate to think of them
as intelligent students of world affairs. The land empire of Charlemagne
was crumbling before their eyes; surely among them there was one who
could envisage the hegemony of the Northmen in an empire of the sea."

the whole to have been little in accordance with the national character, as the treatment of the early missionaries shows.

If the establishment of a great pagan empire in the West was indeed the ultimate aim of the Viking raids, and if the subjugation of England was essential for its accomplishment, then Alfred's victory at Edington [23] may well be included among the decisive battles in the world's history, for the saving of Wessex from absorption into the Danish dominions would then have meant the salvation of Western Europe as a whole; but while the apparent hatred displayed by the Northmen for the Christian religion cannot be denied, [24] it seems difficult to believe that a carefully thought-out plan for the universal establishment of heathenism on the ruins of Christianity would have allowed an Archbishop of York to retain his position at all, [25] or suffered the Christians to remain, even if only as a poor and impotent minority; or that Guthrum and his followers would so easily have agreed to adopt Christianity as an alternative to leaving the country. [26] The terrible fate of the religious houses seems quite sufficiently accounted for by the fact that they offered a rich and easy prey, and so became the chief objects of attack by the invaders, who no doubt thoroughly despised the, to them, inexplicable mode of life of their inmates. [27]

[23] Asser, c. 56; "A.-S. Chron.," sub anno 878; William of Malmesbury, II., c. 6.

[24] There is, however, some difference of opinion as to how far this hatred was real, and in what proportions greed and dislike for Christianity accounted for the exploits of the Vikings. See Lavisse et Rambaud: "Histoire Générale," II., p. 733; Fletcher: "Making of Western Europe," I., p. 293; Cruttwell: "The Saxon Church and Norman Conquest," p. 9; Kendrick: "History of the Vikings," pp. 12–15, 38–40; Fisher: "History of Europe," I., pp. 179, 180.

[25] After the sack of York in 867, Archbishop Wulfhere fled first to Wharfedale, and later on to a king whom the Danes had set up beyond the Tyne. He was allowed to return to York in 874.

[26] "A.-S. Chron.," sub anno 878. William of Malmesbury, II., c. 4, speaks very unfavourably of Guthrum's conduct after he became a Christian. "However, as the Ethiopian cannot change his skin, he domineered over these tributary provinces (i.e. East Anglia and Northumbria) with the haughtiness of a tyrant for eleven years."

[27] Cp. Stomberg: "H.S.," p. 78. "The early Vikings took a special delight in robbing monasteries and killing monks; this was, no doubt, for the simple reason that in these monasteries they could make their easiest and richest hauls; the inoffensive and peaceable dwellers within the cloister walls also aroused the special contempt of these fierce pagan warriors."

Brave though the Vikings undoubtedly were, and romantic as their exploits appear when viewed at this distance of time —more particularly the discovery and colonization of Iceland,[28] Greenland and America—there can be no doubt as to the barbaric cruelty of these sea rovers and the wide-spread misery caused by their ravages. Their war customs well serve to show that such civilization as they possessed did nothing to restrain their natural fierceness. The impaling of captives, or the carving of the blood-eagle on them as an act of revenge,[29] the tossing of children on their spears, and the "roller-reddening" or launching of their boats over the bodies of living victims, when they were about to set out on some fresh expedition,[30] show that cruelty is not invariably associated with cowardice, and that men who in their home life displayed many excellent and even kindly qualities could delight in their warfare in exhibiting unmitigated ferocity.

One other of the Viking characteristics ought to be mentioned here, a characteristic that displayed itself fully when

---

[28] Strictly speaking, Iceland was not discovered by the Vikings, as it had been visited by Irish monks many years before its discovery by the Swede, Gardar Svavarsson, about the year 861. ("Landnáma Bók," I., 2, 1) "M.H.N., Theodorici Monachi Historia," c. 2, speaking of Ingulf settling there says "et tunc primum illa terra inhabitari cœpit, quam modo Islandiam vocamus, præter quod paucissimi ex Hybernia, insula, id est Britannia minori, ibi creduntur antiquitus fuisse ex quibusdam indiciis, repertis videlicet libris eorum et nonnullis utensilibus." "Islendingabók," I., 3. "þa vǫro hér menn cristner, þeir es Norþmenn calla Papa; en þeir fóro sithan á braut, af því at þeir villdo eige vesa hér við heiþna menn, oc léto epter bøcr írscar oc biǫllor oc bagla. Af því mátte scilia, at þeir vǫro menn írscer." Cp. also the Prologue to the "Landnáma Bók."

It seems quite possible that the Irish, in the persons of St. Brendan and his companions, also anticipated the Vikings in the discovery of America.

[29] We have a description of this punishment in the Saga of Harald the Fair-haired, c. 31. It is said to have been inflicted on Ella of Northumbria, after his defeat at York by Ingvar and Hubba in 867, in revenge for the death of their father, Ragnar Lodbrok, at his hands. Ragnar Lodbrok's Saga, c. 17. The "A.-S. Chronicle," however, says with regard to the battle "Both the kings (i.e. Ella and his former rival, Osbert) were slain on the spot." Cp. Matthew of Westminster, sub anno 867.

[30] "C.P.B.," II., p. 349. The Ragnar Cycle, line 56, "ok hildingar haofðo hlunn-roð." The words were spoken by Aslaug, the second wife of Ragnar Lodbrok. Cp. Ragnar Lodbrok's Saga, c. 10. Simeon of Durham, s.a. 1070, mentions that the Scots were guilty of the atrocity of tossing infants on pikes during the invasion of King Malcolm.

their marauding expeditions gave place to attempts at settlement and colonization—their remarkable power of adapting
themselves to different forms and states of society and of
fusing with the people among whom they settled. When they
made their home in a country they adopted its language,
religion and customs, and soon lost their individuality, so that
eventually there remained little to witness to their original
settlement save the place names of the occupied territory.
Thus in Normandy they became Frenchmen; in East Anglia
and Lincolnshire, Englishmen; in Apulia, Italians; only in
Iceland, where they founded a republic, do we find an exception to this rule, and that can hardly be said to be a real one,
for the Irish monks who visited that island seem to have fled
on the arrival of the Northmen and so gave them no opportunity of being influenced by them. But though the Vikings
lost so easily their national individuality, they exercised a deep
influence on the various peoples with whom they fused,
imparting new life to them and aiding greatly in the development of both their political and social organization, as well as
stimulating their intellectual and artistic activities.

Though we read much about the Vikings and their exploits
in the various contemporary chronicles, and so can form a
good idea of the external activities of the Swedes, and more
particularly the foundation by them of the great state of
Russia, to which reference has already been made, we know
but little about the internal state of affairs in their land. We
have, indeed, in the Ynglingasaga an account of the successive
kings of the line of Odin, but even the later ones are but
shadowy figures, though recent archæological researches have
shown that much more historical fact is enshrined in the Saga
than was at one time thought, and real Swedish history can
hardly be said to begin before the time of the coming of
Anskar, while even after that there is more than one period
about which our knowledge is extremely scanty.

The land was apparently generally ruled by a single
monarch, though there were occasionally joint sovereigns, [31]

[31] Ynglingasaga. Alrek and Erik, c. 23; Yngve and Alf, c. 24. There
were two kings—Björn and Emund—at the time of the arrival of Anskar.
When two kings were thus ruling one seems to have had his seat at
Uppsala, the other at Birka.

but in certain respects his authority was very limited. [32]   He
was above all the leader in war, and then his powers were
great; he offered the sacrifices at Uppsala on certain great
occasions; possibly, too, he acted as judge; but he had not
the right to levy taxes and derived his income from the royal
estates scattered over his domains, and he and his bodyguard
travelled from one to another of these in order to use their
produce. [33]   He probably presided at the "things" in the
original Swedish provinces, but these lands, as well as the more
outlying ones, were to a large extent self-governed, each having
its own peculiar laws, [34] though there was, of course, as yet no
written code in any one of them.   He had a bodyguard
(hird), and there was also a well-organized navy which he
had the right to call out every year to undertake a plundering
expedition, the so-called ledung or leding.   The country along
the coast was divided up into a number of districts, each of
which had to furnish its quota of ships and men, the latter
including both rowers and warriors. [35]

Most of his subjects were bonder or free peasant farmers,
living in village communities, and the cultivation of the land
and the rearing of cattle and other animals were the principal
occupations followed.   The chief crops grown were oats,
barley, rye, flax, hemp, beans and peas.   Bees were kept, and
in addition to the animals required for home use, horses were
reared for export. [36]   All the bonder were of equal rank in

[32] Rimbert: "V.A.," c. 23.   "Sic quippe apud eos moris est, ut quod-
cunque negotium publicum magis in populi unanima voluntate, quam
in Regia consistat potestate."   Adam Br., IV., c. 22.   "Reges habent ex
genere antiquo, quorum tamen vis pendet in populi sentencia; quod in
commune omnes laudaverint, illum confirmare oportet, nisi ejus decre-
tum pocius videatur, quod aliquando secuntur inviti.   Itaque domi pares
esse gaudent.   In prælium euntes omnem præbent obedentiam regi,
vel ei qui doctior ceteris a rege præfertur."   The lagman Thorgny in
his speech to Olov Skötkonung at Uppsala "thing" reminded him how
five kings had been thrown into a marsh because they displeased the
bonder by their pride.   "Heimskringla, S.O.S.," c. 81.
[33] Cp. Ynglingasaga, c. 39.
[34] It was not until the thirteenth century that a common law for the
country came into existence.   The provincial codes are given in
Schlyter: "Corpus Juris Sveo-Gotorum Antiqui."
[35] Nerman: "S.R.U.," pp. 21–3.
[36] Horses were used in Sweden itself for sacrificial purposes, on which
occasions their flesh was eaten.   The Angles and Saxons when they came
to Britain would seem to have had the same custom, for we find the
eating of horseflesh forbidden in several Anglo-Saxon penitentiaries.

time of peace, and in each of the different districts they chose one of their number, well versed in the law, to act as *lagman* or judge and explain it as the holding of the "thing" or general assembly, when all disputes that had accumulated were settled. As already mentioned, the different provinces had each its own laws, and though we have no written code earlier than the West Gothic, compiled by the lagman Eskil in the early part of the thirteenth century, it is probable that the various collections when reduced to writing enshrined much that had been customary from quite early times, and so they help us to form a picture of the state of affairs prevailing during the Viking period, though, of course, Christianity had totally changed, or at least modified considerably, some of the ancient practices at the time when the laws came to be formally codified. [37]

With regard to home life, [38] the father, as head of the family, had great authority. He was responsible for its religion and acted in some respects as a kind of priest, and in the house he had a special seat of honour, the high seat, separated by sacred pillars from the other benches. If he possessed wealth his household probably consisted of several servants and slaves in addition to the members of his family. Over the slaves [39] he had absolute power of life and death, but their lot does not seem to have been harder than in other lands and they had the opportunity of gaining their freedom. He had also the right to expose any child born in his house if he did not wish to acknowledge it as his; but if he decided to

[37] As showing the profound influence of Christianity on Swedish medieval provincial legislation we may notice the opening words of the West Gothic code: "Kristær ær fyrst i laghum warum, þa ær kristna war ok allir kristnir, konungær, böndær ok allir bokarlær, biskupær ok allir boklærdir mæn." "U.Ä.B.," p. 68.

[38] We get a glimpse of home life in Viking times in the Eddic poem Rigsþula.

[39] There are several references to slaves and slavery in the Sagas. In Egil's Saga, c. 80, Steinar buys a slave named Thrand for three marks, and the same price—which was reckoned a high one—was paid by Höskuld for a female slave (Laxdæla Saga, c. 12). Cp. "Heimskringla, O.T.S.," c. 58; "Landnáma Bók," IV., 4, 2. Slaves seem to have been more numerous among the Goths than among the Swedes. In Christian times slavery apparently came to an end by the beginning of the fourteenth century.

recognize it he took it up in his arms, water was sprinkled on it, and a name was given to it.[40]   A wife was obtained by negotiations with those of the lady's male relatives who had the right to bestow her in marriage, her own consent being unnecessary[41]; but although much respect was paid to marriage, it was thought no disgrace for the head of the household to have children by his maidservants or slaves. Drunkenness was a very common fault, and seems to have been taken so much as a matter of course that no stigma attached to it. As the head of the house the father dispensed hospitality freely, for no virtue was more highly regarded in Sweden, and it was considered a great disgrace to refuse to entertain travellers. The breaking of an oath likewise brought great shame on the perjurer, though public opinion would seem to have been quite satisfied as long as the actual letter of the promise was observed, even if its spirit were completely disregarded.[42]   The series of Eddic poems known as the Hávamól[43] gives us a good idea of the ethic code of the Vikings, insisting, as it does, on the importance of showing hospitality, of pitying the poor and wretched, of winning the friendship of the good, of avoiding the conversation of foolish men and taking care to find no pleasure in what is evil, of showing courage, and of realizing that though cattle die, and relatives die, and oneself must also die, yet a good name won is deathless.

Apart from their household duties, knitting, sewing and weaving were the principal occupations of the women, though

[40] Saga of Haakon the Good, c. 12; Saga of Halfdan the Black, c. 7; Saga of Harald the Fair-haired, c. 40; Egil's Saga, c. 31; Gunnlaug Ormstungu's Saga, c. 3; "Landnáma Bók," V., 8, 2. Olrik: "Viking Civilization," p. 129, thinks that the custom of sprinkling the child with water was borrowed from Christianity.

[41] Cp. Njal's Saga, cc. 2, 9, 10, 26, 27.

[42] A good example of this is afforded by the part played by Ivar the Boneless in the revenge taken on Ella of Northumbria for the death of Ragnar Lodbrok. Ivar swore never to take arms against Ella, and kept his promise literally, although he was mainly instrumental in bringing about his downfall. See Ragnar Lodbrok's Saga, cc. 16, 17.

[43] The Hávamól consists of six poems, the first and fourth of which contain instructions as to right conduct. In the fourth they are addressed to a young man whom the author styles Loddfafne. Bellows: " The Poetic Edda," p. 29, writes " Few gnomic collections in the world's literary history present sounder wisdom more tersely expressed than the Hovamol."

sometimes they are found undertaking the practice of medicine or of divination,[44] and occasionally trading at markets, or acting as rune-cutters, or even as priestesses. Life was not all toil, for in addition to the break in its routine afforded by attendance at the " things " and the greater sacrifices, special forms of recreation were not unknown. Outdoor sports, in particular, were extensively indulged in, while the games of draughts and chess had made their way to the northern land,[45] and games of chance seem also to have been popular.[46]

It has been asserted that " the religions of heathenism had taken deep root neither in the intellect, the conscience, nor the affections of mankind,"[47] but this statement would seem to require some modification when applied to the beliefs of the Northern nations and more especially to those of the Swedes, otherwise it is difficult to account altogether for the fact that the struggle between Christianity and heathenism in Sweden lasted for over three hundred years, for it seems very improbable that this could have been the case unless the adherents of the ancient faith had entertained a considerable degree of affection for it. Certainly it had deteriorated from the simple Nature worship of more primitive times and had in it " little that was beautiful and much that was repulsive "[48];

[44] Cp. Ynglingasaga, c. 7; also the story of Katla and Geirrida in the Eyrbyggja Saga, cc. 15–20. See further for the occupations of women, Williams: " Social Scandinavia in the Viking Age," pp. 118–20.
[45] Sigurd and Hvitserk, the sons of Ragnar Lodbrok, were playing chess when the news of their father's death arrived. Ragnar Lodbrok's Saga, c. 16. Cp. Gunnlaug Ormstungu's Saga, c. 4. The " Vǫluspǫ́," v. 8, makes the gods play chess in the golden age. Figures of chessmen are given in Du Chaillu, II., p. 354.
[46] The dice were numbered one to six as now, but were oblong instead of cubical in shape. Montelius: " S.H.," I., p. 387. On one occasion St. Olav of Norway cast lots by means of dice with Olov Skötkonung as to who should have certain property. " Heimskringla, S.O.S.," c. 97.
[47] Maclear: " The Apostles of Medieval Europe," p. 3. For a very different view, see Strinnholm: " S.F.H.," IV., p. 2. He considers that with the old Swedes their belief in and worship of the protecting Æsir did more than anything else to brighten their lives and bring them success and happiness in their domestic affairs, freedom and independence in public ones. Cp. Phillpotts: " Germanic Heathenism " in " Camb. Med. Hist.," II., p. 495. " The gods . . . were at any rate occasionally the objects of real trust and affection."
[48] Wordsworth: " N.C.S.," p. 86.

certainly, too, its sacrificial system was a hideous one; but in spite of these things its hold on its votaries was strong,[49] nor was it altogether devoid of beliefs that were capable of being transfigured and ennobled by the teachings of Christianity.

The religion of the Swedes and Goths at the time of the appearance of the first Christian missionaries was practically the same as that of the other Scandinavian nations. Our knowledge of it is derived mainly from the older Edda, a collection of songs of the skalds, supposed to have been made by the Icelander Sæmund the Wise about the year 1100, but probably also due largely to the labours of others[50]; from the younger Edda, a prose version of the old songs, made by another Icelander, the lagman Snorri Sturluson, the author of the "Heimskringla"[51]; from various references to it in the sagas and in Adam of Bremen's history of the archbishops of the Hamburg-Bremen see[52]; and from archæological investigations.

It must not be thought, however, that in the minds of the people there existed a clear and definite belief in the Northern Pantheon as portrayed for us by the Icelandic skalds, but rather that in various places one or more of the deities received special worship and honour, and that there existed a very general belief in such beings as giants, dwarfs, elves and

---

[49] Bang: "Udsigt," pp. 24, 25, gives instances of the worship of the old gods in Norway enduring till quite recent times.

[50] The oldest of this series of thirty-three alliterative poems only dates back to the end of the ninth century, the latest may be a production of the thirteenth. Cp. Dawson: "Making of Europe," pp. 248, 249. The manuscript collection of them was discovered in 1643 by Brynjulf Sveinsson, bishop in Iceland, who styled it "Edda Sæmundi multiscii." The meaning of the term "Edda" is unknown, though various derivations have been suggested. Perhaps the most probable is that which derives it from Oddi in Iceland, the residence of both Sæmund and Snorri. For criticisms of the "Vǫluspǫ," see Phillpotts: "Edda and Saga," pp. 129ff.; Olrik: "Viking Civilization," pp. 131–9.

[51] This Edda was discovered in 1628 by Arngrim Jónsson, and is assigned to Snorri Sturluson (1179—1241). It consists of three parts, the first of which, the Gylfaginning, gives the stories of the old gods. The second and third parts treat of the art of poetry and the system of prosody respectively. Though it may be mainly the work of Snorri it has been revised and amplified.

[52] The "Gesta Pontificum Hammenburgensium" was written about 1075. In addition to the ecclesiastical chronicle it gives a valuable geographical description of the northern lands.

nixies, which lasted to a certain extent far on into Christian times, as it also did in England.[53] Even in the Eddas many contradictory statements and conflicting ideas are to be found, while sometimes the utterances of the poets would seem to indicate that they, or the stories they related, had been influenced more or less by contact with Christian teaching. There is too the difficulty that the northern deities were in some cases not only personifications of moral ideas or of the various forces of Nature, but also represented ancient tribal heroes and leaders,[54] who had been transformed after their death by a gradual process of deification into objects of worship; while it may be further noted that there was a superior race of gods—the Æsir[55]—who were endowed with those moral qualities that appealed most to the Northern peoples, as well as with power over the forces of Nature, and who held sway over the various human activities, and an inferior race—the Vanir—who were originally personifications of natural forces but came eventually to be included among the gods.[56]

The three principal gods worshipped in Sweden would seem to have been Odin, Thor and Freyr, though the cult of certain others, as Ullr and Njǫrðr, was also apparently fairly widespread. Odin was revered as the highest divinity. Not only was he the god of battle, giving victory to those whom he favoured, but he was equally the god of wisdom, skilled in both song and sorcery; while as the All-Father[57] he was in a

---

[53] E.g. "De Gestis Herwardi Saxonis," c. xxiv., where Hereward hears two witches conversing with a nixie in a spring. For belief in trolls, fairies, etc. in Sweden, see Wijkmark: "Svensk kyrkohistoria," I., c. 5.

[54] E.g. Odin himself, Freyr, etc., Ynglinga Saga, cc. 2–13.

[55] The name seems originally to have implied strength. Cp. þrimskviða, v. 20. It was interchangeable with that of gods. Vǫluspǫ́, vv. 6, 7. Snorri Sturluson in the Ynglinga Saga derives the word from Asia.

[56] The Vanir were specially renowned for their wisdom. þrymskviða, v. 15; Skírnismǫ́l, vv. 17, 18.

[57] Odin had many other names, as Lord of Hosts, Spear Lord, etc. They are given in Pr. E., c. 3. Cp. Du Chaillu, I., p. 56, where a list of fifty-one from the Eddas and Sagas is given. The giving of these names was in accordance with the scaldic custom of using *kennings;* that is, the description of a person or thing otherwise than by his or its ordinary name. Thus Thor is the Wielder of the Hammer, the Slayer of Giants, etc.; the sea is the Heaving Plain, the Road of the Sea Kings; and a ship the Wolf of the Billows.

special degree the benefactor of men, whom he did not disdain to visit from time to time apart from his appearances in battle. [58]   In Sweden, however, the memory of his worship has been perpetuated in place names to a much less extent than that of Freyr and Thor or even Ullr. [59]

Freyr would seem to have been the god to whom worship was most extensively offered.   To him was attributed the bringing of spring and summer, rain and sunshine, buds and blossoms; under his protection the pastures were verdant, the cattle throve, the earth yielded bountiful crops and peace prevailed [60]; and so we can understand that his cult would appeal to the Swedes, a people fond of ease and plenty.   The worship of Thor probably went back to far earlier times than that of Odin.   Like the latter he was said to visit the earth, but instead of choosing the homes of the great it was to the farms of the peasants and huts of the poor that he went.   He was called the friend of man, for he brought seed-time and harvest, gave children to the home, guarded against witchcraft and magic, and cared for the ashes of the dead. [61]   Ullr was apparently largely a winter god, renowned for his skill in running on snow-shoes and also in archery, while he was also a brave warrior, and as such was invoked by those about to

---

[58] Tradition assigned the last appearance of Odin to the battle of Bråvalla, where he helped to bring about the defeat of Harald Hildetand of Denmark by Sigurd Ring of Sweden.

[59] Such place-names often end in *lund* (grove), *harg* (altar), or *vi* (sanctuary), showing that originally they were specially connected with the worship of the god.   Thus we have Ullalund, Odensharg, Torsvi, etc.   We may note that while we have also in England many place-names derived from these divinities (e.g. Thoresway, Ulleskelf, Frisby), in the case of Odin they usually incorporate the German form Woden, rather than the Scandinavian Odin; e.g. Wednesbury, Wednesfield. Montelius: "S.H.," pp. 395, 396, and Hildebrand: "S.M.," III., pp. 5–10, give a large number of place-names in Sweden derived from Odin, Thor, Ullr, etc.   For place-names in England derived from Wodin, see Mawer: "Problems of Place Name Study," pp. 60, 61.

[60] Grímnismól, vv. 5, 43; Skírnismól, vv. 3–9, 40–2; Pr. E., c. 24; Ynglingasaga, cc. 12, 13.   For the cult of Freyr, see Schück: "Studier i nordisk religions-historia," pp. 248–306; Wessen: "Studier," pp. 122–9; Dawson: "Age of the Gods," pp. 281, 282.

[61] The references to Thor in the Eddas are far too numerous to be cited.

engage in battle.[62] Njǫrðr was probably originally identical with the earth-goddess Nerthus, described by Tacitus,[63] but had evolved into a male deity, who ruled the sea with the winds that blow over it, and was the protector of sailors.[64]

The only other male divinities that need be mentioned are Týr, the god of courage, who was probably of far more importance in earlier times[65]; Baldr, the god of piety, purity and gentleness[66]; and the evil Loki[67]—begetter of the Fenris-wolf, the World-serpent and Hel—whose treachery brought about the death of Baldr, and who, with his terrible offspring, was eventually to play a prominent part in the coming Ragnarǫkr, the twilight of the gods, which was to precede the renewal of all things. There were also many goddesses, of whom the chief was Frigg, the wife of Odin, the goddess of the home, the giver of gifts to those women who looked to her for help, and the shielder from danger of those who invoked her. She also foresaw the destinies of men, but never revealed them.[68]

Originally the Swedes probably offered worship to their gods in the open air, on a hill-top or in a grove, but as time went on, and the simpler worship of earlier ages became more and more polytheistic, temples were erected to the honour of the various deities. Adam of Bremen has given a short description of the famous one at Uppsala in his history of the

[62] Grímnismǫl, vv. 5, 42; Atlakviða, v. 30; Pr. E., c. 31. It would seem that he was originally one of the Vanir, and husband of Njǫrðr, the earth-goddess, before the latter was transformed into a male deity.

[63] Germania, c. 40.

[64] Vafþrúðnismǫl, v. 33; Grímnismǫl, v. 16; þrymskviða, v. 22; Pr. E., c. 23; Ynglingasaga, cc. 5, 11. His rule over the sea was shared with the Jǫtun Ægir, from whom the name "eagre," given to the bore in the Trent, is apparently derived.

[65] Hymiskviða, v. 8; Lokasenna, vv. 37–40; Pr. E., c. 25.

[66] Vǫluspǫ, vv. 31–3, 62; Vafþrúðnismǫl, v. 55; Vegtamskviða, vv. 1, 7–11; Grímnismǫl, v. 12; Pr. E., cc. 22, 49. For possible Christian influence on the Baldr myth, see Wijkmark: "Kyrko-historia," I., pp. 89–92; "E.R.E.," VI., p. 305.

[67] Vǫluspǫ, vv. 35, 51; Hymiskviða, v. 37; Vegtamskviða, v. 14; þrymskviða; Pr. E., cc. 33, 34, 46, 49, 50. Mogk, in "E.R.E.," VI., p. 305, expresses the opinion that Loki is in reality evolved from the chthonic elves.

[68] Vǫluspǫ, v. 33; Vafþrúðnismǫl, vv. 1–4; Lokasenna, vv. 25–7; Pr. E., c. 35.

Description of Temple

archbishops of Hamburg,[69] while that built by Thórólfr of Mostr at Thorsness in Iceland is described in considerable detail in the Eyrbyggja Saga.[70] From these descriptions and from scattered allusions in the sagas a fairly good idea of the general structure and appearance of a Scandinavian temple can be formed. Square or rectangular in shape, it contained seats around the walls, including special seats of honour, which had pillars at their sides with spikes in them that were regarded as holy. It was the custom for families to take these pillars with them when sailing to Iceland, throw them overboard, and settle where they came ashore.[71] Both outside and inside the temple was adorned with gold and silver, while the altar inside was formed of wood or stone,[72] and on it were the gold or silver ring on which oaths were sworn,[73] a bowl for holding the blood of the sacrificed victim, and a small twig brush for scattering the blood in the shrine and on the worshippers.[74] There were also the images of the gods, often in standing or sitting posture around the altar, but occasionally placed in niches, and well adorned with jewels and bracelets.[75] In the Uppsala temple, which was situated near a great evergreen tree, there were three—Thor in the centre, as the most powerful, seated on a couch and holding a sceptre in his right hand, and Odin and Freyr on either side of him.[76]

[69] Bk. IV., cc. 26, 27.

[70] Ch. IV. Vigfusson and Powell in "Origines Islandicæ," I., p. 252, say that this description is a gloss put in from another work.

[71] Eyrbyggja Saga, c. 4. "Then Thorwulf cast overboard his porch pillars that had stood in the temple . . . and as he did so he declared that he would settle in Iceland at the place where Thunder let them come ashore." Cp. Laxdæla Saga, c. 3.

[72] Hyndluljóð, v. 10.

[73] Hávamól, v. 110; Atlakviða, v. 30. In the latter it is styled the ring of Ullr. One of these rings was carried off from Dublin by King Mælsechnaill II. in 994; see Walsh: "Scandinavian Relations with Ireland during the Viking Period," p. 53.

[74] Hyndluljóð, v. 10; Ynglinga Saga, c. 18; Haakon the Good's Saga, c. 16.

[75] Njal's Saga, c. 87.

[76] In "C.P.B.," I., p. 401, doubt is thrown on the statements of Adam of Bremen about these idols, for Professors Vigfusson and Powell seem to question that they were used at all by the Northmen. "In the famous passage of Adam of Bremen about Uppsala, for instance, we have a tolerably careful writer about the time of the Norman Conquest, when heathendom in Sweden was but half a century dead, putting down his

The worship in the temple would seem to have been connected chiefly with the presentation of offerings [77]—cattle, horses, dogs. This may have been preceded by a kind of procession, for we read of King Adils riding round the Disa hall at the time of sacrifice. [78] The victim was probably slain in front of the altar, its blood caught in the special bowl and then sprinkled by means of the twig brush on the walls, images and worshippers, while its flesh was cooked and distributed. [79] Horned cattle seem to have been most usually offered [80]; but cows, horses, swine and dogs were also chosen as victims, [81]

knowledge at the instance and with the help of King Sweyn Estrithson; but still far removed by land and sea from the place of which he is treating. Accordingly, while he gives us true accounts of the functions of the gods, the site of the temple, the worship of the deified heroes, and mentions the ' sceptrum ' of Thor . . . yet in the midst of all this valuable information we have the usual medieval commonplace of a ' templum auro paratum,' ' statuas trium deorum,' ' solium medio in triclinio,' ' Wodanum sculptare secut nostri Martem solent '; for is it not natural that ' pagani ' should ' colere ydola? ' '' The value of this criticism is greatly diminished by the extraordinary statement that heathenism had been dead in Sweden for half a century when Adam wrote. So far from this being the case it was still powerful in his time, and almost certainly the temple at Uppsala was not destroyed till much later. The great heathen reaction under Blot-Sven, in which St. Eskil suffered martyrdom, evidently occurred after he wrote his chronicle, for he does not mention it. The Hervarar Saga (c. 20) speaks of the image of the god being sprinkled with the blood of the horse sacrificed by that heathen usurper, and idols are also mentioned in the description of Thorolfr's temple in the Eyrbyggja Saga. See further for the Uppsala Temple, Wessen: " Studier till Sveriges mytologi," pp. 169–87.

[77] Cp. " Heimskringla, O.T.S.," c. 28, " Earl Hakon made a great blood sacrifice, and judged his offering to have been accepted by the appearance of two ravens flying which croaked loudly."

[78] Ynglinga Saga, c. 33. The Disar were female guardian spirits of individuals or families to whom formal sacrifice was made under the name of Disablot.

[79] Haakon the Good's Saga, c. 16.

[80] Cp. Ynglinga Saga, cc. 18, 30.

[81] Cp. Hervarar Saga, c. 10. " King Heidrek sacrificed to Frey; the biggest boar he could get he was wont to give to Frey. They accounted this beast so holy that on his bristles they would swear in all great cases, and they used to sacrifice the boar as a Soma-blot after Yule." Quoted in " C.P.B.," I., pp. 405, 406. Animals were not only offered for sacrifice, but were occasionally worshipped. In the " Heimskringla, O.T.S.," c. 71, we read of a certain King Angvald who worshipped a cow, and in the " Landnáma Bók," I., c. 2, of Floki Vilgerdarson sacrificing to three ravens who were to show him the way to Iceland. Eystein, King of Uppsala, is also said to have sacrificed to a cow named Sibilia, which in a battle with the sons of Ragnar Lodbrok killed many men, but was eventually slain by Ivan the Boneless. (Ragnar Lodbrok's Saga, cc. 10, 12.)

and on special occasions human beings were sacrificed. [82] We read of one king, named Aun, offering one of his sons to Odin every ten years in order to procure a prolongation of his life, [83] while King Domald, after the continued failure of the crops, was sacrificed by his subjects in the hope of procuring a year of plenty, [84] and a similar fate befell Olov the Treefeller, [85] who is said to have been remiss in sacrificing to the gods.

There were three great yearly sacrifices—one in October, before the winter, for a good year; one at midwinter (January), for peace and good crops; and a third, in mid-April, for victory in battle. [86] At Uppsala the winter festival was attended from all parts of Sweden, while each ninth year there was a special offering, when men were sacrificed and their bodies hung up in a grove beside the temple together with those of various animals of the male kind. [87]

Apparently there was no special priesthood in the ordinary sense of the word, and the builder of a temple might act as its priest or *gode*. [88] Simple individual sacrifices would seem to have been made by the one who brought the gift but on certain great occasions the duty of offering sacrifice devolved

[82] Eyrbyggja Saga, c. 10, where a description of the sacrificial stone is given.

[83] Ynglinga Saga, c. 29. Nine of his sons were sacrificed in this way, but the Swedes refused to allow him to sacrifice his tenth and last son.

[84] "C.P.B.," I., Ynglinga-tal, ll. 23–8; Ynglinga Saga, c. 18; "Chron. Pros., S.R.S.," I., i., p. 243.

[85] "C.P.B.," I., Ynglinga-tal, ll. 137–43; Ynglinga Saga, c. 47. The "Chronicon Prosaicum," however, says "Olaffwer trætelge . . . doo aff rættom aller." "S.R.S.," I., i., p. 244. Cp. "Minsta Rimchrönikan," lines 268, 269.

[86] Ynglinga Saga, c. 8; "Heimskringla, S.O.S.," cc. 113, 115, 123; "O.T.S.," c. 28.

[87] Adam Br., IV., c. 27. "Ex omni animante, quod masculinum est, novem capita offeruntur, quorum sanguine deos placari mos est. Corpora autem suspenduntur in lucum, qui proximus est templo. . . . Ibi etiam canes et equi pendent cum hominibus." Cp. "Heimskringla, S.O.S.," c. 76; "S.R.S.," I., i., "Minsta Rimchrönikan," ll. 20–35.

[88] See e.g. Hrafnkels Saga, c. 1, iii. "But when Hrafnkell had hallowed for himself the land of Aðalból, he held a great sacrificial feast, and a great temple, too, he reared up there. Hrafnkell loved no other god before Frey, and to him he made offerings of all the best things he had, going half-shares. Hrafnkell settled the whole of the valley, bestowing lands on other people, on condition of being their chief; and thus he assumed priesthood over them. From this it came to pass that . . . he was called Freysgoði." Also Eyrbyggja Saga, c. 12, where there is an account of Arnkill, who was a great lagman and also a temple-gode.

upon the king, and much importance was attached to his performance of it. Haakon of Norway, after a vain attempt to persuade his subjects to adopt Christianity, only retained his kingdom by agreeing to offer the customary sacrifices,[89] and two centuries later the refusal to do this caused Inge I. of Sweden the temporary loss of his throne.[90]

It has already been said that the religion of the Northmen, fierce and cruel as it was in many ways, contained elements that were capable of being used in a modified and ennobled form by the Christian teachers, as, for example, the Baldr myth and the predictions of the Vǫluspǫ. It may be well doubted, however, if any of the Christian missionaries pointed out to their converts that with some of the old teachings it was not their utter abandonment that was necessary, but rather their purification and re-orientation; for to the medieval missionaries in general Odin and Thor and their fellow Æsir were not mere powers of Nature, poetically personified and deified, nor ancient tribal heroes, exalted during the passing centuries by the amplification of their legendary exploits into actual divinities; in their view they were malignant demons, the allies of the devil, the determined and irreconcilable enemies of the White Christ, whose kingdom for its establishment required their utter overthrow, and who in consequence must be wholeheartedly renounced by the converts to the new faith.[91]

Nor must we judge the missionaries too harshly for adopting

---

[89] Haakon the Good's Saga, cc. 15–19.

[90] Hervarar Saga, c. 20.

[91] Some of the converts would seem to have retained a certain amount of reverence for the old gods. In the " Landnáma Bók," III., c. 14, 3, we are told about a certain Helgi, " He was very mixed in his faith. He put his trust in Christ and named his homestead after him, but yet he would pray to Thunder (Thor) on sea voyages." The missionaries seem to have been willing to use the heathen temples, when purified, for Christian worship, and to adopt the old heathen festivals to Christian ones, when possible. The celebrated stone cross at Gosforth has, in addition to a representation of the Crucifixion, sculptures depicting Yggdrasil, the world tree, Viðarr, rending the jaws of the Fenris-wolf, etc., but these do not necessarily imply a retention of the old faith by the Christian Danes, who are credited with its erection. See Calverley: " Early Sculptured Crosses in the Diocese of Carlisle," pp. 139, 146, 148, 156, 169.

such a standpoint. They witnessed the deeds of the followers of Odin and Thor, and the terrible hatred apparently borne by them for all connected with the Christian faith; they saw the destruction of churches and monasteries, the torture and slaying of clergy and monks, and all the manifold horrors that gave rise to the petition in the Gallican Liturgy, " From the fury of the Northmen, Good Lord, deliver us "; and well might they reckon such things as the works of the devil, and believe that for their unrepentant perpetrators there was naught to hope. But although they may have failed to some extent to realize that the pagan Vikings must be judged according to their lights and opportunities, yet none the less when we think of their fearlessness, self-sacrifice, humility, faith, and above all, of their intense desire to win for the kingdom of God those who dwelt in the realms of darkness and of the shadow of death, they claim and receive our deep respect and profound admiration. Occasionally we may find among them one like " swaggering, drunken Thangbrand," [92] whom Olav Tryggvessön employed to help to bring about the conversion of Norway and Iceland, [93] who by his manner of life brought shame on the faith that he professed; while later on, when the profession of Christianity was an advantage rather than otherwise from a worldly point of view, many unworthy men held high places in the Churches of the North; but of the pioneer missionaries on the whole we may well say that they counted not their lives dear unto them, if only they could share in helping the kingdoms of the North to become the kingdoms of the Lord and His Christ.

[92] Longfellow: " Saga of King Olaf," IX. Of him we are told in the Cristne Saga, c. 3, iv., that while at Moster " he was a great spendthrift . . . he got him a ship of war, and harried the heathen, and plundered far and wide." In Iceland he and his men were responsible for the death of two of his opponents (c. 4, iv.).

[93] Ari, VII., i.; " M.H.N., Historia Norwegiæ," p. 115. " . . . Thangbrandum presbyterum, quem ad Glaciales misit prædicare." Cp. Cristne Saga, c. 3, vii.

CHAPTER II

THE MISSION FIELD : FINLAND

THE country now called Finland seems in earlier times to have been occupied by the Lapps, but during the period of the Folk-Wanderings the Karelians, Tavastians and Finns invaded it, formed settlements, and gradually drove the Lapps farther and farther north. A similar fate eventually befell the Quens, a race closely allied to the Finns, who also had their home in the land,[94] but who, braver and more warlike than the Lapps, for some time held their own, not only against the Finns but also the Swedes, who had attacked them. Gradually, however, they were dispossessed of their territories, and became scattered amongst, and in process of time absorbed by, Norsemen, Swedes and Karelians.[95]

The civilization of the Finns when they first settled in their new territories was of a very primitive type, but in their fresh home great changes took place. Dwelling-houses took the place of tents, woods were cleared away and the land put to agricultural uses, working in metals was developed to a high degree, and a trade with foreign lands sprang up. The principal occupations of the people at the time of the invasion of King Erik IX. of Sweden, which took place about the middle of the twelfth century, were very similar to those of the Swedes themselves when Christian missionaries first appeared in their land. The tilling of the soil, the rearing of cattle, hunting, fishing, trading and working in metals occupied the men, while the women were engaged in household duties, and also often helped in the care of the cattle. The Finns had also a very bad reputation for piratical exploits, though it is possible that their activities in this direction may

[94] Quenland is mentioned in the narrative of Othere appended to King Alfred's " Orosius." See the edition of Sweet, pp. 16–18.
[95] Schybergson, I., pp. 2–5.

Finns'
state

have been somewhat exaggerated.[96] In respect to its internal organization Finland differed greatly from Sweden. Not only was there nothing to correspond to the provinces of the latter country, but the Finns possessed no king; indeed, the only units seem to have been the family and the clan, and it was this lack of organization that made them such an easy prey when attacked by their more powerful neighbours.[97]

The earliest account we have of Finnish heathen worship is that given by Bishop Michael Agricola, the father of Finnish literature,[98] in 1551, in the form of a metrical description of the gods of the Tavastians and Karelians prefixed to the Psalter. The other principal sources of our knowledge are the old folk songs of which Dr. Lönnrot formed the epic poem "Kalevala,"[99] and the results of archæological investigations. The songs, however, of which the epic is composed have undergone considerable modifications through having been influenced by the traditions of the surrounding nations and also by the teachings of Christianity; consequently they have in recent years been carefully studied with reference to their geographical distribution and also with a view to differentiating between their primitive elements and later accretions. These investigations have served to restore largely the trust placed in Bishop Agricola's account, which had for a time lost the original value attached to it, owing to certain scholars attributing the contradictions between it and the Kalevala to the untrustworthiness of the bishop's state-

[96] Koskinen, I., p. 19. Like the Vikings they also made trading voyages to various lands.

[97] Schybergson, I., pp. 9, 10.

[98] Michael Agricola became Bishop of Åbo when in 1554 that see was divided by Gustavus Vasa into two—Åbo and Viborg. He had previously been master of the school at Åbo and had also for some years acted as a kind of assistant to the Bishop, Martyn Skytte. His literary work which included the translation into Finnish of the New Testament and the Psalter, was accomplished before his consecration to the see of Åbo. He only held the latter for a short time, as he died in 1557, on his return from a mission to Russia, with which he had been entrusted by the king.

[99] There are two English translations of the "Kalevala," those of Crawford and Kirby. There is also an English epitome of the narrative given in Comparetti: "The Traditional Poetry of the Finns," pp. 74–115. Longfellow seems to have borrowed the metre of Hiawatha from that of this poem.

ments instead of to the outside influences which had deeply modified the original contents of the old folk songs. The view is also now generally accepted that the very numerous magical songs practically all date from after the time when the Finns had been brought into contact with Christian teaching. [100]

To what extent, if any, the Finns had been brought into contact with Christianity before the crusade of St. Erik, about the middle of the twelfth century, can only be vaguely surmised. It is possible that there may have been some Finns associated with the Swedish traders using the Austvegr in Viking times, and that they may have come in touch with Christian merchants from other lands; the Finns in the course of their piratical expeditions may have captured some Christian slaves and from them have learnt something of the doctrines of Christianity; or again, the Swedish conquests in Finland in the time of Erik Segersäll may have introduced the inhabitants of the country to a form of Teutonic heathenism that had already had its beliefs modified to a limited extent by Christian influences. We know that Finnish heathenism shows decided traces of having incorporated ideas that were probably borrowed from the dwellers in the Swedish settlements founded in the land, [101] and it may thus have acquired at second-hand the first faint traces of Christian ideas.

During the course of St. Erik's expedition and Bishop Henry's missionary work many of the Finns accepted Christianity, if only nominally, and when the land again relapsed almost entirely into heathenism it is possible that the old faith became more or less coloured by the Christian teaching that had been received from the missionaries. If this were so, then Bishop Thomas, when undertaking the work of re-christianizing the land, had to encounter a heathen cult, which had come to contain a considerable admixture of its

[100] There is a prose translation of many of these songs in Abercromby: "The Pre- and Proto-historic Finns," II., pp. 65–389.

[101] Such place-names as Odensö, Torskulla, Friggesby, etc. apparently date back to the time of pre-Christian Swedish settlements. For Swedish immigration into south-west Finland, see Schütte: "The Gothonic Nations," pp. 408, 409.

D

Finns'
religion

opponents' beliefs. In giving then a brief account of Finnish
heathenism allowance has been made for this possibility, and
certain beliefs have been mentioned which were unknown to
the primitive cult, but were borrowed at some time from
Christianity, and which naturally underwent considerable
transformation in the course of their absorption.

The original religion of the Finns seems to have consisted
of a worship of departed spirits, and great respect was paid to
those persons who claimed to be able to communicate with
them by falling into a trance. Then it came to be thought
that the spirits could give information by means of certain
signs. Sieves with their bottoms divided into sections, each of
which corresponded with some particular meaning, were
largely used for the purpose of divination; a chip was placed
inside the sieve, which was then shaken, and according to the
section into which it fell, so was the answer to the enquiry.[102]
A further development, due almost certainly to Christian
influence, was the use of magical words and spells by means
of which evil spirits were rendered harmless; for to control
and banish an evil power it was only necessary to repeat to it
its name and to relate to it its history to render it impotent,[103]
and thus song gradually became the chief means employed in
all magical art, especially among the Karelians. So, too, the
belief in the activities of the spirits of the departed also underwent development, and eventually there came to be recognized
a very large number of divinities, controlling the lands, the
woods and the waters, and often confining their activities to
some very limited sphere, such as that of a particular homestead or a special species of tree[104]; in fact, every object in
Nature was supposed to have a protecting divinity, and each
homestead had also its *haltia,* with its supposed residence in
the roof tree. Each homestead, too, was the scene of the

---

[102] Saxén: "Finsk Guda- och Hjältetro," p. 5. In "Kalevala," XLIX.,
ll. 83ff., we have an example of divination by means of alder rods.

[103] Cp. "Kalevala," IX., ll. 270ff., where the flow of blood from the
wound of Väinämöinen is stayed by an aged man, who reviles the iron
of the axe that caused the wound, and relates to it its origin.

[104] E.g. Hongatar was the goddess of the fir-trees; Katajatar, nymph
of the juniper; and Pihlajatar, nymph of the mountain ash, a tree that
was held in special reverence.

activities of a *tonttu,* a capricious sprite, dwelling in the garrets or outhouses, and needing to be propitiated with offerings. [105]

The Finns believed in a god of the air, who was originally called Jumala, but afterwards was given the appellation Ukko (the Aged One). [106] He ruled the elements, letting his voice be heard in the thunder, having the lightning-flash for his sword, and sending the snow that mantled the earth in winter. On him depended the growth of the crops and the well-being of the cattle; but the later belief in him as creator of the universe seems to owe its origin to Christian influences, as in earlier times the conception of a supreme god was apparently absent from Finnish ideas of the universe. Partly responsible for the formation of the visible world were Väinämöinen and Ilmarinen, two beings whom it is difficult to classify, since they seem to represent either one-time divinities humanized into heroes, and then identified more or less with certain shadowy personages of the far past, or else simply men whose remarkable qualities caused them to be celebrated in song and then gradually to be endowed with yet loftier characteristics. [107]

As we might expect in a heavily forested land like Finland there were many woodland divinities, the chief of whom were Tapio, [108] with his tall pine hat and skin of tree moss, and his

[105] Belief in this sprite was evidently due to Swedish influence, the Finnish *tonttu* corresponding to the Swedish *tomte.*

[106] Among the old Finns the name Jumala seems to have been used in more than one sense—sometimes as equivalent to heaven, sometimes as the name of the god of heaven, and sometimes of deity in general. In the "Kalevala" Jumala and Ukko seem often to be used as synonyms: E.g. IX., ll. 403, 404. Ukko is given many titles, as The Thunderer, The Heavenly Father, The Golden King of the Air, etc.

[107] Castrén and Collan were of the opinion that Väinämöinen and Ilmarinen were originally gods, but Lönnrot thought otherwise, and it is now generally agreed that they were only heroes. For a discussion as to whether the "Kalevala" has a historical or a mythical foundation, see J. Krohn: "Finska Litteraturens Historia," I., pp. 439–46. His own judgment is that there is a small amount of historical matter in the poem, but less than in any other national epic. The more recent researches of Kaarle Krohn and others have served to strengthen belief in the importance of the historical element in the epic and have even caused it to be compared with Beowulf for the helpful light it throws upon the past.

[108] "Kalevala," XIV., ll. 153–72.

wife Mielliki, [109] who when she wished the hunter well showed herself decked with golden ornaments, but when unpropitious wore instead mere withes of twigs.   Not only did they grant success in hunting, but they acted as protectors to the cattle in their summer pasture grounds, and possessed a whole band of serving spirits who guarded the various objects in the woodlands.   In olden times, too, the bear, " the honey-pawed king of the forest," was greatly venerated by the Finns, as it was also by the Lapps; it was regarded as the holiest of all animals and special feasts were held in its honour. [110]   The waters, like the forests, had their special divinities, while a third group included those who were connected with the tilling of the soil or with pastoral occupations.   We need only mention Ahto, the waves' red-bearded lord, who with his foam-mantle-veiled wife, the good and beautiful Vellamo, ruled the sea and granted success in fishing, [111] and Kekri, who gave his blessing to cattle. [112]

The chief evil divinity was Hiisi, also called Lempo or Keitolainen. [113]   He was a mighty being who was first thought of as dwelling in dreary mountain caves, but afterwards came to be associated with the woodlands where he drove the bears and wolves as though they had been lambs.   It was possibly the great respect paid to him that led Christian missionaries to be particularly emphatic in denouncing his worship, and so eventually caused him to be regarded as the chief evil spirit.

Most of these woodland and kindred divinities would seem to date from a late period, possibly that in which the struggle between Christianity and heathenism was being carried on, and the same must be said of Päivätär and Kuutar, [114]

[109] " Kalevala," XIV., ll. 45–152.
[110] Holmberg: "Finno-Ugric and Siberian Mythology," pp. 97–8; and for the bear feasts of the Lapps, pp. 85–95. Cp. "E.R.E.," VI., p. 23.
[111] " Kalevala," V., ll. 23–34; XLII., ll. 531–4; XLVIII., ll. 123–50.
[112] Castrén: "Finsk Mytologi," p. 98. He is not mentioned in the "Kalevala."
[113] " Kalevala," IX., ll. 231–44; XII., ll. 273, 274.
[114] " Kalevala," IV., ll. 137–54; XLVIII., ll. 33, 34. They are said to have been invoked as protectors against wasp stings. Päivätär is identified by Ganander (p. 67) with the dawn.

daughters of the sun and moon respectively, for there are only the very faintest, if any, traces of worship of the heavenly bodies among the primitive Finns, although Agricola says that divine honour was paid to them in his time. The influence of Christianity upon the beliefs of the heathenism it encountered, and on the contents of the old folk-songs, has possibly been exaggerated; it seems, for example, rather difficult to believe that the account in the Kalevala of the flow of blood from Väinämöinen's wound is only a distortion of the Gospel narrative of the blood that issued from our Lord's side when pierced by the spear of the Roman soldier[115]; but recent investigators are probably right in their belief that not only the celestial divinities Luonnetar, Päivätär, Kuutar and Otavatar, but also Sukkamieli, the goddess of love, and Kiputytto,[116] the maiden of pain, derived ultimately from the great devotion paid in medieval times to the Blessed Virgin Mary under the differing aspects of Queen of Heaven, the Mater Dolorosa, etc., which naturally influenced the votaries of paganism when incorporating Christian ideas, though in a distorted form, with their own beliefs.

The Finnish conception of the universe included many other beings in addition to actual divinities. Mention has already been made of the *tonttu,* the capricious household sprite, whose activities contrasted so unfavourably with those of the *haltia;* there were also numerous giants, dwarfs, gnomes, nymphs, elves and such-like beings, some of them helpful, others harmful. There was also a widespread belief in the power of men to take the form of some animal. If a bear attacked cattle its action was attributed to some person having taken up his dwelling within it; if a man were changed into a wolf the creature was known as a *viron susi,* a term corresponding to the Swedish *var-ulv* and the old English were-wolf. [117]

Not much is known about Finnish heathen worship. Idols

---

[115] K. Krohn in " E.R.E.," VI., p. 640.
[116] " Kalevala," XLV., ll. 269–80. Sukkamiela is not mentioned in the poem.
[117] Saxén, pp. 17, 18.

seem to have been but little used, and, as in Sweden, there was no special class of priests. Worship, which consisted partly of prayers, partly of offerings, took place in the open air, though apparently there were enclosures set apart for it, as we find Pope Gregory IX. confirming the Church in the possession of groves and sacred places which had been given to it by converts.[118] When the worship of the dead was the outstanding characteristic of Finnish religion offerings to the departed were placed beside the place of their burial. Clothing, household utensils, and more particularly food supplies were thus provided. A later development was the holding of a sacrificial meal in the homestead and afterwards placing the remains of it on the grave so that the deceased person should have in the world in which he was now dwelling the use of an animal corresponding to the one that had been slaughtered to provide the meal. Such meals had to be repeated at intervals for the space of a year, after which the memorial of the dead person was transferred to the general feasts in honour of the dead, which were held on certain days of the year.[119]

When belief in woodland and similar divinities became general, sacrifices deemed appropriate were made to them, and the god of the forest received the first victim of the hunter's skill, the river spirit the fisherman's first catch. Certain trees, wells and stones were considered holy and offerings were placed beside them. As in Sweden, horses, and sometimes men, were offered in sacrifice.[120] Among the special feasts held in later times were one at the time of the spring sowing; another at harvest, when an unshorn lamb was killed and much feasting took place; and a third in late autumn, which was not only observed in memory of the dead, but also in honour of Kekri, the protector of cattle.[121]

[118] Sv. Dip., No. 251; Celse: "Bullarium," p. 62; Åbo D.S., No. 6; Spegel: "Skriftelige Bewis," No. 94; Potthast, No. 8329. Dated Jan. 31, 1229. Perugia.

[119] Saxén, pp. 6, 7.

[120] See letter of Pope Gregory IX. to the Archbishop of Uppsala. Sv. Dip., No. 298; Sv. Tr., No. 86; Celse: "Bullarium," p. 67; F.M.U., No. 82; Potthast, No. 10486. Dated Dec. 9, 1237. Lateran.

[121] For the Kekri feast, see Holmberg: "Finno-Ugric and Siberian Mythology," pp. 64–6.

Although influenced to some extent by its contact with Swedish heathenism, Finnish mythology had comparatively little in common with it. Of the Finnish divinities it has been said that " as persons they are rigid and lifeless, having neither loves, nor hatreds, nor wars. There is no society of gods and hence no place where they come together." [122] There are no counterparts in the Finnish system to the everyday life of the Æsir in the golden age and their meetings for counsel by the fountain of Urðr; to the feasting in Valhalla; to the adventures of Odin and Thor in the world of men; to the overwhelming of the gods on the fatal field of Vígríðr; and to the coming of a new heaven and earth wherein would dwell peace and righteousness. Whether this difference in the character of pagan beliefs in Finland made the work of the Christian missionaries there less difficult than it had been in Sweden cannot be said, for we have very few details of the struggle between the old and the new Faiths[123]; but the nominal conversion of Finland to Christianity was certainly accomplished in a far shorter space of time than was that of Sweden. In both lands, however, heathenism died hard, and we find belief in the old gods lasting down to quite recent times. [124]

[122] Comparetti: " The Traditional Poetry of the Finns," p. 182.

[123] There seems to be no mention of Finland in the Swedish chronicles after the expedition of St. Erik, about the middle of the twelfth century, until the time of the crusade of Birger Jarl, nearly a hundred years later.

[124] Lencqvist: " De Superstitione Fennorum," p. 82, gives an eighteenth century example of a man at Savolax, who, in order to secure success in hunting, cut his finger, collected the blood from the wound in an egg-shell, and buried the latter in an anthill as an offering to Tapio, god of the woods.

Dawson: " Age of the Gods," p. 282, note 1, mentions that Freyr actually appears by name in a trial that took place in 1720, as the central figure in the witches' assembly at Blåkulla, in Sweden.

CHAPTER III

THE INTRODUCTION OF CHRISTIANITY AND THE
HAMBURG-BREMEN MISSION

CHRISTIANITY was late in coming to Sweden, as indeed it was
to all the Scandinavian lands, and the tardiness of its arrival
was by no means compensated for by a speedy acceptance of
its truths, for, as has been already pointed out, the struggle
between the adherents of the old faith and those of the new
was a very lengthy one. Well over three hundred years had
elapsed since the time when the Gospel was first proclaimed
by the shores of Lake Mälar before its victory was completely
secured; and even then heathenism lingered for some time in
the more remote districts,[125] while it retained its hold over the
wandering Lapps of the far north for centuries longer.[126]

[125] We find, for example, that Pope Lucius III., when writing in 1181
to King Knut with regard to his appointment of Egidius to the see of
Västerås, says that he sends the bishop "ut eradicet paganismum,
exstirpet nociva, plantet Christianismum et similia salutaria, prout
quæque, secundum datam sibi a Deo prudentiam, viderit facienda et
omittenda." Sv. Dip. No. 94; P.L. 201, Lucius III., E. and P., No. 12;
Jaffé, No. 14544. Dated Dec. 30, 1181, Lateran.
  A few years previously Sverre of Norway when travelling through
Dalarne had found heathenism still prevailing there. "Sverris Saga,"
c. 12. "Jarnberaland is under the rule of the Swedes, and was at that
time a heathen band."
  [126] Various attempts to convert the Lapps were made from time to time.
In August, 1389, Queen Margaret, jointly with Archbishop Magnus of
Lund, addressed a Latin letter to them, urging them to give up
heathenism and embrace Christianity, the leading tenets of which were
clearly set forth. The Archbishop of Uppsala, too, was urged to undertake mission work among them, though it is not known if he actually did
so. The letter is given in Von Troil, I., p. 368.
  A little later, in the reign of Erik of Pomerania, we hear of a certain
Toste devoting his life to their evangelization, while the "Diarium
Wazstenense" under the year 1525 has the entry: "Eodem anno die
S. Gereonis (Oct. 10th), ex mandato Regis nostri Dni. Gostavi, exivit
frater Benedictus Petri, ad inducendum populum Lapponicum ad
divinum cultum." "S.R.S.," I., i., p. 319. Later efforts were made by
the Russian monks of the island monastery of Solowetzkoij, and by
King Charles IX., but met with only partial success. Even in 1873,
Von Duben ("Om Lappland och Lapparne," p. 426) could write that
the only traces one could find among the Lapps of the influence of the
Roman Catholic priests were the representation on their magical drums
of the Trinity, the Virgin Mary, and some of the saints, and obscure
hints of purgatory in their religion. Cp. Wijkmark: "Svensk kyrkohistoria," I., c. 7, and article on Lapp Mythology by Holmberg in
"E.R.E.," Vol. VII.

The lateness of the arrival of Christianity in the northern land was, however, natural enough, for missionaries could not be expected to visit the realms of the Swedes and the Goths while all their Baltic neighbours remained unevangelized and Norway was still heathen. We may wonder that the early missionary zeal of the Anglo-Saxon Church should have expended itself so largely on efforts in Western and Central Europe, and have left unapproached the land that, inhabited by a race near of kin to the conquerors of Britain, could be reached so easily across the waters of the North Sea. Had Norway been christianized early by English missionaries it is probable that the Swedes would have gained their first knowledge of the new faith from the same source. As it was, however, although the Anglo-Saxon Church could eventually claim—and claim with justice—to be the Mother Church of that of Norway, [127] Sweden had for over a century and a half contained within its borders a Christian community before the first English missionaries made their appearance there. Its position, however, with regard to both numbers and influence was so very insignificant as compared with that of heathenism, and the christianization of the land was so largely the work of English missionaries, that the indebtedness of Sweden to their labours, although they were not pioneers, is almost as great as that of the sister country. [128]

The Swedes seem to have become acquainted with the teachings of Christianity from three separate sources—from

[127] Willson: "History of Church and State in Norway," p. v. " The Church in Norway was the only daughter of that of England to be found in Europe."

Norwegian ecclesiastical historians fully acknowledge the indebtedness of their Church to that of England. Keyser: "Den norske kirkes historie under katholicismen," I., p. 31, "Den norske kirke var hel og holden en datter af den engelske." See also Taranger: "Den angelsakiske kirkes indflydelse paa den norske," p. 1 ; Bang: "Udsigt over den norske kirkes historie under katholicismen," pp. 37f. Some small share, however, in the conversion of Norway must be credited to the German missionaries, for Adam Br., Schol. 142, says "Licet ante illum (i.e. Bishop Sigurd) ex nostris Lifdag, Odinkar et Poppo gentem illam predicaverint. Possumus hoc dicere, quod nostri laboraverunt, et Angli in labores eorum introierunt."

[128] Porthan: "Juusten-Chronicon, Annot.," I., p. 105, speaks of the English Church as the mother of the Swedish ("illius matrem "). Cp. Lagerbring, I., xvi., 26.

captives taken on their plundering expeditions; from Frisian merchants, who, for purposes of commerce, either visited them or actually settled among them; and from certain of their own people, who, while sojourning in foreign lands as traders or military adventurers, had learnt something of Christian doctrine, and on their homecoming had imparted —though possibly with a certain amount of secrecy—their recently acquired knowledge to their friends and relations. [129]

Although on the whole the attachment of the people to their religious system was apparently both sincere and deep, in spite of the fact that scepticism had made a certain amount of headway, yet there were doubtless many among both Swedes and Goths who longed for a purer and more satisfying faith than that afforded by the old nature worship, with its semi-human deities and hideous sacrificial system, and so lent ready ears to the story of the White Christ and His teachings, with the result that they became anxious to acquire a fuller knowledge of the new faith. Thus it came about that in the year 829 [130] there came to the court of the Emperor, Louis the Pious, son of the great Charles, ambassadors from Sweden, [131] who told him how the doctrines of Christianity had reached their land, and expressed their desire for missionaries to be sent. [132] They had certainly made a wise choice in proffering their requests to Louis, for he had for some time been keenly interested in the conversion of the northern peoples, though he had no intention of trying to accomplish it by using the forcible methods that his father had employed

---

[129] "Camb. Med. Hist.," III., p. 313. "The earliest knowledge of Christianity probably came . . . with the extension of trade." See also Arup: "Danmarks Historie," I., pp. 120, 121, for the part played by merchants in the spread of Christianity, and cp. Kendrick: "History of the Vikings," p. 136.

[130] The year is not given by any of the old chroniclers, but it fits in well with certain recorded dates.

[131] Reuterdahl: "S.K.H.," I., pp. 198, 199, doubts if a formal embassy were sent, and thinks it probable that a viking or merchant ship happened to come to some place where the Emperor was staying. According to one account, the ambassadors were sent by King Emund, who at that time was reigning jointly with Björn, the king who actually received the first missionaries.

[132] Rimbert: "V. A.," c. 8.

in the case of the Saxons.[133]   It was in pursuance of this
desire that some years previously, in 822,[134] he had sent his
foster-brother, Ebo, Archbishop of Reims, to Rome in connection with the matter, and the latter had obtained from
Pope Paschal I. a bull by which he was appointed legate to
the Swedes, Danes, Slavs, and other northern nations, with a
view to their evangelization.[135]

Papal authority having been thus secured, Ebo betook
himself to Denmark, where he succeeded in forming the
beginnings of a Christian Church, and the work was further
helped by the appearance, about the year 826,[136] at the
Emperor's court at Ingelheim, near Mainz, of the Danish
Prince, Harald, who had come to ask the help of Louis against
his enemies, who had driven him from his principality.[137]
While at Ingelheim he, as well as his wife, his brother, and
several of his retinue, embraced Christianity, and at their
baptism the Emperor himself stood godfather to Harald.[138]

[133] Einhard : " Vita Caroli," cc. 7, 8.
[134] This seems to be the most probable date, though sometimes the
following year is given.   Ebo, however, would then seem to have been
already working as a missionary in Denmark. " Mon. Germ., II., Annales
Xantenses," " Anno 823, Ebo episcopus pergit partibus Danorum, una
cum Wildericho episcopo."
[135] Sv. Dip., No. 1 ; Sv. Tr., No. 1 ; Celse : " Bullarium," p. 5 ; Spegel :
" Skriftelige Bewis," p. 1 ; Hamb. U.B., No. 6 ; P.L. 129, Paschal I.,
Ep. No. 4 ; Jaffé, No. 2553.   No date. The Pope gives his reasons for
entrusting the mission to Ebo as follows : " Quia in partibus aquilonis
quasdam gentes consistere, quæ necdum agnitionem Dei habere, nec sacra
unda baptismatis sunt renatæ, sub umbra mortis existere, et magis crea-
turæ quam creatori ignava mente servire cognovimus ; idcirco præsentem
reverendissimum fratrem ac co-episcopum nostrum Ebonem sanctæ
Rhemensis ecclesiæ archiepiscopum, necessarium cum consensu fidelium
Dei duximus, illis in partibus pro illuminatione veritatis dirigendum."
[136] The Annales Esromenses (" S.R.D.," I., p. 228) give 826. The
Necrologium Lundense (" S.R.D.," III., No. 90) has the entry " Anno
Domini DCCCXXVII Haraldus Rex Dacie primus, Maguntie baptizatus
est."
[137] Rimbert : " V. A.," c. 6. " Post hæc vero contigit, ut Herioldus
quidam rex, qui partem tenebat Danorum, ab aliis ipsius Provinciæ
Regibus, odio et inimicitia conventus, regno suo expulsus est."   Harald
would seem to have ruled part of southern Jutland.
[138] Rimbert : " V. A.," c. 6 ; Adam Br., I., c. 17 ; " S.R.D.," I., No. 27.
Ermoldus Nigellus : " Narratio metrica de baptismo Haraldi Danorum
Regis."   This poem, which seems to have been written about a year
after the event, gives a full account of Harald's baptism. It is taken
from Book IV. of the author's " Carmen Elegiacum."   See also
" S.R.D.," I., Nos. 4, 5, 13.

Louis was anxious to send back with him a number of Christian missionaries, but he was emphatic that they must be volunteers, and so must have been delighted when he was informed by Walo, Abbot of New Corbey,[139] that one of his monks, named Anskar, was the very man for the task, as he was eager to win the crown of martyrdom.

On being summoned to the court Anskar expressed his willingness to undertake the mission,[140] and shortly afterwards, accompanied by a fellow monk named Autbert, went back with Harald to his native land.   The latter, however, seems to have been unable to secure recognition north of the Eider, and so had to content himself with the rule of southern Jutland and the Frisian district of Rüstringen, which had been conferred on him by the Emperor, nominally to secure him a place of refuge if he needed one, but possibly to attach him more closely to Louis and also to secure the region against Viking attacks.   It seems probable that Anskar laboured at the important trading town of Hedeby, situated not far from the modern Schleswig.[141]   He set up a school for which he procured pupils by purchasing them, but before very long the work was interrupted by Autbert falling ill and having to return to Corbey, while a little later Anskar was again summoned to the Emperor's court in order to be asked to undertake the mission to Sweden which was called for in response to the request of the recent embassy.[142]

[139] Walo was a grandson of the famous Frankish king, Charles Martel. The monastery of New Corbey in Westphalia was founded by monks from the parent house of Corbie, near Amiens, during the time of St. Adelhard, the ninth abbot.   Corbie monastery was founded in 657 by St. Bathilde, widow of King Clovis II. of Neustria.   See "Cath. Enc.," IV., p. 355, Art. "Corbie."

[140] Rimbert: "V. A.," c. 6; Adam Br., I., c. 17.

[141] For Hedeby, see Arup: "Danmarks Historie," I., pp. 119–21; Wadstein: "Norden och Väst-Europa i Gammal Tid.," pp. 54–62.

[142] Rimbert: "V. A.," c. 8. Later on the monk Gislemar was sent to take his place with Harald (Porro cum Herioldo esse disposuit Patrem devotissimum Gislemarum).   Certain old writers assert that Harald apostatized. Annales Esromenses, "S.R.D.," I., p. 238, "DCCCXXXII. Tunc Haraldus rediit in Daciam, et dimisit cristianitatem, et accepit regnum suum." Ericus Olai: "Chronica, S.R.S.," II., i., p. 26, "Demum Harallus apostatavit a fide, videns se non posse temporaliter prosperari."   Petrus Olai: "Annales, S.R.D.," I., No. 16, has the entry, "846. Haraldus Klag Rex Danorum obiit, regnavit annis XX."

Anskar, undeterred by his small success in Denmark, and the thought of the far more formidable journey now necessitated, agreed to make this further missionary effort.[143] Again he was successful in securing a fellow monk, Witmar, as a companion, and after an adventurous journey—partly by sea, partly by land, and partly by lake—in the course of which they were attacked by pirates and robbed of almost all their possessions, including the gifts of the Emperor,[144] they succeeded in reaching Birka, the great trading port on Lake Mälar.[145]

The king, Bero or Björn,[146] received Anskar kindly, and, with the consent of his chief men, permitted him to preach and baptize, while the missionaries also ministered to the numerous captives in the towns.[147] Björn himself does not seem to have accepted the new teaching,[148] but Anskar made a number of converts, among them Herigar, the chief of the district and a trusted counsellor of the king,[149] who built a

---

[143] Rimbert: "V. A.," c. 9; Adam Br., I., c. 17. According to some of the older Swedish ecclesiastical historians Anskar was not the first Christian missionary to visit Sweden, but a certain Herbert is said to have been sent there by Charlemagne, about the year 813, and to have worked with great success among the East Goths. He is even credited with having founded the cathedral of Linköping. See Johannes Magni: "Hist. Met., S.R.S.," III., ii., p. 6; Messenius: "Chronicon Episcoporum," p. 2; Vastovius: "Vitis Aquilonia," p. 1; Baaz: "Inventarium," I., iv., p. 88; Örnhjälm: "H. E.," I., iii., v.; Rameen, c. 1; Olaus Petri, writing at an earlier date than any of these authors does not mention him. The mistake probably arose through antedating the work of Herbert, the first bishop of Linköping, who seems to have lived towards the end of the eleventh century. See Benzelius: "Mon. Vet.," pp. xxx.–xliv.; Rhyzelius: "Epis.," I., p. 100; "Chronicon Rhythmicum Episcoporum Lincopensium, S.R.S.," III., ii., p. 104.

[144] Rimbert: "V. A.," c. 9.

[145] See Note 18.

[146] He seems to have reigned jointly with another king named Emund.

[147] Rimbert: "V. A.," c. 10. "Multi etiam apud eos captivi habebantur Christiani, qui gaudebant jam tandem se mysteriis divinis posse participare."

[148] Johannes Magni: "Gothorum Sveonumque Historia," XVII., c. 16, says: "Cum tamen compertum sit, Beronem ejus nominis secundum . . . fidē Christi (ut dictum est) suscepisse, & in ejus vera confessione animam exhalasse. . . ." But if this had been indeed the case surely Rimbert would have recorded the fact.

[149] Rimbert: "V. A.," c. 10. He styles him "Prefectus vici ipsius et Conciliarius Regis."

church on his lands and did all in his power to further the spread of Christianity.

After a stay of about a year and a half[150] Anskar returned to Germany in the year 831,[151] in order to acquaint the Emperor with the progress of the mission, and to report favourably on its prospects for the future. Louis was greatly pleased, and, after a consultation with his chief advisers, decided to erect a see at Hamburg, whose occupant would have general oversight of the missions in northern lands, and to appoint Anskar, whose character would seem to have greatly impressed his contemporaries,[152] as the first archbishop.[153] The latter was then consecrated the same year,[154] by Drogo of Metz, assisted by the Archbishops of Reims, Mainz and Trier, and the Bishops of Bremen and Verden, after which he journeyed to Rome, where the pallium was conferred on him by Pope Gregory IV. who, in his confirmatory bull,[155] while urging him to work for the conversion of the northern peoples, does not withdraw the legatine authority previously given to Ebo, but joins him with Anskar in the exercise of it,

[150] Rimbert: "V. A.," c. 11. "Peracto apud eos altero dimidio anno."

[151] This seems the most probable date. Ericus Olai: "Chronica, S.R.S.," II., i., p. 24, gives the date of Anskar's visit to Sweden as 845. Johannes Magni: "Hist. Met., S.R.S.," III., ii., p. 7, gives his reasons for thinking this incorrect, and puts the date about 816. Baaz: "Inventarium," I., iv., p. 88, follows him in doing this. Örnhjälm: "H.E.," I., v., p. 13, points out how Johannes Magni has been deceived by the authority of Lupoldus and himself suggests 831. Messenius: "Chronicon Episcoporum," gives 828, and in his "Scondia Illustrata," I., p. 64, places his return in 830. Lagerbring: "S.R.H.," I., 16, 7, gives 829.

[152] The author of the "Vita Rimberti, S.R.D.," II., No. 49, c. 2, styles him "summæ Sanctitatis vir." Robinson: "Anskar, The Apostle of the North," p. 7, says that "in the character presented to us by his biographer we have a singularly attractive combination of transparent humility, unflinching courage, complete self-devotion and unwavering belief in a loving and over-ruling Providence."

[153] Rimbert: "V. A.," c. 11 ; Adam Br., I., c. 18.

[154] Adam Br., I., c. 18, says, however, "Hoc factum est anno Domini 832, qui est Ludvici imperatoris 18, Willerici Bremensis episcopi 43."

[155] Sv. Dip., No. 3 ; Sv. Tr., No. 3 ; Celse: "Bullarium," p. 11 ; Spegel: "Skriftelige Bewis," No. 1 ; Hamb. U.B., No. 9 ; Curschmann, No. 1 ; Jaffé, No. 2574: Undated ; probably 832 (Sv. Dip. gives 835). There is a Danish translation in Jörgensen, p. 107.

though without assigning different regions to each.[156] The Emperor also in 834 issued a diploma entrusting the northern mission to Anskar and assigning to him as an endowment for the diocese the estate of Turholt in Flanders.[157]

The two archbishops seem to have worked harmoniously together during the time that Ebo retained his see,[158] and as Anskar's new office did not at present permit of his return to Sweden they joined to consecrate Gautbert,[159] the nephew of Ebo, who took the name of Simon, as bishop for Sweden.[160] At first Gautbert's mission seemed likely to be successful, for he too was kindly received by Björn and his subjects, and a church was built at Birka; possibly the one built by Herigar had suffered destruction, or, if still existing, was not considered suitable for the new mission.

But before long an insurrection broke out, possibly owing to the anti-Christian bias of the joint king, Emund; possibly, as Örnhjälm conjectures,[161] fomented by *bonder* acting as priests, who were willing to admit Christ among the gods, but refused to allow sole honour to be paid to Him. Gautbert's nephew, Nithard, was murdered, thus becoming Sweden's

[156] "Ipsumque filium nostrum, jam dictum Ansgarium, legatum in omnibus circumquaque gentibus Suenonum sive Danorum nec non etiam Slavorum, vel in cæteris ubicunque illis in partibus constitutis divina pietas ostium aperuerit, una cum Ebone Rhemensi archiepiscopo, statuentes ante corpus et confessionem sancti Petri, publicam evangelizandi tribuimus auctoritatem."

[157] Sv. Dip., No. 2; Sv. Tr., No. 4; Celse: "Bullarium," p. 8. Dated May 15, 834. "Et ut hæc nova constructio periculosis in locis cœpta subsistere valeret, nec prævalente barbarorum sævitia deperiret, quandam cellam Turholt nuncupatam tam huic novæ constructioni perenniter servituram, quam suæ successorumque suorum in gentibus legationi ad nostram nostræque sobolis perpetuam mercedem divinæ obtulimus majestati."

[158] He was deposed by the Synod of Thionville (Diedenhofen) in 835 for disloyalty to the Emperor, and placed in solitary confinement in the Abbey of Fulda. Later he recovered his see for a short time (840–1), and eventually died Bishop of Hildesheim, 851. See Mann: "P.M.A.," II., p. 246; Cath. Enc., Art. "Ebo."

[159] Other forms of the name are Gauzbert, Gozbert, Gosbert and Gosbrecht.

[160] Adam Br., I., c. 19. "Hic (Ebo) seu fatigatione itineris, sive corporis debilitate impeditus, sive potius occupatione seculi delectatus, vicarium pro se dedit Ansgario nepotem Gaudbertum. Quem ipsi ambo consecrantes episcopum vocaverunt Symonem, eumque divinæ gratiæ commendatum in Sueoniam miserunt." See also Rimbert: "V.A.," c. 13.

[161] Örnhjälm: "H. E.," I., x., p. 24.

first Christian martyr, [162] and he himself, though against the will of the king, was driven from the country. [163] He became Bishop of Osnabrück, one of the sees founded by Charlemagne in the eighth century, [164] and as he could not be persuaded to return to Sweden, though retaining his rights as bishop and legate, the little Christian community was left for seven years without a priest. Herigar, however, still laboured nobly, and eventually Anskar found another agent in the person of a hermit named Ardgar, who worked at Birka until the death of Herigar, when he too withdrew, [165] and the Christian community was again left shepherdless.

Meanwhile Anskar in his diocese had experienced much trouble. The estate of Turholt was taken from him on the death of Louis, and in 845 Danish pirates under King Horik of Jutland sailed up the Elbe and burnt Hamburg. Cathedral, monastery, and library all perished in the flames, and Anskar himself barely escaped with his life. [166] In consequence of this disaster it was decided to unite the bishoprics of Hamburg and Bremen, [167] making the latter the see city, but keeping the name of Hamburg for the diocese, and although some opposition to the scheme was offered by the Archbishop of Cologne, who was reluctant to lose one of his suffragan sees,

[162] Johannes Magni: "Hist. Met., S.R.H.," III., ii., p. 8, makes Gautbert also killed, an evident error.

[163] Rimbert: "V. A.," c. 15; Adam Br., I., c. 23.

[164] Lavisse: "Hist. de France," II., i., p. 291. Osnabrück was apparently the first bishopric founded by Charlemagne among the Saxons, and had as its first bishop St. Wiho (785—804). The see, however, does not seem to have been properly organized till the time of his successor, Meginhard. See Hauck: "K. D.," II., p. 675, note 6; "Cath. Enc.," XI., p. 341, Art. "Osnabrück."

[165] Rimbert: "V. A.," cc. 16, 18. Schmid: "Sveriges Kristnande," p. 38, points out that Ardgar is the only hermit ever mentioned in connection with the history of the Church in Sweden.

[166] Rimbert: "V. A.," c. 14; Adam Br., I., c. 23. The "Annales Islandorum, S.R.D.," II., No. 45, give 842 as the date.

[167] The see of Bremen was founded by a decree of Charlemagne dated July 14, 787, Spires. It is given in the "Bremisches Urkundenbuch," No. 1. See also "S.R.D.," I., No. 24, "De Ecclesia Bremensi." On the death of Leuderich, about 846, Anskar became Bishop of Bremen. The archbishopric of Cologne was vacant at the time, but after Gunther had been appointed to it in 850, Anskar requested his approval of the union of the sees, and his refusal to grant it caused the Emperor's interference. See Adam Br., I., c. 29; Rimbert: "V. A.," c. 19.

it was eventually overcome, and as a result Pope Nicholas I. issued a bull,[168] by which he confirmed the union,[169] and gave to Anskar and his successors authority over the Swedes, Danes, Slavs, and other northern peoples.[170]

Some years before this took place Anskar had found time, in spite of his many cares of office, to pay a second visit to Sweden.[171] This time he came not merely in his capacity of overseer of the Church in the North, but also as a messenger of the rulers of Denmark and Germany.[172] Again it was to Birka that he made his way, but he was not as favourably received by King Olov as he had been by his predecessor Björn on his first visit. Before deciding on his attitude

[168] Sv. Dip., No. 6; Sv. Tr., No. 8; Celse: "Bullarium," p. 13; Örnhjälm: "H. E.," I., xxvi., p. 98; Hamb. U.B., No. 14; Bremisches Urkundenbuch, No. 5; Curschmann, No. 4; Jaffé, No. 2759. Dated May 31, 858, (864) Rome. It is difficult to say which year is the true date. Mann: "P.M.A.," II., p. 220, note 2, says "That this bull was issued in 864 is clear from its chronological data." This is certainly true, provided that these dates have not been tampered with. The difficulty is to make the date 864 agree with the statement of Adam of Bremen who says the bull was issued seven years before the death of Anskar (I., c. 36), and the latter is almost universally acknowledged to have taken place in 865. For a full discussion of the claims of the respective dates see Rydberg: Sv. Tr., I., pp. 26–9.

[169] "Quamobrem auctoritate omnipotentis Dei et beatorum apostolorum Petri et Pauli, et hoc nostro decreto, decernimus secundum reverentissimi regis Hludouuici votum, ipsas predictas diœceses, Hammaburgensem scilicet et Bremensem, non deinceps duas, sed unam esse et vocari subdique sedi, quæ predecessoris nostri decreto archiepiscopali est munere sublimata, restituta dumtaxat et Bremensis ecclesiæ rebus episcopatui Ferdensi parte inde ante ablata. Nullus vero archiepiscopus Coloniensis ullam sibi deinceps in eadem dioecesi vindicet potestatem."

[170] ". . . ipsumque filium nostrum, jam dictum Anskarium, legatum in omnibus circumquaque gentibus Sueonum sive Danorum nec non etiam Slavorum, vel in ceteris, ubicunque illis in partibus constitutis divina pietas ostium aperuerit, publicam evangelizandi tribuimus auctoritatem; ipsamque sedem Nordalbingorum, Hammaburch dictam, in honore sancti Salvatoris sanctæque ejus intemeratæ genetricis Mariæ consecratam, archiepiscopalem deinceps esse decernimus, atque ut strenui predicatoris episcopi post decessum crebro dicti Anskarii archiepiscopi personæ tantoque officio apta eligatur semper successio, sub divini judicii obtestatione statuimus."

Anskar had been previously confirmed in his authority by Pope Leo IV. in March, 848. Sv. Dip., No. 5 (dated 849); Sv. Tr., No. 6; Celse: "Bullarium," p. 12; Hamb. U.B., No. 13; Curschmann, No. 3; P.L. 129, Leo. IV., E. and P., No. 1; Jaffé, No. 2579.

[171] Rimbert: "V. A.," cc. 22–7; Adam Br., I., c. 28. The date of this second visit is uncertain, but as it was some time before the death of Gautbert it was probably undertaken about the year 848.

[172] Rimbert: "V. A.," c. 23.

E

towards the archbishop, the king, together with his nobles, resolved to ascertain the will of the gods by means of casting lots.[173] However, the oracle gave a favourable answer, and after twice consulting his subjects, the king gave leave for the continuance of the mission, and gave a hall for use as a church.[174]

One thing that helped largely to procure the favourable decision was the speech of an old man, who reminded the assembly that the God of the Christians had already shown Himself helpful to seafarers in distress, and it would be useful to have another God as helper in time of need in case the old gods should at any time refuse their assistance—a speech that from its utilitarian selfishness calls to remembrance that of the priest Coifi at the council summoned by Edwin of Northumbria in 627 to hear Paulinus declare the Christian Faith.[175]

Anskar, however, was naturally unable to make a lengthy stay in Sweden, so after placing in charge of the mission a priest named Erimbert, another nephew of Gautbert,[176] he returned to Germany. He still retained a keen interest in the little Christian community at Birka, and seems to have sent to it at least three further missionaries.[177] The first of these, a Danish priest named Ansfrid, returned to Germany on hearing of the death of Gautbert; Raginbert, who was next sent, was murdered by Danish pirates on his way to Sweden; but the third, Rimbert, another Dane, who seems to have been consecrated bishop by Anskar before his departure, and who must not be confused with his namesake, the biographer and successor of the archbishop, was still working there at the time

---

[173] Rimbert: "V. A.," c. 24. There is an interesting excursus on sortilage in " C.P.B.," I., p. 411. Divination by rods seems to have been the most usual mode of enquiry in the North, but at Uppsala it was apparently carried out by means of twigs dipped in a bowl containing the blood of a sacrificed victim, and afterwards thrown on a white sheet.

[174] Rimbert: "V. A.," c. 25.

[175] Bede: " Eccles. Hist.," II., c. 13 ; Henry of Huntingdon, sub anno 627.

[176] Rimbert: "V. A.," c. 25 ; Adam Br., I., c. 28. The old Swedish version of the " V.A." calls him the nephew of Anskar.

[177] Rimbert: "V. A.," c. 29.

of his death.   This took place at Bremen in 865,[178] and shortly after it the " Apostle of the North," the title by which Anskar is perhaps best known, was canonized by Pope Nicholas I.

Not long before his death Anskar had sent to the different bishops in German territories a short account of the Swedish mission, at the same time asking for their sympathetic help in the extension of the work.[179]   But in spite of this, very little interest seems to have been shown in the matter either in Germany or at Rome.

The period following the death of Anskar was one of the darkest in the history of Christianity and of civilization in Europe.   The division of the empire of Charlemagne among his three grandsons by the Treaty of Verdun in 843 had been followed by further sub-divisions,[180] and the various kingdoms that had eventuated—precursors partially of the national monarchies that were presently to develop—in the brief intervals of war one with another were often engaged in repelling the ravages of the Danish pirates, the Hungarians, or the Saracens, tasks that were largely accountable for the rapid rise of the feudal system, which though it provided the different lands with efficient defenders against external foes, was later to be responsible for much internal anarchy.   The Popes, too, were at first not only busy in endeavouring to extend their power in Germany, but were called on to take part in the work of defending southern Italy from Moham-medan aggression;   while with the death of John VIII. (872 —882), the last able pontiff of this period, the Papacy was within a few years of entering on the time that was to bring to it indelible disgrace.

Many factors had combined to raise the Papacy to the exalted position it now occupied :   the world-wide importance of Rome, which naturally increased the prestige of its bishop, especially when the fall of the Western Empire left him the

---

[178] Rimbert : " V. A.," c. 34.

[179] Sv. Dip. No. 7 ; " S.R.S.," II., i., p. 260.   Undated.   There is an English translation in Wordsworth ; " N.C.S.," p. 56.

[180] For the disruption of the Carolingian Empire, see " Camb. Med. Hist.," III., cc. 1–3 ; Lavisse and Rambaud : " Histoire Générale," II., i., pp. 358–94.

most important person in Italy; the fact that he was regarded as the successor of St. Peter, the Prince of the Apostles; the record of the part played by the Roman patriarchate in doctrinal controversies; the acquirement of territorial juris-diction, together with the clever way in which Papal policy had balanced one Italian power against another; the increasing practice of appealing to Papal arbitration for the settlement of disputes; and the growth of feudalism, with its reaction on contemporary ideas in regard to the hierarchy of the Church.

But for a century and a half this exalted position—gradually won by the efforts of such pontiffs as Leo I., the first three Gregories, Stephen II. and Nicholas I.—was to suffer severe degradation, and the head of Western Christen-dom—unless himself a violent, unscrupulous man—was to become as a rule little more than the protégé, first of one or other of the factions at Rome, then of the German emperor, and finally of the Counts of Tusculum, while the state of the Papal court was to make it the scandal of Christendom.[181]

The shadows of the period may indeed have been unduly deepened by many historians[182]; the condemnations of the

---

[181] For the Popes of this period (891—1046) see Mann: "P.M.A.," IV., V; also "Camb. Med. Hist.," III., c. 7; V., c. 1.

[182] E.g. Gregorovius: "History of the City of Rome," III., p. 227. "The Popes, clergy, nobles and people of Rome lived in a state of barbarism, than which nothing more shocking can be imagined." Bryce: "The Holy Roman Empire," p. 527. "Rome relapsed into a state of profligacy and barbarism to which, even in that age, Europe supplied no parallel. . . . For more than a century the chief priest of Christendom was no more than a tool of some ferocious faction among the nobles. Criminal means had raised him to the throne; violence, sometimes going the length of mutilation or murder, deprived him of it."
Some Roman Catholic writers are equally emphatic. Fortescue: "The Orthodox Eastern Church," p. 172. "During [the] long period of a century and a half there is hardly one, perhaps not one, Pope who was even an ordinarily good bishop. It is a long story of simoniacal elec-tions, murder and violence of every kind, together with shameless lust." Dawson "The Making of Europe," p. 272. "The Holy See had become the puppet of a demoralized and truculent oligarchy. . . it reached the lowest depths of degradation."
Compare these statements with that of Mann: "P.M.A.," V., p. 295. "Thirty-seven pontiffs filled the chair of Peter from the death of Stephen (891) to the accession of St. Leo IX. (1049). Of these, con-sidering them strictly as Popes and not taking into account what they may have been before they became such, the impartial verdict of history cannot condemn as really a disgrace to their sacred calling more than four at most."

occupants of the Papal chair may have erred by their sweeping nature and their failure to distinguish sufficiently between the characters of the individual popes, for if the Papal line included such utterly unworthy persons as John XII. and Benedict IX., it also included the " holy, wise and virtuous " Gregory V. and Sylvester II., the most remarkable prelate of his age; due allowance may not have been made for the fact that none of the popes, however unworthy, used his position to promulgate heresy or to deny the cardinal doctrines of the Christian Faith; nor must it be forgotten that even in the worst times the Papal office still inspired respect in distant lands. But the shadows were deep enough, the lowering of prestige real enough, the state of ecclesiastical affairs at Rome disreputable enough, to make this period, with one possible exception, the worst in the whole history of the Papacy. In circumstances such as these what wonder that an obscure mission in a little-known northern land—a mission, too, that had never thoroughly taken root—should suffer badly.

And so between the time of the death of Anskar and the later years of the reign of Erik Segersäll, the father of Olov Skötkonung, the first Christian king, we not only know little of the general history of Sweden, but even less about the Christian Church there. Now and again shadowy figures— at one time a king, at another time a bishop—emerge for a brief space of time from the general obscurity, but the chronology of the period is terribly confused, and it is not always easy to say how much there is of truth in the few accounts that have come down to us of the events of these times.

Rimbert, the friend and biographer of Anskar, and like him a Frank by birth, was chosen to succeed him as archbishop, and was appointed to the see in December, 865, by a bull of Pope Nicholas I. [183] A few years later Adrian II. made him legate for the whole North, and urged him to work for the

---

[183] Sv. Dip., No. 8; Celse: "Bullarium," p. 13; Hamb. U.B., No. 19; Curschmann, No. 6; P.L. 119, Nicholas I., E. and P., No. 87; Jaffé, No. 2798. See also "Vita Rimberti," c. 11.

conversion of the Swedes, Danes and Norwegians, [184] and it would seem that he visited Sweden, [185] though the language of his biographer is so vague that it may merely refer to his having accompanied Anskar on his second missionary journey. [186]   After his death at Bremen in 888, [187] nothing was

[184] Sv. Dip., No. 9; Sv. Tr., No. 9; Celse: "Bullarium," p. 14; Hamb. U.B., No. 20; Curschmann, No. 7; Jaffé, No. 2953 (in first edition, Lit. Sp., No. 346). Dated, Nov. 872, Rome. The genuineness of the bull has been questioned, and we may note here that several others of the bulls relating to the confirmation of the archbishops of the Hamburg-Bremen see are placed by Jaffé among the *Literæ Spuriæ* at the end of his work.   On the other hand, Mann: "Lives of the Popes," VI., pp. 84–5, says: "Although objections are urged against the Hamburg-Bremen series of papal bulls, from that of Gregory IV. to the one in question (of Leo IX.), there can be no doubt that, if some of them have been interpolated in the matter of details as to the exact countries subject to the united see, they are substantially authentic."   The interpolations referred to by Dr. Mann would seem to have been inserted at a time when the archbishops saw their authority in northern lands seriously threatened, and so falsified existing documents in order to strengthen their claims.   For instance, the bull of Gregory IV. in 832 making Anskar legate "in omnibus circumquaque gentibus Sveonum sive Danorum, nec non etiam Slavorum," has been interpolated to read "Ansgarium et successores ejus legatos in omnibus circumquaque gentibus Danorum, Sueonum, Norvehorum, Farrie, Gronlondan, Halsingalondan, Islondan, Scridevindun, Slavorum, necnon omnium septentrionalium, et orientalium nationum, quocunque modo nominatarum, delegamus, et posito capite et pectore super corpus et confessionem sancti Petri apostoli sibi suisque successoribus vicem nostram perpetuo retinendam publicamque evangelizandi tribuimus auctoritatem."   That Greenland was first discovered by either Gunbjörn or Erik the Red over a century later shows the falsity of the interpolation; while although there were Irish monks in Iceland before this time, it is very doubtful whether the Pope was acquainted with the fact.   Schmeidler: "Hamburg-Bremen und Nordost-Europa," II., pp. 128–59, thinks that Archbishop Adalbert may have been responsible for the falsification of the bulls of Gregory IV. and Nicholas I.   F. Curschmann in "Die älteren Papsturkunden des Erzbistums Hamburg" has critically examined twenty-five of these papal letters from that of Gregory IV. to that of Alexander II. with respect to writing material, the agreement of the style with that of the Curia's "Liber Diurnus," and the facts recorded as compared with other sources, as Adam of Bremen's "History of the Archbishops of Hamburg."   For a convenient summary of his principal conclusions see Schmid: "Sveriges Kristnande," pp. 28–32.

[185] Adam Br., I., c. 62.   "Bircam . . . post obitum sancti Ansgarii annis LXX. nemo doctorum ausus est pertingere præter solum, ut legimus, Rimbertum."

[186] "Vita Rimberti," c. 20.   "Fertur etiam antiquorum more sanctorum quædam fecisse miracula, frequenter videlicet, dum iret ad Sueoniam, tempestatem maris orationibus suis sedasse. . . ."   Reuterdahl: "S.K.H.," I., p. 172, well remarks about the anonymous "Vita Rimberti" that it is more of a panegyric than a history, more a description of the services rendered to mankind by the worthy archbishop than a detailed account of his life.   Cp. also Schmid: "Sveriges Kristnande," p. 41.

[187] "Vita Rimberti," cc. 22, 23; M.G.H. SS. III. Annales Corbienses, "888 Rimbertus archiepiscopus obiit."

apparently done to aid the little Christian community at Birka. Adalgar, his successor, after having been confirmed in the rights of his see by Pope Stephen V., [188] seemed likely to be deprived of them a few years later by a bull of Pope Formosus. [189] The Archbishop of Cologne had again brought forward his claim to jurisdiction over the see of Bremen, and at a synod held at Frankfort, which was presided over by Hatto, Archbishop of Mainz, [190] all the suffragan bishops declared unanimously that until the time of Adalgar the see of Bremen had always been dependent on that of Cologne. Formosus was informed of the synod's findings, and as Adalgar neither went to Rome himself, nor sent any representative to state his side of the case, the Pope compromised; for the present matters were to remain as they were, but the diocese of Bremen was to return to its old position as a suffragan see of Cologne as soon as Christianity had made such progress among the heathen that the see of Hamburg would have its own suffragan bishops. But the old archbishop lived to recover his original privileges, for Pope Sergius III. reversed the decree of his predecessor by confirming what Nicholas I. and other popes had decreed with regard to the authority of the Church of Hamburg over the Danes, Northmen, Swedes and other northern peoples, and reaffirming the union of Bremen and Hamburg. [191]

---

[188] Sv. Dip., No. 10; Sv. Tr., No. 10; Celse: "Bullarium," p. 14; Hamb. U.B., No. 24; Curschmann, No. 9; P.L. 129, Stephen V., No. 1; Jaffé, No. 3461 (1st ed., Lit. Sp., No. 351). Dated May, 891, Rome (Jaffé, 885–91). In Sv. Dip., Sv. Tr., Celse and Jaffé the Pope is styled Stephen VI.

[189] Sv. Dip., No. 11; Celse: "Bullarium," p. 14; Örnhjälm: "H.E.," II., i., p. 109; Hamb. U.B., No. 25; Curschmann, No. 10; P.L. 129, Formosus, No. 5; Jaffé, No. 3487. Dated 892 (Örnhjälm, Jaffé, 893; Sv. Dip., Hamb. U.B., 895).

[190] This is the famous Hatto, who, according to the German legend, was eaten by mice which swam across the Rhine to his castle. He had been a strong supporter of the Emperor Conrad I. and of the union of the German states under one head, and according to another account, died of a broken heart on hearing of the triumph of Henry, Duke of Saxony. For the Synod see Mann: "P.M.A.," IV., pp. 64–6.

[191] Sv. Dip., No. 12; Sv. Tr., No. 11; Celse: "Bullarium," p. 14; Hamb. U.B., No. 26; Curschmann, No. 11; P.L. 131, Sergius III., E.

We have only a vague general statement that Adalgar performed his duties in regard to the northern nations, and of his successors, Hoger [192] and Reginward, we know nothing in this respect, but Archbishop Unni, whose pallium was sent him by Pope John X., [193] and who, like Anskar, Rimbert, Adalgar and Hoger, had been a monk of Corbey, after working successfully in Jutland and the Danish islands came to Sweden, and with considerable difficulty made his way to Birka, where he found that Christianity had almost completely died out. [194] We have very few details of his mission, but he seems to have preached with success, making a number

and P., No. 4; Jaffé, No. 3537. Dated Feb. 2nd, 905, Rome (Jaffé, Feb. 1st; Curschmann, 906-8).

"Quicquid autem a beato Nicolao papa et ceteris predecessoribus nostris Hammaburgensi ecclesiæ concessum est, scilicet habere archiepiscopalem potestatem in regna Danorum, Noruenorum, Suenorum et omnium septentrionalium nacionum, et Bremensem ecclesiam et ipsam Hammaburgensem ecclesiam non duas, sed unam esse ecclesiam et parrochiam, decernimus et confirmamus."

[192] The confirmatory bull of Pope Sergius III. for Hoger (Sv. Dip., No. 13; Celse: "Bullarium," p. 15; Hamb. U.B., No. 27; Curschmann, No. 12; P.L. 131, Sergius III., E. and P., No. 8; Jaffé, No. 3549. Dated May 19th, 911, Rome. [Jaffé, Curschmann, June 1st]) is interesting because the Pope gives an explanation of the importance of the Pallium. "Pallium autem sanctitati tuæ ad missarum solemnia celebranda, ex more, transmisimus, quod tibi non aliter, Ecclesiæ tuæ privilegiis in suo statu manentibus, uti largimur, nisi solummodo in die sanctæ ac venerandæ resurrectionis domini nostri Jesu Christi, seu in Natalitiis Sanctorum Apostolorum atque beati Baptistæ Johannis, nec non in assumtione sanctæ Dei genetricis Mariæ, simulque in dominicæ domini nostri Jesu Christi nativitatis die, pariterque in solempnitatis Ecclesiæ tuæ die, et natalicii tui die, sicut a prædecessore nostro domino Gregorio, hujus almæ sedis præsule sanctitum est. In Secretario vero induere tua Sanctitas pallium debeat, et ita ad missarum solempnia proficisci, et nihil sibi amplius temerariæ præsumptionis adrogare, nedum in exteriori habitu inordinate aliquid arripiatur. Cujus quam indumenti honor modesta actuum vivacitate servandus est, hortamur, ut et cuncta ornamenta conveniant, quatenus auctore Deo recte utrobique possis esse conspicuus. Itaque tua filiis tuis sit regula, in ipsa, si qua fortitudo illis injecta est dirigatur, in ea quod imitantur aspiciant, in ipsa, se semper considerando proficiant, ut tuum, post dominum, videatur esse bonum, quod vixerint."

[193] Sv. Dip., No. 14; Sv. Tr., No. 13; Celse: "Bullarium," p. 15; Hamb. U.B., No. 29; Curschmann, No. 14; P.L. 132, John X., E. and P., No. 15; Jaffé, No. 3562 (1st ed., Lit. Sp., No. 357). Dated Oct. 29th, 920, Rome. Wrongly dated 913 in Sv. Dip. and Celse. John became Pope in 914.

[194] Adam Br., I., c. 63.

of converts. [195]   He was about to return to Germany when he
sickened and died, and was buried at Birka, 936. [196]

Adam of Bremen says that a king named Ring was ruling
at the time of Unni's visit, [197] but according to the Icelandic
Chronicles, Erik Segersäll would seem to have begun his reign
in 922. [198]   As he ruled till about 995 he was probably very
young at this time, and Ring may have acted as regent;
possibly, however, he was only a minor king, ruling over
Birka and its immediate neighbourhood, though this seems
very improbable in such a centralized state as Sweden.
Erik Segersäll and his brother Olov were the sons of a king
named Björn the Aged, of whom we know practically nothing
except that he is said to have reigned fifty years, and that his
rule was a successful one. [199] It seems most probable, however,
that in one or both cases the chronology is erroneous.

Erik and Olov ruled jointly till the death of the latter, when
Erik became sole king.   This displeased Styrbjörn, son of
Olov, who would be one of the most remarkable characters in
early Scandinavian history, if the exploits attributed to him
could be regarded as facts and not merely as legends.   He
claimed a joint share in the rule of the kingdom, but as Erik
wished to wait longer before granting this, he was given a
fleet of sixty long-ships so that he might occupy himself with
Viking expeditions.   After various other adventures he succeeded in making himself master of the Baltic pirate

---

[195] Adam Br., I., c. 63.   "Sveones . . . et Gothi a sancto Ansgario
primum in fide plantati, iterumque ad paganismum relapsi, a sancto
patre Unni sunt revocati."

[196] M.G.H. SS., III., Annales Corbienses.   " 936.   Unni archiepiscopus
Hammaburgensis profectus in Scithiam prædicandi gratia verbum Dei,
ibique defunctus ac sepultus est."
    Adam Br., I., c. 64.   His head was brought to Bremen and buried
before the altar in the Church of St. Peter.   Jörgensen, p. 192, remarks
with regard to this fact that it seems to show that there was no longer
any principal church on the island in Lake Mälar.

[197] Book I., c. 63.

[198] Annales Reseniani.   " 992.   Anlat Biarnar Svia konongr.   Eiricr enn
Sigrseli oc Olafr toko riki synir hans."

[199] Harold the Fairhaired's Saga, c. 29;   "Heimskringla, S.O.S.,"
c. 81.

stronghold of Jomsborg,[200] and then is said to have terrorized Harald Gormsön,[201] King of Denmark, into accompanying him on the expedition to Sweden, which he had planned with a view to wresting the throne from Erik. On landing he burnt his fleet so that his men should have no means of retreat, whereupon Harald, with the ships which he had brought to Styrbjörn's aid, promptly sailed back to Denmark, while Styrbjörn marched towards Uppsala, and a terrible battle took place at Fyrisval, outside the city.[202] Erik, who is said to have dedicated himself to Odin after a period of ten years, was victorious, while Styrbjörn, who on the advice of his uncle Ulv had sacrificed to Thor, was slain.[203]

Erik, a few years later, invaded Denmark, where Svend Forkbeard[204] had succeeded his father Harald, possibly in

---

[200] Saxo X., c. 479. Jomsborg was not far from Wollin. For the Jomsviking Saga, see "Flateyjarbok," I., cc. 123–64. The importance of Jomsborg has been much over-rated. L. Weibull in "Kritiska undersökningar i Nordens historia omkring år 1000," pp. 178ff., even comes to the conclusion that Jomsborg and the Jomsvikings never existed, while Kendrick: "History of the Vikings," p. 179, note 1, p. 183, thinks that the whole story must rest under suspicion, and that the adventures of Styrbjörn in Sweden cannot be historical. But while acknowledging that the accounts of the Jomsvikings are largely legendary, it seems impossible to deny that there was such a community. Jarl Thorkill, who became an ally of Ethelred II. of England, and figured largely in the history of his reign, was a Jomsviking; see "A.-S. Chron." and Florence of Worcester, sub annis 1009, 1013, and cp. Oman: "England before the Norman Conquest," pp. 570–7. Jomsborg was burnt by King Magnus in 1043 according to the Annales Reseniani.

[201] He is perhaps better known as Harald Blaatand (Blue Tooth). Schück: "S.F.H.," I., p. 232, thinks it may have been the Danish king's intention to make Sweden a tributary land with Styrbjörn as jarl.

[202] Adam Br., II., c. 21; Saxo X., c. 479; Cp. "Heimskringla, S.O.S.," c. 71. "C.P.B.," II., p. 62, gives the verse of Thorwald Healtisson, who had himself taken part in it. "Let every charger of the ogress (wolf) that hungers go to Fyrisfield. There (it is no vaunt) Eric has cut down in battle quarry enough for every one of them."

[203] Cp. Adam Br., IV., c. 22. "Se quando viro præliantes in angustia positi sunt, ex multitudine deorum quos colunt, unum invocant auxilio; ei post victoriam deinceps sunt devoti, illumque ceteris anteponunt"; also Earl Haakon's Saga, c. 6. For a critical discussion of the fight see C. Weibull: "Sverige och dess nordiska grannmakter," pp. 54–75. He is of opinion that if the battle actually took place it was merely the defeat of a Viking chief by Erik.

[204] This was the Svend (Sweyn) who harried England in the time of Ethelred II., and died at Gainsborough. See "A.-S. C." and Florence of Worcester, sub annis 994—1014; William of Malmesbury, II., c. 10. The runestones show that many Swedes took part in his expedition.

order to revenge himself for the help the latter had given, though unwillingly, to Styrbjörn. He was successful in conquering the country, [205] and retained possession of it till the time of his death. [206] While in Denmark he is said to have been much impressed by the miracles of Bishop Poppo of Schleswig, who carried a piece of glowing iron in his hand without taking harm, and also allowed a garment coated with wax to be burnt on his body. He accepted Christianity and was baptized, [207] but on his return to Sweden, though his conversion had caused several more Christian missionaries to cross into that country, he relapsed into heathenism. [208] What happened to the missionaries we are not told.

Adaldag, Archbishop of Hamburg, died in 988, after an episcopate of over fifty years' duration. He was a member of the chapter of Hildesheim, and chancellor of the Emperor Otto I., when through the influence of the latter's mother, Matilda, widow of Henry the Fowler, the conqueror of the Hungarians, he was chosen to fill the vacancy caused by the death of Unni. [209] He proved to be an able, if ambitious, prelate, and during his rule the jurisdictional rights of Hamburg and its union with Bremen were again confirmed,

[205] "Chronicon Sveciæ Prosaicum, S.R.S.," I., i., p. 244; Saxo X., c. 495.

[206] Erik's son, Olov Skötkonung, is also said to have conquered and driven out Svend, but afterwards to have restored the kingdom to him. Svend had married his mother, Sigrid Storråda. Annales Esromenses, "S.R.D.," I., pp. 234, 235.

[207] Adam Br., II., c. 33. He says that he had the account of Erik's conversion from Svend Estridsön, King of Denmark, who also gave him much other information about Sweden. Cp. Annales Esromenses, "S.R.D.," I., p. 234.

[208] Adam Br., II., c. 36. "Hericus igitur Suedorum rex in Dania conversus ad christianitatem, ibidem baptizatus est. Qua occasione prædicatores in Suediam transeuntes a Dania, fiducialiter agebant in nomine Domini. Audivi ego a prudentissimo rege Danorum (Svend Estridsön), Hericum, post susceptam christianitatem, denuo relapsum ad paganismum."

[209] Adaldag was also connected with Corbey, as he had been a student there. Chron. Corb. quoted by Reuterdahl; "S.K.H.," I., p. 235. He was sent the pallium by Pope Leo VII. in 937. Hamb. U.B., No. 33; Curschmann, No. 15; P.L. 132, Leo VII., E. and P., No. 13; Jaffé, No. 3612 (dated 937–9 in P.L.). A confirmatory bull was issued by Pope Marinus II. Sv. Tr., No. 14; Hamb. U.B., No. 34; Curschmann, No. 16; P.L. 133, Marinus II., No. 1; Jaffé, No. 3630 (Lit. Sp., No. 259). Dated May, 946, Rome (Curschmann, 943–5).

this time by Pope Agapetus II., in a bull issued January 2nd, 948.[210] Adaldag, possibly for political reasons, seems to have shown more interest in the spread of Christianity in Denmark than in Sweden, though he consecrated a Dane named Odinkar to be bishop in the latter country,[211] and we also read of one of the Danish bishops, Liafdag of Ripa, working there.[212]

Yet when at the close of Adaldag's long episcopate he was succeeded by Libentius,[213] Sweden was still almost entirely heathen. The Hamburg-Bremen mission had now lasted more than a hundred and fifty years, and though it cannot be called a complete failure, the meagre impression that it had made on Swedish heathenism was extremely disappointing. The various missionary bishops and priests who had worked in the country had certainly made a number of individual converts, but nothing in the way of a properly organized Church can be said to have been established, and it is necessary to emphasize this condition of affairs in order to appreciate properly the achievements of the English missionaries, who were now about to commence their labours in the

---

[210] Sv. Dip., No. 15; Sv. Tr., No. 15; Celse: "Bullarium," p. 16; Hamb. U.B., No. 35; Curschmann, No. 17; P.L. 133, Agapetus II., E. and P., No. 5; Jaffé, No. 3641 (Sv. Dip. wrongly dated 952). The authenticity of this bull seems generally acknowledged. Note the reference to the Emperor, also the anathema pronounced on opponents. "Et hoc nostro decreto decernimus secundum prenominati bone memorie Nicolai pape sanctionem et reverentissimi regis Ludowici votum, ipsas predictas dioceses, Hammaburgensem scilicet et Bremensem, non deinceps duas, sed unam esse et vocari. Omnem quoque adversantem vel contradicentem atque piis nostris studiis quolibet modo insidiantem anathematis mucrone percutimus, perpetueque ultionis reum diabolica sorte dampnamus, ut culmen apostolicum, more predecessorum nostrorum, causamque Dei pio affectu zelantes ab adversis hinc inde partibus muniamus."

[211] Adam Br., II., c. 23.

[212] Adam Br., II., c. 23; Adam says "in Sueonia vel Norwegia." Ripa is the modern Ribe.

[213] The confirmatory bull was sent by John XV. Sv. Dip., No. 17; Sv. Tr., No. 17; Celse: "Bullarium," p. 18; Hamb. U.B., No. 52; Curschmann, No. 18; Jaffé, No. 3835. Dated Nov. 8th, 989, Rome (Sv. Dip. and Celse, dated 988). The bull issued by the Anti-Pope John XVI., June 1st, 996 (Sv. Dip., No. 18; Sv. Tr., No. 18; Celse: "Bullarium," p. 19; Hamb. U.B., No. 53; Curschmann, No. 19; Jaffé, No. 3854) is sometimes assigned to John XV., but that Pope died at the beginning of April, 996.

land. Mainly as the result of their evangelistic efforts the next hundred and fifty years witnessed a remarkable change in the situation. At the end of that time instead of a heathen monarch there was a Christian one; instead of the Christians forming a tiny minority existing on sufferance, they were decidedly in the majority; instead of one or two scattered congregations there was a national Church with a definite, if somewhat rudimentary, organization. The Viking raids had become a thing of the past, while the era of the Crusades had commenced; and so overwhelming had been the triumph of the religion of the White Christ over that of Odin and Thor that the very stones of the heathen temple at Uppsala had helped to build the church of the new faith there. Much indeed still remained to be done, but a magnificent work had been accomplished, and under God it was mainly the achievement of the band of missionaries who— partly by way of Norway or Denmark and partly directly— had found their way to Sweden from England.

CHAPTER IV

THE ENGLISH MISSIONARY BISHOPS

ONE of the chief characteristics of the early Anglo-Saxon Church was its zeal for missionary work. Even before the whole of England had been evangelized this had made itself apparent, for ere the exiled Bishop Wilfred had gained the hearts of the men of Sussex by teaching them in time of famine how to catch fish, and had then gone on to win for Christianity the last stronghold of heathenism in Britain, he had laboured for a short time, when on his way to Rome, to spread the Gospel among the Frisians, who dwelt along the shores of the North Sea, between the mouth of the Scheldt and the Elbe. [214]

His example had been followed by the Northumbrian, Willibrord, who with eleven companions took up the work in which Wilfred had been the pioneer. With the support of King Pepin, who had recently annexed part of the Frisian territories to the Frankish dominions, and was later to acquire the remainder, and encouraged by Pope Sergius, who appointed him Archbishop of the Frisians, he laboured for many years in these lands, winning numerous converts and establishing an organized Church with its archiepiscopal see at Utrecht, the old Roman station of Trajectum, the crossing-place of the Rhine. [215]

Even more renowned than Willibrord is the West Saxon Winfrid, better known as Boniface, of whom it has been said that no other Englishman has ever played so great a part in Central Europe. [216] After having helped Willibrord for a

---

[214] Eddi: Vita Wilfridi, cc. 26, 27; Bede: "H.E.," V., c. 19.

[215] Hauck: "K.D.," I., pp. 433–46; Hunt, pp. 212–14. The life of Willibrord was written by Alcuin, the English scholar, who settled at the court of Charlemagne.

[216] Hodgkin: "History of the Anglo-Saxons," I., p. 327. For the work of Boniface in Germany, see Hauck: "K.D.," I., pp. 448–590; Browne: "Boniface of Crediton." The Life of Boniface by Willibald is given in M.G.H. SS., II., pp. 331–53.

time he became Archbishop of Mainz, and earned the title of
Apostle of Germany, so much did he do for the evangelization of the Bavarians, Thuringians and Hessians, before in
755 he met a martyr's death at the hands of the Frisians,
among whom he had returned to labour after having
relinquished his archbishopric.

Other names that come to mind in connection with early
Anglo-Saxon missionary enterprise on the Continent are
those of Swidbert, Wigbert and Werenfrid, members of the
band that accompanied Willibrord; the two Ewalds, who
laboured in Old Saxony, and who both sealed their faith with
their blood; Willebald, Winnebald and Walburga, sons and
daughter respectively of the West Saxon Prince Richard, and
founders of the religious house of Heidenheim; Burchard,
who rendered much assistance to Boniface in his work, and
Lul, who succeeded the archbishop in the see of Mainz when
he returned to Frisia; Lisba and Tecla, respective heads of
the communities of nuns at Bischoffsheim and Kitzingen;
and Willehad, who was employed by Charlemagne for the
conversion of the Saxons and became the first Bishop of
Bremen. [217]

With mission work of so extensive and so intensive a
character it seems somewhat strange, as we have already
noticed, that efforts were not made earlier for the conversion of Norway, but when eventually the English missionaries did turn their attention to that country [218] so largely

[217] For Swidbert see Bede: "H.E.," V., c. 11; for the two Ewalds,
Bede: "H.E.," V., c. 10, and Florence of Worcester, sub anno 692; for
Willehad, his life by Anskar in M.G.H. SS., II., pp. 378–90. For a short
general account of the activities of the missionaries, see Hunt, pp. 211
–21, and for Willebald, Winnebald and Walpurga, see Browne:
"Boniface of Crediton," c. 6.

[218] The missionaries to Norway would seem to have come largely from
the Danish part of England. Worsaae: "Danes and Norwegians in
England, Scotland and Ireland," pp. 134, 135, says "The English priests
or missionaries with Scandinavian names—as, for instance, Eskild,
Grimkild and Sigurd—who went over to Scandinavia in the tenth
century, for the purpose of converting the heathen, were, as their names
show, of Danish origin, and undoubtedly natives of the Danish part of
England. Sprung from Scandinavian families, which, though settled in
a foreign land, could scarcely have so soon forgotten their mother tongue,
or the customs which they had inherited, they could enter with greater
safety than other priests on their dangerous proselytizing travels in the

were they responsible for its conversion that its Church may be said to owe its origin directly to their labours. [219]

Then came the turn of Sweden, where they were to accomplish almost as notable a work as they did in Norway; but as St. Sigfrid, the greatest of all the English missionaries who laboured there, as well as several of his fellow-country-men, did not come directly from England, but by way of Norway, it will be well to glance briefly at the history of that country during the half-century preceding the commencement of their work.

The many small states of which Norway was composed were united into a single powerful kingdom by Harald Haarfagre about the middle of the tenth century. [220] His son, Erik, who, possibly from his bravery but more likely from his cruelties, got the name Blodökse (Blood-axe), succeeded him, but ruled so tyrannically [221] that his half-brother Haakon, foster-son of Athelstan of England, [222] was offered the throne. After a short struggle Erik Blodökse was driven from the country [223] and Haakon became king. He had received

heathen North; where, also, from their familiarity with the Scandinavian language, they were manifestly best suited successfully to prepare the entrance of Christianity." There seem to have been several Danish archbishops in England, and at one time both the archbishops—Odo of Canterbury (942–58) and Oskytel of York (958–70) were of Danish extraction. The former had previously been Bishop of Rams-bury, the latter of Dorchester. See Stubbs: "Registrum Sacrum Anglicanum." The life of Odo is given in "S.R.D.," II., pp. 401–11.

[219] Bang: "Udsigt over den norske kirkes historie under katholicismen," p. 37, after acknowledging the indebtedness of Norway to the Anglo-Saxon Church goes on to say "Af alle de mange folkeslag, der i förste halvdel af middelalderen antog den kristne tro, var der maaske ingen nationem, hos hvem en saa dyb, varm og skjön kristendom slog rod som hos angel-sachserne."

[220] Harald the Fairhaired's Saga, c. 3.

[221] Ágrip, V.; Harald the Fairhaired's Saga, cc. 44–7.

[222] "M.H.N., Theodorici Monachi Historia," c. 2, p. 7. "Prædictus vero Haraldus (i.e. Harald Haarfagre) miserat unum ex filiis suis Halstano regi Anglorum, Hocon nomine, ut nutriretur et disceret morem gentis." See also Ágrip, V., i.; Flateyjarbok: O.T.S., c. 9; Harald the Fairhaired's Saga, cc. 42–3.

[223] He came to England and was taken as king by the Northumbrians, but on Edred invading their land they abandoned him (948). He re-covered his authority in 952, but was finally driven out in 954. See Anglo-Saxon Chronicle under these dates; also Ágrip, VII., i.; Egil's Saga, c. 59. Florence of Worcester gives different dates for his rule in

NB. He does not seem to be acquainted with the recent controversy about the chronology of Eric.

THE ENGLISH MISSIONARY BISHOPS   59

baptism in England, and after he felt himself firmly established on the Norwegian throne he set to work to introduce Christianity. He sent to England for a bishop[224] and clergy, built churches for them,[225] and himself at Frosta "thing" set the claims of the Christian Faith before the assembled bonder. But he gradually found that he was not only unable to induce them to accept Christianity, but that they were determined that their king should keep up the old blood-offerings for plenty, and eventually he gave way and ate of the sacrificial horse-flesh.[226]

After Haakon's death there followed a period of confusion, and then in 995 there came to Norway the famous Viking chief, Olav Trygvessön,[227] who with boundless energy and tremendous enthusiasm set to work, not only to get himself acknowledged by all as king, but also to make his country a Christian one. On one of his Viking voyages he had embraced Christianity,[228] and when he was in England he

Northumberland; Henry of Huntingdon makes him king there for three years. He is said to have died in battle in Spain; see Ágrip, VII., iii.; Egil's Saga, c. 67. Another account makes him fall when engaged in conflict with Oswulf of Bamborough on Stainmoor. See Bugge: "N.H.," I., ii., p. 186; Gjerset: "H.N.P.," I., p. 162.

[224] It seems not unlikely that this is the bishop mentioned by William of Malmesbury: "De Antiquitate Glastonienis Ecclesiæ" (Gale: "Scriptores," p. 325). He gives a list of monks "qui . . . fuerunt episcopi tempore Edgari regis in diversis locis." The fourth entry runs "Nonas Aprilis obiit Sigefridus Norwegensis Episcopus Monachus Glastoniæ." Haakon's attempt to christianize Norway took place some years before the accession of Edgar, and so the expression "in the time of King Edgar" would not be strictly accurate; but the same may be said with regard to two other bishops in the list—Almer, Bishop of Sherborne (1017—c. 1022) and Livingus, Bishop of Wells (999—1012) and afterwards Archbishop of Canterbury (1013–20). Jörgensen, p. 502, thinks this bishop was the court-bishop of Knud the Great, who stirred up opposition to St. Olav in Norway; Bishop Wordsworth suspects that he was possibly the Swedish St. Sigfrid, "N.C.S.," p. 74; Bugge: "N.H.," I., ii., p. 191, identifies him with Haakon's court bishop.

[225] Saga of Haakon the Good, c. 15.

[226] Saga of Haakon the Good, cc. 17, 18, 19.

[227] Annales Reseniani. "995. Vphaf rikis Olafr Tryggvasonar." For his early life see "Heimskringla, O.T.S.," cc. 1–30; also Flateyjarbok: O.T.S.

[228] Fagrskinna, c. 69. "Olafr var kristnade vestr i Syllingum." Cp. Cristne Saga, c. 3, 3; "Heimskringla, O.T.S.," c. 32. The historians Bang (p. 44), Taranger (p. 125), Jörgensen (p. 390) and Hodgkin (p. 384) however, all think that he was probably baptized just before his confirmation at Andover.

[margin notes: NB re death of Eric Bloodaxe; Malmesbury in Norway; NB]

F

was confirmed at Andover by Bishop Ælfeah of Winchester in the presence of Ethelred II.   He promised then that never again would he join in any Viking raid on England, and this promise he kept faithfully. [229]

Although very different views have been taken of his character, [230] it is difficult to believe that his zeal for

[229] No mention is made of his confirmation in the Saga, nor of his previous ravages on the east coast of England and victory over the English at Maldon; there is only the bare statement in Chapter 31, "Thereafter Olaf Trygvesson sailed to England and ravaged wide around the land."   There is, however, a full account of his doings in England in the "Anglo-Saxon Chronicle," sub annis 993, 994.   Cp. Florence of Worcester and Henry of Huntingdon, sub anno 994.   Ælfeah in 1005 became Archbishop of Canterbury.   The story of his murder by the Danes in 1012 is well known.   His life, written by the order of Lanfranc, about 1080, is given in "S.R.D.," II., No. 64.

[230] Adam Br., II., c. 38, says, "Narrant eum aliqui illum christianum fuisse, quidam christianitatis desertorem; omnes autem affirmant peritum auguriorum, servatorem sortium et in avium prognosticis omnem spem suam posuisse.   Quare etiam cognomen accepit, ut Olaph Cracabben diceretur.   Nam et artis magicæ, ut aiunt, studio deditus omnes, quibus illa redundat patria, maleficos habuit domesticos, eorumque deceptus errore periit."   Cp. Annales Esromenses, "S.R.D.," I., p. 125; Ericus Olai: "Chronica, S.R.S.," II., i., p. 29, "Sed hic fuit solo nomine christianus."   Gjerset: "History of Iceland," p. 56.   "(Olaf Trygvessön) was so little familiar with the inwardness and true character of Christianity that he regarded baptism as conversion, and imposed no restriction on the subsequent life and conduct of those who had . . . given their allegiance to the Christian Church."

A completely different view of his character is given in "C.P.B.," II., p. 83.   "The greatest of all the northern kings, his life is an epic of exceeding interest.   Coming out of the darkness he reigns for five short years, during which he accomplishes his great design, the christianizing of Norway and all her colonies; and then in the height of all his glory, with the halo of holiness and heroism undimmed on his head, he vanishes again. . . . All bear witness to the wonderful charm which his personality exercised over all that were near him, so that, like the holy king Lewis (who, however, falls short of Olaf) he was felt to be an unearthly superhuman being by all those who knew him."

A truer view than any of the preceding would seem to be that expressed by E. M. Almedingen: "The English Pope," p. 35.   Speaking of Olav Trygvessön and St. Olav she says: "Their personal convictions were doubtless absolutely sincere, but they did not seem to demand an equal sincerity from their people."   Cp. also Smith: "The Northmen of Adventure," p. 180.   "Why should (Olaf) have risked losing (his crown) by forcing a new religion upon his subjects, whether they wanted it or no? . . . the simplest explanation is that Olaf's conversion by the holy man of the Scilly Isles was a genuine one, and that he came to Norway as a Crusader of the Cross."   There is an interesting comparison between the two Olavs in Metcalfe: "Passio et Miracula Beati Olavi," pp. 20–3.

Christianity was a mere pretence.   Wherever he travelled in
his dominions he was accompanied by missionaries, and
among them we meet for the first time the English bishop
known in Norway and Iceland as Sigurd or Jón-Sigurd, and
in Sweden as Sigfrid, [231] who was to become the best known
of all the English missionaries to Sweden, and who after
Anskar certainly deserves the title " The Apostle of the
North." Olav's vigorous crusade met with great apparent
success, for before long not only Norway itself, but Iceland, [232]
the Faroes, the Orkneys, and even Greenland, had become
Christian, at any rate in name. [233]   If this seems surprising in
view of the very slow progress made by Christianity in Sweden
full allowance must be made not only for the temperamental
difference in the inhabitants of the two lands, but for the
forceful personality of Olav and his satisfaction with little
more than a nominal acceptance of the new faith.   Willingly

Olaf Tryggvason Saga

[231] I have followed the Icelandic tradition that Olav's bishop Sigurd,
(called Jón Sigurdr by Oddr: " O.T.S.," cc. 16, 32, 38, 44), was the same
person as the Swedish bishop Sigfrid, but there is much difference of
opinion in regard to this.   Rhyzelius: "Epis.," I., p. 293, Note A,
asserts that they were two distinct persons, and Strinnholm: "S.F.H.,"
II., p. 657, Note 1196, endeavours to explain how they came to be confused with each other, but thinks that they both worked in Sweden; cp.
also H. Hildebrand: "S.H.," II., p. 89; "S.M.," p. 56.   On the other
hand Wordsworth: "N.C.S.," p. 83, says "The fact that Adam of
Bremen clearly knew of only one Sigfrid, and that a famous man, makes
it probable that there was one man bearing the name of Sigurd in
Norway and Sigfrid in Sweden."   See also Reuterdahl: "S.K.H.," I.,
pp. 314f.;   Taranger, pp. 146–57;   Jörgensen, pp. 413f.;   Keyser, I.,
p. 62;   Willson: "History of Church and State in Norway," p. 356;
Schmid: "Den helige Sigfrid," c. 1.   Bang (" Udsigt, " p. 45, note 1)
says it is impossible to decide with any certainty whether the Norwegian
Sigurd is also the English Sigfrid, and Stubbs: "Registrum Sacrum
Anglicanum," p. 194, suggests that he may be identical with a Sigfrid
who was Bishop of Lindsey at the end of the tenth century.
[232] "Heimskringla, O.T.S.," cc. 80, 88–91, 103; "M.H.N., Theodorici
Monachi Historia," c. 12.   Iceland was apparently discovered by the
Irish monks some time before the year 800.   The Irish monk Dicuil in
Chapter VII. of his "De Mensura Orbis-Terræ," written in 825, says
that thirty years earlier some monks told him of their stay in the island;
and when later it was colonized by Norwegian settlers, the latter found
books, bells and croziers left by the monks who fled at their approach.
See Note 28.
[233] Oddr: " O.T.S.," c. 39, " Olafr konungr cristnaðe Noreg ok Ork-
neyiar, Grenland ok Island, Hialtland ok Föreyiar ok allt fólkit."   Cp.
Fagrskinna, c. 71;   "M.H.N.," X., p. 183;   "Heimskringla, O.T.S.,"
c. 104.

or unwillingly his subjects had to embrace it.   The king
certainly preferred that they should be won by peaceful
persuasion, but if that failed he did not hesitate to use force—
and force of a terrible kind, as witness the horrible tortures
inflicted on Eyvind Kinnrif and Raud the Sorcerer. [234]

Sigurd would seem to have been present on both occasions,
for we are told that he used many suitable arguments in the
endeavour to persuade Eyvind to accept Christianity, though
without success; while when Olav's visit to Raud, who lived
on the island of Godö in Salten Fjord, seemed to be made
impossible owing to the terrible weather prevailing at the
entrance of the fjord, which was attributed to the magical
powers of the sorcerer, Sigurd " took all his mass robes and
went forward to the bow of the king's ship; ordered tapers to
be lighted and incense to be brought out.   Then he set the
crucifix upon the stem of the vessel, read the Gospel and many
prayers, besprinkled the whole ship with holy water, and then
ordered the ship-tent to be stowed away, and to row into the
fjord.   The king ordered all the other ships to follow him.
Now when all was ready on board the Crane to row, she went
into the fjord without the rowers finding any wind; and the
sea was curled about their keel track like as in a calm, so quiet
and still was the water; yet on each side of them the waves
were lashing up so high that they hid the sight of the
mountains." [235]   Olav was thus able to capture Raud while
asleep, and being unable to win him over by promises or
persuasion, is said to have tortured him to death by forcing
an adder down his throat.

We may wonder that Sigurd, who seems to have been a
mild and humane man, did not try to restrain the king from
subjecting his opponents to such inhuman treatment.   That
it was not from fear of occurring the royal displeasure his

[234] "Heimskringla, O.T.S.," cc. 83, 87. Vigfusson and Powell, "C.P.B.,"
II., p. 83, refuse credence to these accounts as well as to those of the
massacre of the wizards by fire in the hall at Nidarnes, and of the
drowning of the warlocks at the Reef of Wailing (Troldeskjoer).   They
think that they are due to ecclesiastical interpolations in the story of his
life, and that the Latin Chronicle of Sæmund the Wise is largely responsible for them.

[235] "Heimskringla, O.T.S.," c. 87.   Cp. Flateyjarbok: O.T.S., c. 318.

interference later in the case of Erling Skjalgssön, who had offended St. Olav, would seem to show.[236] Possibly the fact that both Eyvind and Raud were sorcerers kept him from interceding on their behalf; but there is a remarkable passage in the history of Norway written by the monk Theodoric, which shows that Olav Trygvessön's severe dealing with his opponents met with ecclesiastical approval. He says that the king, seeing that the people's hearts were hardened and that with their mothers' milk they had imbibed idolatry, and that words alone would be useless to move them, had to resort to blows; and that in doing so he was but imitating his Master, who poured wine as well as oil into the wounds of the traveller,[237] and was following out the Gospel precept, " Compel them to come in that my house may be full." [238]

It seems not unlikely that in addition to helping Olav Trygvessön to christianize Norway, Sigurd may also have worked in Sweden during the king's lifetime. Olav's sister Ingeborg had married Ragnvald Ulfsson, the jarl of Väster-götland, on condition that he accepted Christianity and caused his subjects to be baptized. In consequence of this, Olav sent a number of missionaries to labour in the jarl's territories, and it is quite possible that Sigurd may have been one of them.[239]

Naturally Olav's proceedings had made him many enemies and his injudicious zeal in the cause of Christianity was largely responsible for his death. He wished to marry Sigrid Storråda, the widow of Erik Segersäll of Sweden and mother of the reigning king, Olov Skötkonung.[240] The lady seems to

[236] " Heimskringla, S.O.S.," c. 127.
[237] Cp. Bede, Twelfth Homily, " Samaritanus Dominum significat."
[238] " M.H.N., Theodorici Monachi Historia," c. 11. " Cernens namque effera corda barbarorum et a viterno squalore perfidiæ et quodammodo congenita cultura dæmonum, quam pæne cum lacte matris ebiberant, nisi in manu valida non posse liberari, et quia minus movebantur ad verba, addidit frequenter et verbera, imitatus dominum suum, qui vulneribus sauciati infudit oleum et vinum, nec non et illud evangelicum; compelle intrare ut impleatur domus mea."
[239] " Heimskringla, O.T.S.," cc. 105, 106.
[240] Oddr: " O.T.S.," c. 35. " Sigridr var moðir Olafs sønska "; Harald Greycloak's Saga, c. 11. Various explanations are given of the name " Skötkonung." Geijer: " History of the Swedes," E.T., p. 37, says " Olave . . . was, it is said, still an infant in his mother's lap when the

have been pleased with the idea of marrying Norway's hero-king, but when she refused to renounce heathenism he struck her with his glove, calling her " an old faded woman and a heathen jade." [241]   The blow cost him his kingdom and his life, for Sigrid now married Svend of Denmark, [242] and bent her energies to the formation of a coalition against her late suitor.   As a result of her endeavours Svend of Denmark, Olov of Sweden and a number of discontented Norwegians under Earl Erik leagued themselves against Olav, [243] and attacked him when he was returning from an expedition to Vendland, which he had undertaken at the instigation of his wife Thyra. [244]   After a heroic fight against overwhelming odds, which took place possibly off Svolder, a creek in the west of the Isle of Rügen, possibly in the Sound, Olav was completely defeated, his famous warship, the Long Serpent, was captured, and he himself perished in the waves. [245]

Illustrates the
uncertainty of
the period.

people offered their homage, and thence received the name of the Lap-king (Sköt-konung). Olaus Petri (Chrönika, " S.R.S.," I., ii., p. 234) and Baaz (" Inventarium," I., vi., p. 99) think he got the name from causing the payment of the Rome tax (skott).   Hans Hildebrand, " S.H.," II., pp. 8of., thinks that the name was derived from a land tax and was connected with his coinage.   The last is perhaps the most likely explana-tion, for Olov brought minters from England to Sigtuna, and as far as is known, the coins that they made were, with one exception, the first issued in Sweden. See Hallendorf and Schück : " History of Sweden," p. 28, and for Skötkonung, Schmid : " Den helige Sigfrid," pp. 175–9.

[241] " Heimskringla, O.T.S.," c. 68.
[242] " Heimskringla, O.T.S.," c. 98.
[243] " Heimskringla, O.T.S.," c. 108.
[244] Thyra was the widow of Styrbjörn, and sister of Svend of Denmark. She was afterwards married to Burislav I. of Poland (992—1025) but ran away from him to marry Olav.   She urged the latter to get Burislav to give up certain property which she owned in Vendland, and at length he sailed with his fleet to Vendland, and there met Burislav and arranged matters satisfactorily.   His enemies lay in wait for him on his return and attacked him when he was separated from the greater part of his fleet.
[245] Ágrip, c. 20 ; Fagrskinna, cc. 73–81 ; " Heimskringla, O.T.S.," 111–23. Adam of Bremen, II., c. 38, puts the scene of the battle in the Sound ; " Hoc factum est inter Sconiam et Seland, ubi solent reges navali bello confligere." Svanström : " Short History of Sweden," p. 20, C. Weibull : " Sverige och dess nordiska grannmakter, pp. 99–115, and Arup, I., p. 133, also favour the Sound as the scene of the battle. There was for some time a story current in Norway, that Olav had escaped by swimming and gone on a pilgrimage to the Holy Land, where he presently became a hermit and eventually died in a Syrian monastery. Cp. " M.H.N., Theodorici Monachi Historia," c. 14. " Ibi tunc quidam dicunt regem scapha evasisse et ob salutatem animæ suæ exteras regiones adisse, quidam vero loricatum in mare corruisse."   In the Flateyjarbok, I., O.T.S., c. 401, there is an account of his spear and helm being seen at Antioch.

After the battle, which was probably fought in the year 1000,[246] Svend of Denmark and Olov Skötkonung divided Norway between them, except a certain part which was given to the sons of that Haakon Jarl who had ruled the country before the time of Olav.[247] They had previously made an agreement that each should not only maintain Christianity in his dominions but should also endeavour to propagate it among other nations,[248] and we presently find Sigurd, or, as we must now call him, Sigfrid, coming to settle at Östrabo,[249] and labouring among the people of the surrounding district.

How long after the battle of Svolder this was it seems impossible to say, as it is difficult to account satisfactorily for his movements after the battle until the time eight years later[250] when he appeared at the court of King Olov and that monarch was baptized by him in the well of St. Birgitta,[251]

[246] Annales Reseniani. "1000 Fall Olafs Tryggvasonar." Skalholts Annales. "1000. Orrosta á Svarldrar vagi. fall Olafs konungs Tryggvasonar." "S.R.D.," II., No. 55, gives 999, while Jörgensen (p. 398) thinks the battle took place on September 9th, 1002. Arup: "Danmarks Historie," I., p. 133, also gives 1002 as the date, but most historians assign it to the year 1000.

[247] "Heimskringla, O.T.S.," c. 123.

[248] Adam Br., II., c. 37. "Feceruntque pactum ad invicem firmissimum, ut christianitatem in regno suo plantatam retinerent, et in exteras effunderent nationes."

[249] "Historia S. Sigfridi, S.R.S.," II., i., p. 350. Östrabo is the modern Växjö.

[250] Various incorrect dates are given by the old chroniclers. E.g. Petri Olai Annales, "S.R.D.," I., p. 173, "Anno Domini 955 Rex Svetia Olavus cognomento Schotkonung baptizatus a Sancto Sigfrido Eboracensi Archiepiscopo"; Minsta Rimchrönikan, lines 376–80:—

> "Jak döptis aff S. Sigfridz hand,
> Ieena Källo i Wästgöthland,
> Sigfridz Källa wider Husaby,
> Swerike Christnades mäst i thy,
> Effter Gudz börd M.C. och VIII. ahr."

Ericus Olai: "Chronica, S.R.S.," II., i., p. 33, gives 956; Olaus Petri: "Chrönika, S.R.S.," I., ii., p. 234, gives 980, or a little later, and Laurentius Petri gives 989; Messenius (Sc. Ill., Bk. XXII.) gives 999, Von Dalin 1001, and Lagerbring: "S.R.H.," I., xvi., 21, is the first to give the correct date, 1008. Geijer, E.T., p. 37, says Olov was baptized before the year 1000, apparently because Adam makes him a Christian before the battle of Svolder. Wahlström: "Om Olof Skötkonungs Dop," pp. 13f., argues strongly in favour of the year 1018.

[251] This is, of course, not St. Birgitta of Sweden, who lived long after the time the narrative was written, but must be the Irish St. Bridget. Olav Trygvesson of Norway had married an Irish princess, and the missionaries he sent into Västergötland after the conversion of Rangvald Ulfsson may have introduced her cult there. Olaus Petri: "Chrönika, S.R.S.," I., ii., p. 234, calls the well Sigfrid's.

Chronology of Olaf Skötkonung

at Husaby, near Skara, Sweden thus getting her first Christian king. [252]   Nor do we know with any certainty how he and the king first came in contact with each other, nor why Olov, who was apparently a Christian before the battle of Svolder, was not baptized until after a lapse of eight years.

According to the Icelandic tradition, Sigfrid, after vainly endeavouring to comfort Queen Thyra, who, not altogether unjustly, blamed herself for the death of Olav Trygvessön, and starved herself to death, [253] came to southern Sweden and worked there as a missionary bishop; but his life, which, however, was not written until the early part of the thirteenth century, [254] though giving us an account of his later years which harmonizes sufficiently well with what is learnt from other sources, assigns the arrival of the bishop to quite different circumstances, and makes no mention at all of his previous association with the King of Norway.

[252] " S.R.S., I., i., p. 7 ; " U.Ä.B.," p. 29.   " Olawaer Skotkonongaer war fyrsti konongaer, sum kristin war i Sweriki.   Han war döptaer i kiaeldu þerre, wið Hosaeby liggaer ok heter Byrghittae, af Sighfriði biskup." Minsta Rimchrönikan, lines 286, 287, gives Stenkil Eriksson as the first Christian king.   Though Olaus Petri (" S.R.S.," I., ii., p. 234) explains this contradiction by saying that Stenkil had become a Christian and then relapsed into heathenism, and mentions another Stenkil, whom he styles " the Younger," the Rhyming Chronicle would seem to be at fault through considerably antedating the reign of Stenkil, which actually occurred in the second half of the eleventh century.   Saxo, X., c. 501, gives a very incorrect account of Olov's baptism.   " Consimilis ejusdem pontificis (i.e. an English missionary, Bishop Bernhard) industria Suetiæ regem Olavum ad Christiana sacra perductum Jacobi nomine venus-tavit, morum profectui decus vocabuli tribuens.   Utrum autem idem rex ab eo, an a Bremensium pontifice Unnone sacrorum usum disciplinamque perceperit, parum comperi."   It was Olov's son Anund who was called Jakob, while Unni had died at Birka in 936.   Jörgensen, pp. 313, 314, though willing to accept the fact of Olov's baptism by Sigfrid, says with regard to Husaby that the well cannot possibly have been used for the purpose of baptism.

[253] Flateyjarbok, I., O.T.S., c. 387.   " Ok þui gafzst sem hon sagde at hon matte huorke eta ne drekka firir trega. spurde hon sidan Sigurd byskup huat manni vaeri lofat firir gude at naeyta minnzst til faedu til lifs naeringar.   Ok sidan bergde hon eftir þui sem hann sagde henni at minnzst vaeri lofat ok med þui hlydne marke andadizst þyry drottning efter. IX. daga."

[254] Apparently about 1205.   In the " Chronicon Episcoporum Wexion-ensium, S.R.S.," III., ii., p. 130, in relation to Bishop Johannes it is stated :   " Hic XII. annis episcopatum Wærendie tenuerat quando gesta beati Sigfridi in scriptis sunt redacta.   Swercone rege filio Karoli nonum annum sui regni agente.   Anno ab incarnacione domini MCCVI : o."

According to its compiler, King Olov of Sweden sent messengers to King Mildred of England, with whom he was in alliance,[255] asking for missionaries to be sent to his land to try to bring about its christianization.[256] On receiving this request Mildred called a council at which he set the needs of the Swedish realm before the assembly, without, however, receiving any offers of service before the third day, owing apparently to the ideas generally prevalent as to the great danger of undertaking any missionary enterprise in Sweden on account of the ferocity of its inhabitants.[257] On the third day of the council, however, Sigfrid, Archbishop of York, volunteered to undertake the mission, and having been provided with a ship set out for Sweden, travelling by way of Denmark, which was now largely Christian.

On landing in the latter country, he was very kindly received by the king[258] and his chief nobles, who welcomed him with the greeting " Benedictus qui venit in nomine Domini."[259] After a stay of some time in Denmark, Sigfrid informed the king of his mission to Sweden, and that monarch, although with reluctance, allowed him to proceed on his way. After a toilsome and difficult journey, across steep mountains and through dense woods, he at length came to Värend, a land abounding in good things, with its rivers full of fish, bees and honey in plenty, fertile fields and meadows, numerous wild animals of many different species and surrounded by thick and wide-stretching forests.[260] There he took up his

[255] " Historia Sancti Sigfridi, S.R.S.," II., ii., p. 346. " Regi quidem Anglorum Mildredo in tantum confœderatus erat, ut exenniis regalibus et donariis ad invicem donarentur, et pacto pacis regnum utriusque foret stabilitum." Cp. Minsta Rimchrönikan, ll. 418–21.

[256] " Hist. S.S.," p. 346.

[257] " Hist. S.S.," p. 346. " Ferocitas quippe gentis illius aures multorum perculerat et idcirco quorumlibet corda formido titillabat." Cp. " Vita Sancti Sigfridi," p. 366.

[258] " S.R.S.," II., i., p. 348, note h, says that this king was Harald Bluetooth, but as he died in 991 this seems impossible. The editor has apparently not allowed for Svend Forkbeard's return to Christianity after his lapse into heathenism.

[259] " Hist. S.S.," p. 350.

[260] " Hist. S.S.," p. 350. " . . . omnibus bonis abundans, piscosis, fluminibus, apibus et melle repleta, agris fertilibus et pratis decorata, feris diversorum generum opulenta, silvis densissimis et magnis circumcincta."

residence at Östrabo, and there he was when summoned to the king's court.

While we may hesitate to pronounce the whole account " a stupid fable," as the historian Lagerbring has done,[261] since it is possible that there is a substratum of truth in it, yet it is obvious that, apart from the difficulty in reconciling it with the Icelandic accounts, some of the details are quite inaccurate. There has been no King of England named Mildred,[262] but there is little doubt that Ethelred II. is the monarch intended,[263] and that he was on friendly terms with Olov would seem to be implied not only by the statements in the old chronicles[264]—which possibly enshrine a well-known tradition—but also by the fact that the coins of the Swedish king—apparently the first to be struck in the country with the exception of some made at Birka when at the height of its prosperity—were made on the pattern of Anglo-Saxon coins by English minters who were brought from Lincoln to Sigtuna.[265]

[261] " S.R.H.," I., xvi., 21.   " Den är intet annat än en dum Fabel."

[262] Mildred, however, is an English name.   It was borne by the Abbess who founded the convent at Minster in Kent in the seventh century, also by a Bishop of Worcester (745–75) and by a Northumbrian king or duke. For other instances of the occurrence of the name in Anglo-Saxon times, see Searle : " Onomasticon," p. 352.   In the Västerås Breviary, Mildred is styled Vuldredus.

[263] Ericus Olai : " Chronica, S.R.S.," II., ii., p. 31, says of Ethelred " forte ipse est Mildredus, de quo in historia S. Sigfridi fit mentio," and almost all later historians agree with this identification, but Baring-Gould : " Lives of the Saints," II., p. 310, seems to prefer Edred to Ethelred.

[264] " Hist. S.S.," p. 346 ;   Minsta Rimchrönikan, ll. 418–21.   Von Dalin : " S.R.H.," I., xx., i., even thinks that Olov went to England on a friendly visit about 998.

[265] There were five of these mint-masters : Godwine, Leofman, Snelling, Ulfhel and Thregr ; possibly also a sixth named Ælfric.   The coins were like the English ones of Ethelred II., but rather heavier. After Anund Jakob succeeded his father he had different mint-masters, and his coins are mostly modelled on the English ones of Knud.   See Cornell : " Sigtuna och Gamla Uppsala," pp. 97, 98.   The coins of Olov Skötkonung are pictured in H. Hildebrand : " S.H.," II., p. 79 ; those of Anund Jakob on p. 91 ; the earlier Birka coins on p. 78.   See also Hildebrand : " S.M.," I., pp. 78of.   The possibility that the mint-masters were sent by Svend, and not by Ethelred, must not be overlooked. Godwine was at one time mint-master to Olav Trygvessön in Norway ; see Bugge : " N.H.," I., ii., p. 254 for an illustration of one of his Norwegian coins.

For illustrations of the Birka coins, see Kendrick : " History of the Vikings," p. 96.   Schück : " Birka," pp. 18, 19, doubts if they were actually minted there.

But although Mildred can be so far satisfactorily accounted for, it seems impossible to give a fitting explanation of why Sigfrid is styled "Archbishop of York," for none of the occupants of the see has borne that name, nor do we find any reference in any of the English chronicles to the council that is said to have been held by the king; the one fact that they do mention about Sweden in connection with Ethelred is that his little grandsons, Edward and Edmund, were some time after his death sent by King Knud to Olov Skötkonung to be murdered. The Swedish king, however, was unwilling to carry out the cruel deed, and sent them to Solomon, King of Hungary, to be brought up at his court. [266] It has been suggested that Sigfrid did not actually occupy the see of York, but was only consecrated archbishop there; but unless he is a different person from the Norwegian Sigurd he had been consecrated several years previously. St. Birgitta in one of her revelations speaks of him as archbishop, [267] but sometimes as an honour a higher title was assigned to an ecclesiastic than he actually possessed; certainly Sigfrid is only called bishop in the list of the occupants of the see of Skara appended to the West Gothic Law, [268] while Vastovius only calls him archdeacon, [269] and Alford says definitely that he was a priest of York and not a bishop there. [270] Another suggestion is that York should really be Cork, and that Sigfrid's three nephews were not Cluniac monks but came from the Irish monastery of Duniacum [271]; but this explanation, if adopted, would seem to increase rather than diminish the difficulties, and

[266] Florence of Worcester: Chronicle; Simeon of Durham, sub anno 1017.
[267] Book VIII., c. 46. The Blessed Virgin says in the vision to St. Birgitta. "S. Sigfridus Archiepiscopus exivit de Anglia et fecit voluntatem Dei in regno Sueciæ. Sic ille Sacerdos, pro quo tu oras, constituat Ecclesiam. . . ." Quoted in "Acta Sanctorum," XI., p. 849.
[268] "U.Ä.B.," p. 47. "Sighfriđaer war fysti biskuper, sum haer kom kristnu a."
[269] "Vitis Aquilonia"; Cp. Von Dalin: "S.R.H.," I., xx., 10, p. 31. Wilson: "English Martyrologe," p. 39, also calls him archdeacon, and says that he was made metropolitan of Götaland.
[270] "Fides Regia Anglicana," III., Index Sanctorum. "Sigfrid Episcopus Uexoviensis in Norwegia. Fuit Eboracensis Præsbyter, non Episcopus ibi, ut multi putaverunt."
[271] See Schmid: "Den helige Sigfrid," p. 135, note 1.

possibly Reuterdahl is right in considering that the writer of
the chronicle may have been influenced by Rimbert's account
of the mission of St. Anskar. He points out what he considers
are the significant similarities between the two narratives.
Olov is a heathen, but sympathetic, generous, kind, and well-
disposed towards the Christians, and is thus like King Björn.
The latter sends an embassy to Germany; Olov is made to
send one to England, as it is an Englishman whose life is to
be related. In the case of both Anskar and Sigfrid there is
held a public assembly to discuss matters [272]; the former
becomes an archbishop, the latter already is one. For both
the journey is long and difficult, while both work for a time
in Denmark before coming to Sweden and stand high in
favour with the Danish king. Further, he thinks that the
natural resources that Sigfrid finds in Värend are reminiscent
of Adam of Bremen's description of Sweden. [273]

When closely examined these similarities do not seem to be
particularly striking, and it ought not to be overlooked that
there is the further possibility that the chronicler has partially
confused Olov of Sweden either with Olav Trygvessön of
Norway, who was certainly on terms of friendship with
Ethelred and who brought Sigfrid with him from England,
or with St. Olav, who in his Viking days was for a time the
ally of Ethelred and as such took part in the famous battle of
London Bridge. [274]

If we now turn to the Icelandic tradition, which has
already been mentioned briefly, we find that Sigfrid after the
battle of Svolder, having vainly endeavoured to prevent
Queen Thyra from starving herself to death, passed over into
Västergötland and made it the seat of his labours. That the
bishop immediately after the death of the missionary king,
with whom he had worked so loyally for several years for the
spread of Christianity, should have thus betaken himself to

[272] In the case of Anskar the assembly discussed the mission to Denmark, which preceded that to Sweden.
[273] "S.K.H.," I., pp. 321, 322. Taranger, p. 150, agrees with Reuterdahl that the narrative has been influenced by that of Rimbert.
[274] Annales Reseniani. "1009 Olafr konongr van Lunnduna borg."
Flateyjarbok: S.O.S., c. 20; "Heimskringla, S.O.S.," c. 12.

O's own sensible conclusions
K. Svend. X'tt or heathen ?

THE ENGLISH MISSIONARY BISHOPS 71

the realm of one of Olav's enemies certainly appears on the
face of it a very unlikely proceeding. If, however, he had
been largely responsible for the missionary work in that
province which had followed the marriage of Princess
Ingeborg to Jarl Rangvald Ulfsson, he would probably feel
tolerably secure among his converts in spite of the changes in
the political situation since he had worked there, while he
could doubtless reckon in addition on the protective influence
of the Princess. It is, however, in Värend and not in Västergötland that we find him settled when messengers arrived to
summon him to the court of King Olov, and we do not know
when he made the change between the two territories, and
whether it was a direct one, or if other travels for missionary
purposes intervened. [275]

It does not seem outside the bounds of possibility that
Sigfrid may after the death of Olav Trygvessön have gone
first to Västergötland, and then, after working there for a
time, have returned to England, to make his way later on to
Denmark, and from there to proceed again to Sweden,
possibly sent by Sven at the request of his son-in-law, Olov
Skötkonung. If this were indeed the case the Icelandic
chronicles and the legendary life of St. Sigfrid are less in conflict than they appear to be. Another possibility is that he
went to Denmark only; certainly he would seem to have
spent some time working in that country. Svend of Denmark,
though baptized in early life, is said to have relapsed into
heathenism and become a bitter persecutor of the
Christians. [276] If this was so, he had apparently again

[275] The account given in Flateyjarbok: O.T.S., c. 400, gives little idea
of the length of time that elapsed between the arrival of Sigfrid in
Sweden and the baptism of Olov Skötkonung. " Efter skilnad þeirra
Olafs konungs Trygguasonar uendi Sigurdr biskup til Suiþiodar at baen
Olafs konungs Aerikssonar er þar var þa med þeirre saett ok samninge at
herra byskup skyllde hafa frialsa yfirferd um allt Suiariki at predica guds
eyrende til rettsnuningar þeirre aumu þiod er þar hafde langan tima
skemdarfullum ok skynlausum skurgodum þionat."

[276] Adam Br., II., cc. 25, 27. "S.R.D.," I., Annales Esromenses.
"DCCCCLXXXV. Cumque cepisset regnare Sven Rex, et persecutionem
cristianorum exercuisset in Dania." Jörgensen, p. 299, is unwilling to
accept the common tradition of Svend's lapse into heathenism. Cp.
Helveg: "Den Danske Kirkes Historie," I., pp. 110f.; Steenstrup:
"D.R.H.," I., p. 362. Previté-Orton, p. 154, calls him a heathen, but
Dawson: "Making of Europe," p. 273, speaks of him as a nominal professor of Christianity who followed in all things the traditions of the
barbarian warrior.

Gotbald

become a Christian before the battle of Svolder, [277] otherwise it is difficult to account for the pact with Olov Skötkonung with regard to the propagation of Christianity in their respective domains, [278] or for his action in sending an English bishop named Gotebald to labour in Skåne, which at that time was Danish territory.   This Gotebald worked also in Sweden and so would seem to have been the first English missionary bishop, with the possible exception of St. Sigfrid himself, to do so.   Unfortunately, we have no details as to the success or otherwise of his labours; we do not know how early they began or in what part of Sweden they were carried on— though this would probably be the territory adjoining Skåne —but have only the bare statement of his working in Swedish as well as Danish and Norwegian lands. [279]   The memory of

---

[277] " S.R.D.," I., Annales Esromenses. Under the year 985 is given in addition to the account of Svend's persecution of the Christians, that of the loss of his kingdom, his penitence, and his restoration by Olov Skötkonung.   L. Weibull: " K.U.," pp. 100, 101, points out the like-ness between Adam of Bremen's description of Svend's repentance and that of Manasseh of Judah given in 2 Chron., c. 33 ; C. Weibull: " Sverige och dess nordiska grannmakter," pp. 76–95, gives reasons for thinking Adam's account of the conquest of Denmark by Erik incorrect.

[278] See Note 248. Svend had perhaps been driven from his kingdom by Erik Segersäll, father of Olov Skötkonung, or more probably it had been conquered by the Swedish king during his absence, and some historians have thought that the latter only restored it to him on condi-tion that he accepted Christianity, but this seems very improbable. Possibly Svend in his earlier years had hated Christianity, but in forming an estimate of his character in later years undue importance must not be attached to the statements of the English chroniclers, who naturally enough viewed him with disfavour.   There is a remarkable passage in the Encomium Emmæ (" S.R.D.," II., No. 66), relating to his last days, which certainly does not represent him as a hater of Christianity.   " Cui (i.e. Knud) dum multa de regni gubernaculo, multaque hortaretur de Christianitatis studio, Deo gratias, illi, virorum dignissimo, sceptrum commisit regale."   Wahlström: " Om Olof Skötkonungs Dop.," p. 9, points out that the arrangement made by the two kings is the first Scan-dinavian diplomatic treaty.

[279] Adam Br., II., c. 39.   " Svein, interfecto Cracabben, duo regna possedit. Ipse igitur mox destructo ritu ydololatriæ, christianitatem in Nortmannia per edictum suscipere jussit.   Tunc etiam Gotebaldum quendam ab Anglia venientem episcopum in Sconia posuit doctorem, qui aliquando in Suedia, sæpe dicitur evangelizasse in Norvegia."   See also " S.R.D.," I., Annales Esromenses, p. 235.   Alford: " Fides Regia Anglicana," III., p. 437.   " Quo etiam anno (i.e. 1004) mortuus ponitur in nostro Martyrologio sanctus Gotebaldus, Norvegiæ episcopus, quem superiori sæculo Swanus Danorum Rex, ad Christianam Fidem con-versus, in Scaniam misit, ad Christianæ Fidei sementem spargendum."

his toils, however, remained, and although he does not appear
to have been included in any of the Swedish medieval
diocesan calendars, he was commemorated at Lund on
August 21st.[280]   His name we may note also appears in the
English Martyrology compiled by the priest, John Wilson, in
the early part of the seventeenth century, but a different day
is assigned for his commemoration.[281]

Whatever, then, may have been the movements of Sigfrid   *Sigfrid*
during the first few years that followed the battle of Svolder,   *in Sweden*
we find him some time before the baptism of Olov Sköt-
konung settled at Östrabo, the modern Växjö, engaged in the
work of evangelizing the surrounding districts.   He had with
him, according to the legend, his three nephews, Unaman,
Sunaman and Vinaman, who were Cluniac monks and were
also respectively priest, deacon and sub-deacon[282]; and even
if we hesitate to accept the complete historicity of these
persons, it is at any rate highly probable that Sigfrid had some
helpers.   In a vision he was directed by an angel where he
should built a church.[283]   He began to preach and won many
hearers, and eventually twelve wise and aged men were
chosen to represent the twelve chief tribes of the land, who

[280] " S.R.D.," III., No. 90.   Necrologium Lundense.   " B XII. Kl.
Sept.   Commemoratio Godeboldi et Bernhardi Episcoporum et Henrici,
qui fuit primus nostræ ecclesiæ Episcopus."   The Bernhard mentioned
here was an Englishman, according to Saxo.   Henry had been bishop of
the Orkneys and court chaplain to Knud the Great before be became the
first Bishop of Lund.   The fact that he died while in a state of intoxication does not seem to have been considered sufficiently serious to prevent
his commemoration.   Alford: " Fides Regia Anglicana," III., Index
Sanctorum, gives April 5th as the day of Gotebald's commemoration.
[281] The compilers of the " Acta Sanctorum " think that Gotebald's
claim to sanctity is insufficiently proved.   Vol. X., pp. 392, 395, sub die
April 5th.   " Gotebaldus Episcopus, ab Anglia, veniens in Scania positus
Doctor, dicitur in Suedia et Norvegia evangelizasse. . . . Hic episcopus
Gotebaldus adscriptus est, ut Sanctus Martyrologio Anglicano Wilsoni
et Calalogo Generali Ferrarii.   Nos certiora ecclesiastici cultus docu-
menta desideramus."
[282] " Hist. S.S.," p. 351.   Old Swedish Version.   The Latin Version
only gives their respective orders.
[283] " Hist. S.S.," p. 352.   " Somno quippe vir Dei citius corripitur,
angelum Dei fulgore nimio amictum sibi cernit assistere, vultu placido
tali exorsum affamine ;   Surge citius Deo dilecte, et sequere me.   Illo
autem in spiritu eum sequente, duxit ad locum procul, juxta stagnum,
quem certis terminis ædificandæ ecclesiæ præfixum ostendit, sicque dis-
paruit."

were to decide about the truth of his teaching, and on behalf of the commonality to determine whether it should be accepted or not.

Sigfrid instructed them in the cardinal truths of Christianity, laying especial emphasis on God's love for the world and the joy in heaven over the repentance of sinners, and insisting, too, on the importance of receiving the sacrament of baptism. The whole twelve after listening to his teaching were convinced of the truth of Christianity and agreed to return for baptism in twelve days time [284]; eleven of them returned in due course for the administration of the sacrament, while the twelfth, who had died during the interval, was given a Christian burial. The conversion of their representatives was followed by that of a large number of the people, and Värend was rapidly becoming christianized when there came a sudden check to the work, caused by the summoning of Sigfrid to attend on the king and the murder of his nephews during his absence at the court.

According to one account, it would appear that Olov, previous to sending the invitation to Sigfrid, had heard of his work in Värend, but had been somewhat uncertain of his identity, and had consequently sent one of his trusted councillors to investigate what was happening and bring back to him a report regarding the actions of the strangers—that is, Sigfrid and his companions. The messenger was present at the celebration of the Mass, and on his return to the king duly reported what he had witnessed. He had seen weaponless men, whose customs seemed more to resemble those of women than of warriors; they had been clothed in curious garments and had performed various ceremonies connected with the rite. When the bishop had elevated the host the people had fallen on their knees. The host had then changed into a young Boy, whom the bishop kissed, and who then dis-

[284] The Latin version of the history implies that the baptism took place on the first occasion. "Mox illi duodecim illuminati a Spiritu sancto, ad veram catholicam fidem conversi, Jesum Christum agnum Dei, tollentem peccata mundi, fermiter crediderunt, et baptizati in fonte, juxta Östrabo montem manante, sua nomina dederunt conscripta." P. 354. The old Swedish version makes the baptism take place on their return.

appeared, while the host remained on the paten. [285] When the king heard all this he knew who it was that had come to his kingdom and sent to fetch him to the court.

As we have seen the Swedish king, accompanied by his servants and bodyguard, was accustomed to stay at the various royal estates in turn, in order to make use of their produce, and Olov seems to have been holding his court at or near Husaby in Västergötland when Sigfrid, in response to the invitation he had sent, came to him. The saint does not appear to have hurried on his journey, for when he passed through Utvängstorp in Vartofta he stopped there for a time to teach and baptize the people of the neighbourhood. The clear spring well, of which he made use, came to be regarded as sacred in later times, and on the hill a church was afterwards built [286]; while the fact that his name is associated with several other places in the neighbourhood would seem to show that his missionary zeal refused to allow him to neglect any opportunity afforded him of preaching the Gospel to the heathen, even though the king might be waiting his arrival with great impatience. It is, however, possible that Sigfrid evangelized this district on some later occasion, after first making its acquaintance while on his way to the court.

At length he arrived, and was received with great honour by King Olov, who shortly afterwards was baptized in the well at Husaby. [287] Why the king had so long delayed his baptism we do not know. Possibly it was owing to the influence of his mother, Sigrid Storråda, who had remained a heathen; possibly, as in the well-known case of the Emperor Constantine, he had shrunk from assuming the greater responsibilities that would come with the reception of the sacrament; possibly fear as to the effect of the action on his heathen subjects in Sweden proper deterred him for a time, and he may have remembered the fate of Haakon the

[285] "Vita S. Sigfridi, S.R.S.," II., i., p. 367. Cp. the accounts in Cæsarius Heisterbacensis: "Dialogus Miraculorum," II., pp. 167-9, of the monk, Godeschalk, who saw Christ under the form of a Child in his own hands, and the priest, Adolphus, who saw in the host, first the Virgin and Child, then a Lamb, and then our Lord crucified.

[286] Götlind: "Saga, Sägen och Folkliv i Västergötland," pp. 140, 141,
[287] See Notes 250, 252.

G

Good in Norway.[288] It may now have been the influence of Sigfrid that caused him to delay no longer, but to take the final step. At any rate it was taken, and as was so often the case when a heathen monarch—though the term is not strictly applicable to Olov in the circumstances—showed his acceptance of the Christian faith by being baptized, a number of his subjects followed his example, including the members of his family and household, and also the whole army,[289] although by the latter phrase it is probable that only his personal bodyguard is meant.

It is perhaps well to mention here that it has been claimed by some German historians that Sigfrid was not an Englishman but a fellow-countryman of theirs, and that he was sent on the mission that resulted in the baptism of Olov by Archbishop Bruno of Querfurt; a view that has also been adopted by certain Swedish historians. The three principal reasons put forward for the adoption of these conclusions are that Sigfrid seems to be a German rather than an English name; that Adam speaks of the bishop in connection with the see of Bremen; and that there exists a copy of a letter written in 1008 by Archbishop Bruno of Querfurt,[290] the Apostle of the Slavs, to the Emperor Henry II., in which he speaks of the conversion of a " senior suigorum," together with a number of his people, in the course of a mission undertaken by a bishop, who is unnamed, and a monk of the name of Robert.[291] The term " senior suigorum " is interpreted to

---

[288] Haakon the Good's Saga, cc. 15–19.

[289] "Hist. S.S.," p. 356. "Omnesque familiares et domestici ejus, universusque exercitus, cum tota ejus familia." The "Vita S.S.," p. 368, simply says "ibidem cum sua familia baptizavit." According to Adam Br., however, his wife and sons were baptized by Thurgot, the first Bishop of Skara (II., c. 57).

[290] Bruno was not Archbishop of Querfurt, but received from the Pope the title "archiepiscopus gentium."

[291] The letter is given in Beckman: "U.Ä.B.," p. 49; also in Lundström: "Fynd och Forskningar," I., p. 13; "Non lateat regem, quod episcopus noster cum egregio monacho, quem nostis, Rodberto, ultra mare in evangelium (prædicandum?) suigis transmiserat. Quomodo venientes nuncii verissime dixerunt, ipsum seniorem suigorum, cujus dudum uxor christiana erat, gratias Deo! baptizavit, cum quo mille homines et septem plebes eandem gratiam mox et receperunt. . . ."

mean " the king of the Swedes," [292] whose wife is said in the letter to have long been a Christian, [293] while the bishop is identified with Sigfrid.

Certain modifications of this theory have been put forward, as, for instance, that " senior " can refer to a chieftain and not to the king [294]; that Sigfrid, although sent by Bruno, was of English birth [295]; or that the mission sent by Bruno was distinct from that of Sigfrid, and probably had Sigtuna and not Västergötland as the scene of its labours. [296] For some time, however, the main contention that the letter referred to a mission to Sweden organized by Archbishop Bruno was widely accepted, either to the exclusion of, or in conjunction with, the relations of the Icelandic annalists and the compiler of the life of St. Sigfrid.

With regard to the points brought forward in support of *O's reply* the theory, the first is soon disposed of, for that Sigfrid was certainly an English name seems to be supported by good evidence. Bede mentions a co-abbot of St. Peter's Convent at Wearmouth, who died in 689, who bore it [297]; Florence of Worcester has several references to a Sigfrid, Abbot of Glastonbury, who in 1125 was made Bishop of Chichester [298]; and later in the same century there was a second occupant of

[292] Voigt: " Brun von Querfurt," p. 122, " Indem ich mit anderen für so gut wie gewiss halte, dass der von Brun erwähnte Fürst der Schweden Olaf Schosskönig war." Cp. H. Hildebrand: " S.H.," II., p. 75; Moeller, p. 142; Hauck: " K.D.," III., p. 630.

[293] Adam Br., II., c. 57, says that the wife of Olov Skotkönung was baptized at the same time as her son Anund Jakob.

[294] Dehio: " Geschichte des Erzbistums Hamburg-Bremen," I., p. 157. " Bruns Ausdruck (senior) lässt mit mindestens ebensoviel Recht auf irgend einen Jarl oder sonstigen Vornehmen schliessen."

[295] Schück: " S.F.H.," I., p. 270.

[296] Jörgensen, pp. 423f.

[297] " D.N.B.," Vol. LII., p. 246.

[298] Florence of Worcester: " Chronicle," sub annis 1125, 1127, 1128, 1130. The " A.-S. Chronicle " also mentions him under the last date as present at the consecration of Christ Church, Canterbury, by Archbishop William; and Henry of Huntingdon, who calls him Bishop of Sussex, says that he attended a council held at London in 1129. He was deposed in 1145, possibly for opposition to King Stephen, and retired to Glastonbury.

the see of the same name. [299] The mention of Sigfrid by Adam in connection with the see of Bremen is also sufficiently accounted for by the fact that its archbishop possessed jurisdiction over Sweden at the time when the English missionary bishop was working there, for it was not until the following century that this jurisdiction was transferred to Lund. [300] The letter is the only really important piece of evidence that favours at all the claims of the German historians, and it is certainly a remarkable coincidence that it should bear as its date the year to which the baptism of Olov Skötkonung is usually assigned.   On the other hand, it may well be asked why Bruno should have thought of sending any mission to Sweden, when he had been specially appointed by Pope Sylvester II. missionary archbishop to the heathen eastern lands, much as Ebo of Reims had earlier received a similar commission from Pope Paschal I. in regard to the North. The term " Suigi " probably refers to some tribe living in the neighbourhood of the Black Sea, [301] but even if this people cannot be definitely identified, it is now generally acknowledged that Olov Skötkonung was baptized by Sigfrid, and that the latter was of English birth. [302]

Sigfrid's successful mission in Västergötland was, however, brought for a time to an abrupt termination by the arrival of sad news. His three nephews, whom he had left behind to carry on the work in Värend during his absence, had been attacked secretly at a place called Gelboberg [303] and slain.

[299] Lundström: "Fynd och Forskningar," I., p. 8, note 2, says that he was informed by Bishop Wordsworth that two bishops of Winchester had borne the name Sigfrid.   It is evidently the two bishops of Chichester who are meant as there has been no Sigfrid of Winchester. See further, Gams: "Series Episcoporum," p. 185; Stubbs: "Registrum Sacrum Anglicanum," pp. 44, 50; Ollard and Crosse, p. 111; and for the name Sigfrid in Anglo-Saxon times, Searle: "Onomasticon," pp. 418, 419.

[300] See Chapter VIII.

[301] This is the opinion of Dean Lundström, who has investigated this matter very fully. See his "Fynd och Forskningar," I., pp. 10, 14–22; II., pp. 64–87.

[302] E.g., O. von Friesen: "Upplands Runstenar," p. 38, says that there can no longer be any doubt about Sigfrid's English birth. Cp. Cornell: "Sigtuna och Gamla Uppsala," p. 93.

[303] "Hist. S. Davidis," Lectio 6, "S.R.S.," II., i., p. 409.   Schmid: "Sveriges Kristnande," p. 138, thinks that the name is taken from Mt. Gilboa in David's lament over Saul and Jonathan.

Their heads had been cut off and thrown into the lake, while their bodies had at first been hidden in a wood under a great heap of stones; but owing to certain prodigies happening at the place of burial—multitudes of crows making their appearance there by day, and a wonderful luminous pillar showing itself in the sky by night—the murderers, fearing lest their crime might be discovered, had removed the remains of their victims to an unknown spot.[304]   The cause of the murder does not seem to have been anger on the part of the heathen at the success of the missionaries in winning converts, but covetousness excited by the value of the vessels used in the service of the Church.[305]   Sigfrid, naturally anxious as to the effect of these happenings on the newly-made converts of the district, having obtained permission from the king, returned to Östrabo and resumed his labours, " watched by night in prayer, preached by day, sorrowed over the unbelief of those who had turned away from the Gospel, but rejoiced over those who wished to become Christians, and spared himself no pains in the service of God."[306]

The story of the finding of the three heads of his nephews is a good example of the miraculous element so prominent in the medieval legends of the saints.   As Sigfrid went from his house at night he saw three star-like lights that hovered over a lake in the immediate vicinity, and as he watched them they moved shorewards.   The bishop made his way to that part of the lake shore for which they appeared to be making, waded into the water, and discovered a wooden pail, weighted down by a stone, in which were the three heads of his murdered nephews, as incorrupt as at the time of their martyrdom.   Clasping them to his breast he appealed to heaven for retribution on their murderers, whereupon the first head gave him assurance that the crime would be avenged. " When? " asked the second head, and the third replied, " In the third generation."[307]

---

[304] " Hist. S.S.," p. 358.   Cp. the brief account in the " Vita S.S.," p. 369.

[305] " Hist. S.S.," p. 356.

[306] " Hist. S.S.," Swedish Version, p. 361.   Cp. " Officium S.S.," Lectiones 2 and 3.

[307] " Hist. S.S.," pp. 360, 362.   Cp. " Vita S.S.," p. 370 ; " Officium S.S.," Lectiones 6, 7, 8. Cp. the story of the speaking head of St. Edmund of East Anglia related by " Matthew of Westminster," sub anno 870.

This legend, which Bishop Wordsworth stigmatizes as " a puerile extravagance," [308] certainly attained wide credence, and one proof of this is afforded by the old seal of the Chapter of Växjö, of which only one example has been preserved. [309] It shows three heads, one larger and full-faced in the centre, the other two smaller and in profile at the sides. The centre head has the tonsure, showing that it represents a cleric, and all three end at the neck, from which blood is dripping. A banner at the top in the centre shows that the heads are those of missionaries, while below is portrayed the surface of a sheet of water. There are also a star and an arm, with three fingers of the hand stretched out.

As it seems to have been usual for the patron saint or saints of a diocese to figure on the seal of its chapter, it would appear that the martyred missionaries, rather than St. Sigfrid, were at first regarded in that light in relation to Växjö, although the latter was looked upon as the founder of the see. It must not be forgotten, too, when considering whether they can properly be regarded as historical personages, that the Icelandic chronicler when relating Sigfrid's sermon at Sigtuna, to which reference will be made later, makes him speak of the martyrs of Växjö, though he does not name them. [310] It was usual, too, when Sigfrid was portrayed in medieval windows to represent him as clasping the three heads to his breast. The simple faith of those times, so far from having difficulty in believing the miraculous, seems rather to have expected it. That there were miracles performed by some of the saints we need not hesitate to believe [311]; that God for His glory and

---

[308] " N.C.S.," p. 73.

[309] The seal is pictured in Örnhjälm: " H.E.," III., iv., 47; and in Schmid: " Den helige Sigfrid," opp. p. 85. It is of wax, and is attached to a letter sent out by the Chapter in 1292.

[310] Flateyjarbok, I., O.T.S., c. 401.

[311] Schück: " S.F.H.," I., p. 275, seems to think that if the relations of the missionaries can be trusted, the power to work miracles was the chief means of the conversion of the heathen. The remarks of Bright on medieval miracles are worth recalling: " Of the medieval stories of miracles the great bulk may be summarily dismissed—not merely, nor indeed mainly, because of the contrast which so many of them present, by their grotesqueness, or puerility, or matter-of-course profusion, to the 'signs' recorded in Scripture, but because the interval between the

the extension of His kingdom, in response to the prayer of
faith, may have directly interposed on various occasions and
allowed signs and wonders to be wrought by His servants
should not surprise us. But in certain cases, the unsaintlike
character when living of those at whose tombs the miracles
were supposed to be wrought, the unsatisfactory nature of
many of the miracles themselves, and the tendency to exalt
the powers of departed saints to an extent derogatory to both
the majesty and mercy of God, may well make us hesitate to
accept the complete truth of many of the happenings related
by the monkish chroniclers. And in this case, while fully
accepting the saintliness of Sigfrid and believing that the
account of the martyrdom of his nephews enshrines an historic
fact, we must certainly be permitted to doubt the literal truth
of the story of the speaking heads.

Some time after Sigfrid's return King Olov himself arrived
in Värend with an army, and imposed heavy fines on the
people on account of the crime, afterwards offering a considerable sum to the bishop in expiation of the wrong wrought
on his relations. Sigfrid, however, thinking of the future needs
of the church, asked that instead of the money some landed
property might be given, with the result that the king made
over to him for its support the estates of Hof and Tjurby. [312]
As we have seen a church had already been built, and so we
get the beginnings of the bishopric of Växjö; but although
Sigfrid is often spoken of as the first occupant of the see, it did
not have a regular succession till much later, and he ought
rather to be looked upon as a missionary bishop, who for a
considerable time made this place the centre from which he
travelled round, preaching and baptizing, building churches
and ordaining priests, [313] and possibly exercising some kind of

alleged occurrence and the account of it is usually long enough to allow
of a rank upgrowth of legend, encouraged by the fixed preconception of
the age, that miracles must always attend upon, and attest, high
sanctity." "Early English Church History," pp. 72, 73.

[312] "Hist. S.S.," p. 362.

[313] "Hist. S.S.," p. 364. "Peragrabat namque partes omnes Sveciæ,
prædicando, baptizando et populum ad fidem Christi convertendo, sacris
etiam monitis hos, quos fide imbuerat, admonebat, ut in illa æterna a
Deo præmia percepturi perseverarent."

general supervision over the whole work of the Christian Church in the country.

It was presumably on one of his missionary journeys, taken not very long after his return from Husaby, that he preached to a great multitude of people at Sigtuna on the shores of Lake Mälar, one of the principal trading places in the country. He reproved the heathen Swedes for their evil deeds, related to them how the king and many of his subjects had been baptized, reminded them of the part that they had played in the expedition that led to the battle of Svolder, [314] and spoke of the Christian missionaries so recently slain at Växjö, ending with an exhortation to repentance and amendment. [315]

It is after this story of the preaching in the saga that we get an account of a conversation between Sigfrid and the Icelander Hūnroðr Vefredsson, which not only tells strikingly in favour of his identity with Olav Trygvessön's court bishop, but shows in what affectionate regard he held his late royal master, while it also calls to mind Bede's story of how St. Aidan gave to a beggar a beautiful horse that had been presented to him by King Oswin of Northumbria. [316]

Hūnroðr was planning a journey eastward and asked the bishop to predict his future astrologically in the way that the wise men of old had been accustomed to do. Sigfrid warned him against such practices and urged him to hold fast to the Christian faith. Hūnroðr then asked the bishop for a loan in order to ensure his success in his undertaking, but the latter had nothing of value except a gold ring which had been given him by Olav Trygvessön. On this he set such great store that he feared that it had become a snare to him, imperilling the safety of his soul, and consequently he gave it to Hūnroðr to help to supply his needs. [317]

good evidence for identity of Sigurd & Sigfrith

---

[314] Before the commencement of the battle Olav Trygvessön had made a scornful reference to the fact that the Swedes were still heathen. " Ekki þurfum vér at óttask Svia hrossaetur, fyrir því at þeim man tiðara at sleikja innan blótbolla sína heldr en ganga upp á Orminn langa undir vápn var." Fagrskinna, c. 79.

[315] Flateyjarbok, I., O.T.S., c. 401.

[316] " Eccles. Hist.," III., c. 14.

[317] Oddr: "O.T.S.," c. 24; Flateyjarbok, I., O.T.S., c. 401.

The fact of Olov Skötkonung having become a baptized Christian must have been of considerable help to Sigfrid in his work, though whether the bishop was often brought in contact with the king we do not know. Shortly before the close of his reign, however, Olov became very unpopular with his subjects, and indeed came near to losing his crown altogether. He was suspected of wishing to destroy the great idol temple at Uppsala, [318] and this naturally angered the Swedes, since they were still for the most part heathen; while his foreign policy with regard to the neighbouring kingdom of Norway was displeasing to both Swedes and Goths.

In Norway Olav Haraldssön, who was later to become the land's patron saint, was now ruling. He was a descendant of Harald Haarfagre, and on coming to Norway in 1015 had succeeded in wresting the rule from the Earls Haakon [319] and Sven, the latter of whom was governing a third part of the country as a vassal of the Swedish king. [320] In the war that ensued Olav invaded Sweden, and when the Swedish king thought he had him safely entrapped in Lake Mälar escaped by cutting a fresh channel for his fleet. [321] In spite of his success, however, Olav of Norway was anxious for peace and friendship with Sweden and wished to marry the king's daughter Ingegard. The Swedish peasants at the Uppsala " thing " secured the unwilling consent of Olov to the arrangement, after a remarkable speech by the lagman Torgny, in which, after blaming Olov for his pride, he offered him the choice between agreeing to the wishes of his subjects and forfeiting his crown and life. [322]

But Olov failed to keep his promise, for he gave Ingegard in marriage to Jaroslav of Russia, [323] and although Olav of

---

[318] Adam Br., II., c. 56. Cp. "S.R.D.," I., No. 18, Annales Esromenses, sub anno 1024. Schmid: "Sveriges Kristnande," p. 56, hints that Olov coveted the wealth of the temple.

[319] Earl Erik, the father of Haakon, had in 1015 resigned his powers and gone to assist Knud of Denmark in the subjugation of England. See Arup: "Danmarks Historie," I., p. 131.

[320] "M.H.N., Theodorici Monachi Historia," c. 14. "Olavus vero rex Svethiæ commendavit partem suam Sueinoni fratri Erici."

[321] "Heimskringla, S.O.S.," c. 6.

[322] "Heimskringla, S.O.S.," cc. 80, 81.

[323] Adam Br., II., c. 37; "Heimskringla, S.O.S.," cc. 92, 95.

Norway espoused instead her half-sister Estrid, [324] Olov's subjects were so incensed at his conduct that, had it not been for the rivalry between Swedes and Goths, he would probably have lost his crown. Though the Swedes had been offended both at the proposed destruction of the Uppsala temple and also at the king's treatment of his brother sovereign, they considered that the Goths were infringing on their prerogative in proposing his deposition, and determined to retain him as king although under changed conditions. After some discussion it was agreed that Olov should choose whatever district he wished for his residence, and should there establish a church, but should make no converts by force. [325] He was also to share his crown with his son, Anund Jakob. [326]

Olov's choice fell on Skara in Västergötland, [327] which about the year 1020 [328] he made the seat of a bishopric, and got Unwan, Archbishop of Bremen, [329] to consecrate for it a priest named Thurgot, [330] who thus became the first diocesan bishop in Sweden, and seems to have met with great success in his

[324] " Heimskringla, S.O.S.," c. 94.

[325] Adam Br., II., c. 56. " Is (i.e. Olov) subditos sibi populos ad christianitatem convertere volens, magno laboravit studio, ut templum ydolorum, quod in medio Sueoniæ situm est, Ubsola destrueretur. Cujus intentionem pagani metuentes, placitum, cum rege suo tale constituisse dicuntur, ut si ipse vellet christianus, optimam Suediæ regionem, quam vellet, suo juri teneret, in qua ecclesiam et christianitatem constituens, nemini de populo vim recedendi a cultura deorum inferret, nisi qui sponte cuperet ad Christum converti."

[326] " Heimskringla, S.O.S.," c. 96.

[327] Skara seems to have become important in quite early times. See H. Hildebrand: " Skara Domkyrka," p. 4. Becoming the seat of the first Swedish bishopric naturally added to its importance and later on it is said to have possessed ten churches and eleven convents, but this is probably an exaggeration. See Lindskog: " Försök till en kort beskrifning om Skara stift," I., p. 5.

[328] Schmid: " Sveriges Kristnande," p. 55, thinks that the initiative for the creation of the see came from Unwan rather than the king, and points out (pp. 56–7) that it must have happened within about the years 1015–22, as it took place when Olav Haraldssön was ruling in Norway and Olov Skötkonung in Sweden.

[329] Unwan succeeded Libentius in the see of Bremen in 1013. His legatine authority over the North was confirmed by Pope Benedict VIII. in April, 1022. Sv. Tr., No. 20 ; Hamb. U.B., No. 64 ; P.L. 139, Benedict VIII. E. and P., No. 37 ; Jaffé, Lit. Sp., No. 377.

[330] Rhyzelius: " Epis." I., pp. 163, 164. Von Dalin, I., xx., 9, following Adam Br., II., c. 57, says that he baptized the wife and children of Olov Skötkonung. See further, Hauck: " K.D.," III., pp. 646, 647.

work of evangelizing the surrounding region, as well as other parts of southern Sweden. [331]   What the relations were between Thurgot and Sigfrid is unknown, and it is strange that in the list of bishops appended to the old West Gothic Law-book neither Thurgot nor his successor, Goteschalk, is named. Sigfrid himself is said to have been the first bishop to introduce the Christian faith into these parts, and mention is made of his having consecrated three churches—those of Friggeråker, Gerum and Agnestad. [332] That he came from England is stated, but no reference is made to any work of his in Norway or Denmark, and as the transference of his labours to Värend is noticed, those in Västergötland must belong to the time before he settled at Östrabo and went to Husaby to baptize King Olov.

According to the compiler the next West Gothic bishop was Unni, whom he calls an archbishop, says that he was consecrated in England and sent out, and that the people were so reluctant to embrace Christianity that they stoned him to death. [333] Here he is badly wrong, for Unni was the Archbishop of Bremen who visited Birka in the first half of the tenth century and died a natural death there in 936. [334] The third bishop, Osmund, he says, moved the bishop's seat to Skara, [335] apparently implying that it had previously been at

[331] Adam Br., II., c. 56. "Ille vir strenue legationem suam perfecit in gentibus; duos nobiles populos Gothorum suo labore Christo lucratus est." This statement must not, of course, be taken too literally.

[332] "U.Ä.B.," p. 47. "Sigfriðaer war fyrsti biskuper, sum haer kom kristnu a. Han for af Aenglandi ok hingaet ok maerkti haer þre kyrkiustaeði ok vighði þre kyrkiugarðae. En aer i Friggiaerone, annar i Girem, þriði aer i Agnistaðum."

[333] "U.Ä.B.," p. 50. "Annar war Unni aerchibiskupaer. Han wighðis i Aenglandi ok saendis swa hingat. þa wildi haer swa nöðoght folk wið kristnu takae, at þer toko biskupin ok tyrfðu til banae maeð stenum."

[334] Of course it is just possible, though extremely improbable, that there was also a bishop of Skara with the name of Unni, who lived in the time of Sigfrid, and that the old chronicler has partially confused him with the archbishop of earlier times.

[335] "U.Ä.B.," p. 51. "þriði war Astmuðaer biskupaer. Han satti fyrst staf oc stol i Skarum." The "Vita S. Sigfridi," p. 368, says of the church at Husaby, "Quae ecclesia postmodum per longa temporum curricula Cathedralis fuit, donec sedes episcopalis exinde Skaris est translata."

Husaby, while he also says of him that he died there, whereas, as we shall see later, he came to England and spent the last years of his life at the monastery of Ely.   It would seem then that at the time of the compilation of the list of bishops Thurgot and Goteschalk had been completely forgotten, [336] but that traditions of the work of Sigfrid, which contained a good deal of actual fact, were still current in the neighbourhood, and that mingled with these were vague traditions concerning Unni and Osmund, which were used in ignorance of their untrustworthiness.   Certainly we cannot but feel that for the early history of the see of Skara, Adam of Bremen, who lived so near to the time of Sigfrid and his immediate successors, and who, moreover, not only had access to the chapter records of the see of Bremen but was personally acquainted with Svend Estridsön of Denmark, who had spent many years in Sweden and gave him much information about that country, is a more reliable authority than the compiler of the Bishops' Chronicle in the West Gothic Law-book.

Olov Skötkonung does not seem to have survived very long the arrangement by which he fixed his court at Skara, for he died about 1022, [337] and was succeeded by his son Anund Jakob, [338] who from being joint ruler now became sole king of the land.   He was, like his father, a zealous Christian, and though he was noted for the severity which he showed towards evil-doers, and earned the name " Kolbränna " [339] from his practice of firing the houses of delinquents, he seems on the whole to have been popular with his subjects.   He was wise enough to make no attempt to impose Christianity on them

[336] In the case of Goteschalk this is hardly surprising, for apparently, though appointed bishop, he never went to Skara.   Adam Br., IV., c. 23.   " . . . secundus vero Godescalcus, vir sapiens et bonus, ut prædicant, nisi quod domi sedens ocium labori prætulit."

[337] Annales Reseniani.   " 1022.   † Olafs konungs Sensca.   Avnvndr toc riki."

[338] The name Jakob was given to him at his baptism.   Adam Br., II., c. 57 ; " Heimskringla, S.O.S.," c. 89.   Later on the Swedes gave him the name Anund.   "S.O.S.," c. 96.   Saxo, X., c. 512, seems to confuse him with his brother Emund.

[339] " U.Ä.B.," p. 29.   " Annar konongaer war Aemundaer Kolbraennae oc het þy Kolbraennae, at war riwaer i raefstum sinum at braennae hus mannae."   Cp. " Chronicon Prosaicum, S.R.S.," I., i., p. 245.

by force, but during his rule it continued to make good progress through the labours of Sigfrid and others.

Unlike his father, Anund was on friendly terms with Olav of Norway—a policy which perhaps helped to account for his popularity—and he allied himself, although not very energetically, with that monarch against Knud of Denmark.[340] This state of friendliness would no doubt make him willingly acquiesce in Sigfrid acting again as a court chaplain to the King of Norway. In that country a heathen reaction had followed the death of Olav Trygvessön, a very natural result of that king's reprehensible methods of introducing Christianity, and Olav had a busy time in carrying out the re-establishment of the Christian faith in those districts where it had been overthrown.[341] In this work he had the help of Sigfrid, and we have more than one reference to the bishop in the Saga, particularly in the contest with the great chief Dale Gudbrand, one of the principal supporters of the old faith. We have a very picturesque account of the events that led up to the destruction of the idol of Thor in which this chieftain put such trust, after which Olav gave his opponents the choice of accepting Christianity or waging battle. Dale Gudbrand then stood up and said, " We have sustained great damage upon our god; but since he will not help us, we will believe in the God thou believest in." He and his son were baptized by Sigfrid, and he built a church in the valley.[342]

There were other English missionaries, too—Grimkel, Rudolf and Bernard—who helped Olav in his task of completing and consolidating the work of his name-sake,[343] and

[340] "Heimskringla, S.O.S.," c. 141.
[341] Oddr: "O.T.S.," c. 39, says with regard to the work of the two kings, " Olafr konungr Tryggva sonr saetti vingardin. en enn helge Olafr konung létt riðlaz vinberin með favgrum blomum ok riðluþum vin viðum af vin berium ok allz kyns aldini ok ferðe sva mikin avoxt sem hann var lenge konungr."
[342] "Heimskringla, S.O.S.," cc. 118, 119. Sigfrid would seem to have returned to Norway some time before the death of Olov Skötkonung, so that monarch was probably still reigning at the time of Dale Gudbrand's conversion.
[343] Adam Br., II., c. 55. Grimkel is again mentioned in IV., c. 33. The anonymous author of the " Historia Norwegiæ " in " M.H.N." makes Olav bring these three as well as Sigfrid with him from England (p. 124).

owing to the friendly relations existing between him and
Anund Jakob, they, like Sigfrid, worked sometimes in Norway,
sometimes in Sweden.   As in the case of Gotebald, however,
we have no detailed account of their work in the latter
country and do not even know in which districts it was carried
on, though in all probability it would be in parts adjoining
Norway.   Grimkel, who was a nephew of Sigfrid, [344] would
seem to have been Olav's principal court bishop, [345] and he
not only helped the king in the evangelization of the people,
but shared with him in the compilation of a code of laws,
intended to embody all the points in which Christianity
affected the life of the people, and which was agreed upon at
a special assembly of the bishops, clergy and other learned
men held at Moster. [346]   In later times when King Olav had
to go into exile in Sweden Bishop Grimkel accompanied him,
and after the king's death at the battle of Stiklestad, when he
was attempting to recover his kingdom, he played a very
prominent part in establishing his right to be regarded as a
saint. [347]   Bernard, after working for a time in Norway, was
sent by Olav to Iceland, where he supervised the preparation
of a Christian code of laws, and saw it put into practice.   After
a stay of five years in Iceland, [348] he seems to have been made
Bishop of Skåne by King Knud, who was very partial to the
employment of Englishmen for high ecclesiastical offices in
his Danish territories, [349] so much so as to cause grave discontent to Archbishop Unwan of Bremen.   The latter caught
one of these bishops, Gerbrand of Roskilde, who had been
ordained by Ethelnoth, Archbishop of Canterbury, and forced
him to promise to recognize his metropolitical rights, while at
the same time he censured Knud, who promised to work with
him in the future. [350]   Rudolf, who is called Bishop of

---

[344] " M.H.N., Theodorici Monachi Historia," c. 19, makes him his
brother's son, but in Flateyjarbok: O.T.S., c. 403, he is said to be his
sister's.
[345] "Heimskringla, S.O.S.," c. 55.   Cp. Flateyjarbok: S.O.S., c. 43.
[346] Keyser, I., c. 12.   Den Norske Kirkes Historie
[347] "Heimskringla, S.O.S.," cc. 258, 259.
[348] Ari VIII., i. Ari styles him " enn bócvíse."
[349] Cp. Jörgensen, pp. 449–51.   Bernard had been consecrated by
Ethelnoth, Archbishop of Canterbury, in 1022 ; see Stubbs: " Registrum
Sacrum Anglicanum," p. 33, and Searle: " Anglo-Saxon Bishops," p. 210.
[350] Adam Br., II., c. 53.

Nidaros, was apparently a relative of Edward the Confessor,
King of England.[351]   About the year 1029 he and Sigfrid
paid a visit to Archbishop Libentius of Bremen,[352] who had
just succeeded Unwan in that see, and were present at the
funeral of Thurgot, Bishop of Skara, who had died of leprosy
at the see city where he had been staying for some time with
the archbishop.[353]   The two prelates were able to relate to
Libentius the story of the progress of Christianity in the two
northern lands, telling him how much God had done for the
salvation of the heathen, and when shortly afterwards Rudolf
returned to Norway he found that the rapid progress made
there by the Faith seemed to render his further stay unnecessary; consequently he made his way to Iceland, where he
spent nineteen years helping to establish the Church,[354] after
which he returned to England and was made Abbot of Abingdon by King Edward, but died two years later in 1052.[355]

We know little of Sigfrid's doings after his return from
Germany.   Probably he resumed his itinerant missionary
work for a time, keeping Växjö as his centre.[356]   We learn
that he gave advice both to St. David and St. Eskil as to the
parts of the country they should try to evangelize,[357] and he
was probably the consecrator of the latter, who is said to have
been related to him and to have acted for a time as his
chaplain.[358]   Apparently he lived to a very great age, the later
part of his life being spent quietly at Växjö, where he died, in
what year is unknown, but probably between 1060 and

[351] The "A.-S. Chronicle" calls him his cousin.
[352] Adam Br., II., c. 62. "Aderant vero tunc cum archiepiscopo prædicatores inclyti, Othingar junior ex Danis, Sigafrid a Suedia, Rodolf a
Normannia episcopi, narrantes ei, quanta fecerit Dominus in salute
gentium, quæ cotidie convertebantur."
[353] Adam Br., II., c. 62. "Illis namque diebus beatissimus Thorgat
episcopus pro labore prædicationis Bremæ cum archiepiscopo diutius con-
sistens, fertur asperrimo lepræ morbo percussus, diem vocationis suæ cum
magna expectasse patientia."
[354] Ari, c. 8. [?] Islandabök
[355] "A.-S. Chron." sub anno 1050. "Anglia Sacra," I., 167. "1052:
Rodulfus episcopus et abbas Abbendonensis ecclesiæ obiit." See further,
"Chronicon Monasterii de Abingdon," in Rolls Series, pp. 463, 464.
[356] Stomberg: "H.S.," p. 136, thinks that his activity was confined to
Västergötland and Småland.
[357] "Historia S. Davidi," Lectio VIII. "S.R.S.," II., i., p. 410.
[358] "Legenda S. Eskilli, S.R.S.," II., i., p. 392.

1070. [359] One incident is related of him just previous to his death. His great age had caused him to become somewhat forgetful and he ordered a bath to be prepared for him on a fast day. A voice reproved him for doing this, whereupon he left the bath and confessed his fault. A few days later he died, [360] and was buried at Växjö under the altar of the cathedral. [361]

Although we know on the whole so little about the details of the life of Sigfrid, and more particularly so with regard to his work in Sweden, yet there seems no doubt that he did more than any other individual—more even than Anskar himself—for the conversion of that country. [362] The results of the mission of the latter were, as we have seen, disappointingly meagre; his successors had done little more than keep alive the single congregation he had founded at Birka; but at the time of Sigfrid's death, if we place it about the year 1068, although the great heathen temple at Uppsala was still standing, and the Swedes themselves were still largely heathen, both Västergötland and Östergötland had been extensively christianized, and even among the Swedes a considerable amount of progress had been made, while the struggle between the two religions was giving clear indications as to how it would ultimately end. For this state of affairs Sigfrid was very largely responsible, and his claim to the title of " Apostle of Sweden " cannot be disputed.

According to some authorities Sigfrid was canonized by Pope Adrian IV. about the year 1158, [363] and he is commemorated on February 15th. It seems very doubtful, however, if he was ever formally canonized, and in those times it often happened that the sainthood of a person was

[359] He was evidently dead at the time when Adam of Bremen wrote his history (about 1075).

[360] Flateyjarbok: O.T.S., c. 402. " . . . ok eftir fa daga fell Sigurdr byskup j saran siuknnat saeliga framlidande af þessu lifue stundligu almenniligan ueg til almatligs guds þeim se lof ok dyrd aeinum j þrenningu um veralldir verallda."

[361] See Baaz: "Inventarium," I., c. 8, p. 105. "Locus sepultura S. Sigfridi est in Cathedrali Templo Wexionensi, sub Altari. . . ."

[362] Cp. Stora Rimchrönikan, l. 43. "Sigfridus aff Wäxiö som christnade Sweriges Land."

[363] Vastovius: "Vitis Aquilonia," p. 32.

established without such process. An impressive life or a martyr's death, reports of miracles wrought at the tomb of the deceased, the invocation of his help in times of trouble that followed such reports, and the sainthood of the person was accepted in the district that had witnessed his labours and death. The sphere of his cult might remain restricted to this district, or it might become enlarged—sometimes gradually, as in the case of Sigfrid; sometimes with great rapidity, as with Olav of Norway—until it came eventually to comprise the whole land and sometimes even the whole of Western Christendom. A formal canonization might follow or the Pope might recognize *de facto* the sanctity of the individual in question.

In the case of Sigfrid, in spite of all that he had accomplished, a long time seems to have elapsed before his sanctity was generally recognized throughout the country of his adoption. This fact can be deduced from the dating of letters or documents written on the day set apart for his commemoration. The first of these bearing Sigfrid's name is one written by Bishop Ysarn of Strängnäs in 1292, granting an indulgence of forty days to those who with due respect visited the relics of St. Botvid. [364] In this he is styled "confessor," while King Birger in a letter of 1312, in which he confirms the gift of the property of Ekeby by his brothers, Erik and Valdemar, to the convent at Riseberga, calls him "bishop and confessor." [365] But the observation of his day was evidently not yet general, for in 1313 we find the Abbot of Alvastra, in the diocese of Linköping, dating a letter of February 15th "in crastino Valentini," [366] while it is not till 1357 that we have a letter from Skara diocese bearing as its date St. Sigfrid's Day. [367] Eventually, however, not only did the observance of the day become general, [368] but it was looked upon as a festival

---

[364] Sv. Dip., No. 1061. "Datum Tælgis anno domini MoCConona-gesimo secundo, die beati sigfridi confessoris."

[365] Sv. Dip., No. 1835. "Datum ørabro. Anno domini MoCCCoXIIo., die beati sigfridi episcopi et confessoris."

[366] Sv. Dip., No. 1902.

[367] Schmid: "Den helige Sigfrid," p. 71.

[368] In the Vadstena Diary it is fully recognized. See entries under years 1409, 1411, 1419, etc. In one case, however,—1460—February 15th is styled the Thursday before Sexagesima.

of such importance that we find letters or documents with such dates as " in profesto Sancti Sigfridi confessoris," [369] " in crastino Sancti Sigfridi episcopi," [370] " feria quarta proxima post festum beati Sigfridi episcopi et confessoris," [371] " die lune, proxime, ante festum beati Sigfridi," [372] and " odensdagen nest firi sancti Sigfridi dagen." [373] Växjö, as we have seen, had been the chief centre of the saint's labours in Sweden. Though it had had a regular succession of bishops from the later part of the twelfth century onwards it had not been made a market town, but in 1342 this privilege was conferred on it by King Magnus Eriksson, to the glory of God and of St. Sigfrid. [374]

St. Sigfrid's Day appears in all the Swedish medieval diocesan calendars, [375] but its festal rank varied considerably in the different dioceses; in Linköping and Strängnäs, for instance, it was " totum duplex," in Västerås " duplex," while in Uppsala it was only " semi-duplex." [376] The original office for St. Sigfrid's Day would appear to have been that in use at Växjö, which with certain modifications was adopted in the other dioceses. The cult of the saint was not confined to Sweden. In Denmark it was probably first popularized by Petrus Johannes, a Dane, who in the last quarter of the

[369] Åbo D.S., No. 275. Dated Räntämäki kyrka, 1392.
[370] Åbo D.S., No. 544. No place named, 1449.
[371] Sv. Dip., II., No. 538. Dated Uppsala, 1405.
[372] Sv. Dip., No. 2133. No place named. Gift to Vårfruberga Convent, 1318.
[373] Sv. Dip., No. 4284. Dated Kumo, 1348.
[374] Sv. Dip., No. 3624. Dated February 13, 1342. Skeninge. "Förty att S. Sigfridus och Domkyrckian i Wexiö hafwa hafft omthålla och misshufft och J sielfwa stora skada och ogång aff ty att Wexiö hafwer eij warit kiöpstader. . . . Tå hafwe Wi för Edra Rättwijsa böön skull . . . och Gudi til heders och S. Sigfrido, att förscriffne Wexiö skall häreffter kiöpstader och heeta."
[375] The seven pre-Reformation sees in Sweden all possessed a printed Calendar with the exception of that of Växjö.
[376] The Festal Grades differed to some extent in the different dioceses. In the Uppsala Missal there were seven: Totum duplex, duplex, semi-duplex, simplex, ix. lectiones, iii. lectiones and commemoratio; in the Strängnäs and Västerås Missals five: Totum duplex, duplex, simplex, iii. lectiones, memoria; and in the Norwegian Missal seven: Summum, majus duplex, duplex, semi-duplex, simplex, iii. lectiones, commemoratio.

fourteenth century was for some time Bishop of Växjö, [377] and who on returning to his homeland to become bishop first of Aarhus and then of Roskilde, founded in the latter place a chapel to the honour of Sigfrid. [378] A century previously at a chapter of the Augustinian Order held at Arboga in 1303 it had been decided that St. Sigfrid's Day, with its octave, was to be observed throughout the whole province of Dacia. [379] How far this decree was carried out we do not know, but in later times, although Roskilde was the only Danish diocese in which St. Sigfrid's festival took high rank, he was also commemorated at Lund, Aarhus and Odense, [380] while relics of him were preserved both at Lund and in the Franciscan monastery at Roskilde. [381] That his cult was by no means negligible in Denmark seems to be witnessed to by the fact that we have at least one important political event chronicled as having happened on his day. [382]

In Norway the calendar in the general missal for the kingdom contained Sigfrid's name, [383] and he is commemorated in the Cologne and other martyrologies, [384] but no English medieval calendar seems to have appointed a day for his remembrance—nor, indeed, for any other of the English

[377] He occupied the see from 1382 to 1386, and seems to have owed his appointment to a Papal provision, the Pope refusing to confirm the Chapter's choice of Henricus Karoli. See Rhyzelius: "Epis.," I., p. 301 ; Brilioth : "Svenska kyrka," pp. 132, 133. He became Bishop of Roskilde in 1395.

[378] "S.R.D.," III., p. 374, note k. Cp. "S.R.D.," I., No. 16. "1408 obiit Dominus Johannes Andree miles de Aesendorp, qui fundavit altare Katherine in Capella Sancti Sigfridi." No. 20. "CIƆCDXIX., vi. Non. Martii Roschildiæ moritur Laurentius Johannis Decanus. Hic fecit librarium in Sacello S. Sigfridi."

[379] "S.R.D.," V., No. 163, p. 644. "In festo beati Sigfridi et per octavas octoginta dies."

[380] Lindberg : "Die Schwedischen Missalien," p. 205, seems to have overlooked this when he says " Der einzige spezifisch schwedische Heilige, der über die dänische Grenze gelangte, ist also, ausser Birgitta, St. Erik."

[381] "S.R.D.," VIII., No. 215, p. 272.

[382] "S.R.D.," I., No. 27. "MCCCV. Concordia facta est inter Regem et Duces die beati Sigfridi."

[383] "XV. kal. Mar. Sigfridi epī et confessoris. simplex."

[384] P.L. No. 123. Usuardus Monachus Sangermanensis : Martyrologium. Auctaria. Editio Lubeco-Col. " Ipso die, sancti Sigfridi, episcopi et confessoris." Molan. "Vexione in Dacia, sancti Sigfridi episcopi, præclaræ sanctitatis viri, qui Sueciam ad Dominum convertit." See also " Acta Sanctorum," V., p. 848.

missionaries who laboured in Sweden—though workers in other continental fields, as, for instance, Boniface and the two Ewalds, were deemed worthy of the honour. [385]

For many years before the death of Sigfrid there had been other English missionaries labouring in the land, but in their case too the details of their lives are disappointingly scanty. One of the earliest of them was a certain Woldred, who would seem to have worked in the early part of Anund Jakob's reign. [386] Of him, indeed, very little is known, not even which part of the country was the scene of his labours, but from the account that we have of his death he was evidently a man whose zeal as a Christian teacher outran his discretion. The Swedes seem to have been willing enough to let the Christian missionaries labour among them so long as they confined themselves to peaceful methods and did not in any way interfere with the heathen worship, or attempt to make converts by force. As Bishop Wordsworth remarks, Sweden " was a country to which forcible conversion was abhorrent," [387] and the martyrdom of the three nephews of Sigfrid, and later on that of Botvid, had in neither case anti-Christian zeal as its motive.

Woldred after an eloquent sermon to his heathen audience, which apparently roused no resentment among them, started to anathematize an image of Thor, and then, supplementing speech by action, with a two-edged axe hewed down the idol. This action so enraged the witnesses of the deed that they promptly fell upon him, slew him, and cast his body into a

[385] " Medii Ævi Kalendarium," I., pp. 454, 458 ; II., pp. 34, 98. In the Exeter Calendar Boniface was commemorated on June 5th, and the two Ewalds on October 3rd. The name of Boniface also occurs in the Sarum Calendar.

[386] Messenius: " Chronicon Episcoporum," pp. 14, 15, says, " Hujus vero tempore, videlicet MXXVIII., Ulfridus zelo cultus divini flagrantissimus Anglicana tellure posthabita, transivit in Sveciam, a quo idolum gentis Thorstan, in frustra comminutum, et Ulfridus extemplo mille confossus mucronibus barbarorum, animam efflavit." In Sc. Ill., I., p. 82, however, he calls him Valtridus, and puts the date of his martyrdom about 1026. Alford: " Fides Regia Anglicana," III., Index Sanctorum, gives 1028 as the year of his death, and January 17th as the day of his commemoration.

[387] " N.C.S.," p. 85. Compare his remarks on p. 81.

neighbouring marsh. [388] This happening afforded an excellent example of the unwisdom of using force in religious matters in Sweden, and Woldred's fellow-missionaries and successors would seem for the most part to have realized that such actions as the destruction of heathen images must follow the acceptance of Christianity, not pave the way for it. It is interesting in this connection to notice the differences in the national characteristics of the Swedes and Norwegians as shown by the attempts at forcible conversion in their respective countries. In Norway the violent measures of Olav Trygvessön and St. Olav succeeded where the peaceful measures of Haakon the Good had failed, while in Sweden the one king—Inge I. —who attempted to make the adoption of Christianity compulsory lost as a consequence his crown for a time, and when he did eventually recover it had profited sufficiently by his experience to change his policy, and trust to peaceful means for the spread of the Gospel. It is true that one Swedish province—Småland—had Christianity forced upon it, but this was the work of a Norwegian king, Sigurd the Jerusalem-Farer, [389] and we must not forget that probably with him, as with his famous predecessor, Olav Trygvessön, a merely nominal acceptance of Christianity was sufficient. [390] The fact that their acceptance of the Faith was a voluntary one should have made the Swedes better converts, but we have one old English writer who contrasts them very unfavourably in this respect with the Norwegians, Danes and Icelanders. The Swedes and Goths, he says, so long as all goes well with them seem to respect the Christian faith; but if there comes any

---

[388] Adam Br., II., c. 60. " Per idem tempus sermo est quendam ab Anglia nomine Wolfredum, divini amoris instinctu Suediam ingressum, verbum Dei paganis cum magna fiducia prædicasse. Qui dum sua prædicatione multos ad christianam fidem convertisset, ydolum gentis nomine Thor, stans in concilio paganorum cœpit anathematizare; simulque arrepta bipenni simulacrum in frusta concidit. Et ille quidem pro talibus ausis statim mille vulneribus confossus, animam laurea dignam martyrii transmisit in cœlum. Corpus ejus barbari laniatum post multa ludibria merserunt in paludem."

[389] Ágrip, LVI., i. " . .ok logþo vistagiald á Smálond, XV. c. nauta, ok tóko við kristni." Cp. " Heimskringla : S.S.J.," c. 28.

[390] Hildebrand : " S.M.," III., p. 62, thinks that the expedition was probably undertaken more for the sake of plunder than for the extension of Christianity.

misfortune—death, drought, stormy weather, attacks of enemies or destructive fires—they attack, not only with words but deeds, the worship of God, which they seemed to honour, punish the Christians in their land, and wish to expel them. [391]

In writing thus the monk Ailnoth had in mind the heathen rising under Blot-Sven and the martyrdom of St. Eskil, for he mentions the latter in support of his statement. It seems hardly fair, however, to give an event of forty years earlier as a proof of the unsatisfactory nature of the Christianity of the Swedes and Goths of his time, nor to draw conclusions of so general a nature from one particular happening. One feels, too, that he is naturally somewhat biased in favour of the Danes, the life of whose sainted king he is writing. The whole history of the introduction of Christianity into Sweden shows that the sweeping judgment of the English monk needs to be considerably modified. As elsewhere, the progress of Christianity was not an uninterrupted one; as elsewhere, men adopted the Christian faith for unworthy motives, and in times of reaction and trial denied it. It must not be forgotten what important changes in manner of life were necessitated by even its nominal acceptance—the giving up of Viking raids; the abandonment of such rights as the possession of more than one wife and the exposure of newly-born children [392]; and the necessity of obeying the laws of the Church, instead

[391] "S.R.D.," III., "Ælnothi Monarchi Historia S. Canuti," p. 331. "Svethi vero et Gothi, rebus ad votum faventibus, prosperisque, succedentibus, christianitatis fidem nomine tenus venerari videntur: At, ubi adversitatis aura, sive terræ infertilitate, ærisve siccitate, aut procellarum densitate, seu hostium incursione, vel ignis adustione, inflaverit, fidei religionem, quam venerari verbo tenus videbantur, non modo verbis, verum etiam rebus, christianorumque fidelium persequotionibus, insequuntur, atque suis finibus omnino expellere conantur."

[392] In Iceland, however, when it was decided to adopt Christianity as the national faith, the old law of the right of exposure of children was allowed to remain, and the eating of horse-flesh was still permitted. See Christne Saga, VIII., 9. With regard to the adoption of Christianity in Iceland, Gjerset: "H.N.P.," I., p. 351, says, "The legislative act of the Althing which abolished the old worship produced no perceptible change in the moral life or the religious views of the people." Compare this judgment with that of Dawson: "Making of Europe," pp. 252–3. "The influence of Christianity on Iceland was not, as some writers would have us believe, a superficial and external element in the life of the people: it was of fundamental importance for their culture. . . . The conversion of Iceland was not merely a matter of political expediency; it was the acceptance of a higher spiritual ideal."

of only national and so self-imposed laws. Since, then, some of the new customs and observances must have entailed considerable hardships on converts as being opposed to life-long usages not easily discarded, it is not surprising that where the acceptance of the Faith was accompanied by no deep and heartfelt conviction of its truth, any additional strain put on outward adherence to it by a temporary loss of popularity, or by its failure to bring any hoped-for temporal blessings, caused numerous lapses into heathenism or a state of practical agnosticism.

In any case, whatever truth there may be in the statements of Ailnoth in regard to the Swedes and Goths, they cannot be taken to invalidate the principle that the acceptance of Christianity should be voluntary, and that such means as those used by Charlemagne in Saxony or the two Olavs in Norway to bring about its adoption as a national faith were thoroughly reprehensible.

CHAPTER V

THE ENGLISH MISSIONARY BISHOPS *(continued)*

THE fact that Anund Jakob was an earnest Christian and was also popular with his subjects no doubt helped considerably to assist the progress made by Christianity in his dominions, for, however limited the power of the Swedish monarch may have been in some respects, his example and influence must have had considerable weight. His friendship with Olav of Norway was another factor in the evangelization of Sweden, for, as we have already seen, the latter was greatly helped in the work of consolidating the accomplishment of his predecessor Olav Trygvessön by a band of English missionary bishops, and these had extended their labours into Sweden, so that in more than one way Anund's rule was more favourable to the progress of the Gospel than that of his father Olov Skötkonung, the first Christian king.

Anund Jakob, however, died about the year 1052, and was succeeded by his half-brother Emund, usually called the Old, of whom the chroniclers speak in very unfavourable terms, [393] although we really know very little about his rule, and it would appear probable that the attempt he made to alter the ecclesiastical state of affairs in his dominions, so that they should be practically independent of the jurisdiction of the Archbishop of Bremen, was responsible for Adam's description of him as " pessimus." [394]

It was another nephew of Sigfrid, named Osmund, [395] who

---

[393] " U.Ä.B.," p. 30. " þriði war Aemundaer Slemae, ok het þy Slemae, þy at war sliskaer ok eigh goðaer at þra i þy mali, han wildi fraemiae." Krantzius, V., c. 11, says "solo nomine Christianus," but Lagerbring, I., xvi., 28, points out that nothing bad is known about him except his dispute with Adalbert.

[394] Adam Br., III., c. 14. It must not be forgotten that although Adam is on the whole a most trustworthy historian he exhibits a tendency to glorify the see of Hamburg-Bremen, and so his judgments on persons who encroached, in his estimation, on its prerogatives must be received with caution. Cp. Schmeidler: "Hamburg-Bremen und Nordost Europa," pp. 108, 109. "Aber wenn man ihn als historische Quelle

was largely concerned in this matter. As a boy he had been sent by his uncle to the school at Bremen,[396] and probably his education there helped to develop the ambition which was such a prominent feature of his character. Not satisfied with the priesthood he determined to obtain episcopal orders, and presently made a visit to Rome, hoping to obtain consecration there. In this endeavour he was unsuccessful, but in the course of his travels he found a Polish archbishop, who was willing to confer on him the desired order,[397] and he then made his way to Sweden to become court-bishop to King Emund, who for some unknown reason seems to have been anxious to free the Church of his country from its dependence on the see of Bremen, and saw in the arrival of Osmund an opportunity of carrying out his wishes. Actually Osmund styled himself archbishop, claimed to have been appointed as such by the Pope,[398] and adopted the state corresponding to the dignity that he claimed. News of his proceedings was brought to Adalbert, who at that time occupied the see of

würdigen will, erwägen, welche Glaubwürdigkeit Nachrichten, die nur bei ihm überliefert sind, beanspruchen dürfen oder nicht, so muss man einmal nicht nur auf seine Vorzüge, sondern auch auf seine Fehler und Einseitigkeiten die Aufmerksamkeit lenken. Dieser sind bisher noch nirgends genügend und in richtiger Weise ans Licht gestellt, die Gesamterscheinung des Werkes in seiner Entstehung, wie sie sich auf Grund der Handschriftenstudien nunmehr verfolgen lässt, ist noch niemals gewürdigt worden ; auch seine schriftstellerische Kunst bei einem hervorragenden Gegenstande, in der Disposition seines ganzen dritten Buches ist noch ganz unbeachtet geblieben." Cp. also the remarks of Schück : " S.F.H.," I., p. 267, and Schmid : " Sveriges Kristnande," p. 45. A further fact to be taken into consideration is that for his knowledge of Swedish affairs Adam was largely indebted to Svend Estridssön, who would naturally view them through Danish eyes.

[395] Adam Br., IV., c. 33.

[393] Adam Br., III., c. 14.

[397] Adam Br., III., c. 14. " Verum is (i.e. Osmund) postea beneficiorum oblitus, pro ordinatione Romam accessit, indeque repulsus, per multa loca circuivit erroneus, et sic demum ordinari meruit a quodam Polaniæ archiepiscopo."

[396] Wordsworth : " N.C.S.," p. 79, considers that there may have been something in Osmund's claim, but this hardly seems to fit in with the " indeque repulsus " in the narrative of Adam of Bremen. Osmund comes third in the list of the Bishops of Skara, and he also appears in the " Chronicon Episcoporum Arosiensium, S.R.S.," II., ii., p. 121, as the second bishop of Västerås. Hildebrand : " Skara Domkyrka," p. 6, does not think that he was a bishop in Västergötland, and it is to be noted that he is also called Bishop of Växjö.

Bremen, and whose naturally haughty disposition made him little likely to endure such an encroachment on his prerogatives with equanimity. To remedy matters he consecrated Adalvard, Dean of Bremen, as Bishop for the Swedes,[399] and sent him with a number of monks to Sweden to remonstrate with Emund for the impropriety of entrusting to Osmund that which of right belonged to the Archbishops of Bremen, and also to protest against the false doctrine which the intruder was said to preach.

Adalvard on his arrival found that in one respect at any rate the reports that had reached Bremen were not exaggerated. He found Osmund acting as archbishop of the country, having a cross carried before him, and claiming to be there as the representative of the Pope.[400] But when he appealed to King Emund he found that monarch by no means willing to acknowledge the right of the Archbishop of Bremen to interfere with the ecclesiastical arrangements in his realm. Probably Emund felt much the same as Harald Haardraade of Norway, who appointed bishops in his land according to his own pleasure, having them consecrated in England or France, and when remonstrated with by Archbishop Adalbert sent his messengers out of the country, saying that he recognized no other archbishop or ruling lord in the kingdom beside himself.[401]

A "thing" was called to discuss the claims of the new arrival, with the result that Adalvard was driven away with insults, while it was possibly mainly owing to the influence of Stenkil, one of the leading nobles, who afterwards became king, that he did not meet a worse fate.[402] But trouble came upon Emund's realm. His son Anund, together with his army,

---

[399] Adam Br., III., c. 14, Schol. 94. This was the older Adalvard, who comes fifth in the list of the Bishops of Skara.

[400] Adam Br., III., c. 14. "Tunc veniens in Suediam, jactavit se a papa consecratum in illas partes archiepiscopum."

[401] Adam Br., III., c. 19. Harald would also seem to have brought Greek bishops to Norway; see Bang: "Udsigt," p. 84; Gjerset: "Hist. of the Norwegian People," I., p. 283. Pope Alexander II. wrote to Harald to reprove him for his methods of appointing bishops. P.L. 146, Alexander II., E. and P., No. 3; Jaffé, No. 4471.

[402] Adam Br., III., c. 14. Stenkil is here called the nephew of Emund.

perished on account of the poisoning of the wells when on an expedition to the country of the Amazons—by which curious appellation some part of Finland would appear to be meant [403]—while drought and famine attacked Sweden itself. The feeling of the time attributed the disasters to the discourteous treatment meted out to Adalvard and it was decided to recall him. [404] This was done and about the same time Emund died, and was succeeded by the jarl Stenkil, who was possibly the son of the old jarl Rangvald Ulfsson of Västergötland, though he is sometimes called the nephew of Emund. [405]

Osmund became reconciled with Archbishop Adalbert, who confirmed him in his office, and for some time he worked faithfully in Skara diocese and in Halland, where he baptized his converts in a well by Sibbarp in Fahrås-härad. Eventually he came to England, and stayed for some time with Edward the Confessor, but having visited the famous monastery at Ely, he decided to make it his home, and spent the remainder of his days there, performing for the monks various episcopal duties. [406] He seems to have been much respected at the monastery, and the character given him by the Ely chronicler

[403] Adam Br., III., c. 15. Cp. IV., c. 19, Schol. 119.

[404] Adam Br., III., c. 15. "Deinde cum aliis cladibus tanta siccitas et frugum sterilitas Sueones afflixit, ut missis ad archiepiscopum legatis, episcopum suum reposcerent, cum satisfactione fidem gentis pollicentes."

[405] Adam Br., III., c. 15. "Post quem (i.e. Emund) levatur in regnum nepos ejus Stinkel." The Hervarar Saga, c. xx., says "han atti dotter Omundar Kongs."

[406] Historia Elyensis, c. 42. "Nunc dicendum est de Osmundo pontifice inter supradictos pridem honorifice translato, qui de Suedtheda regione, ubi Episcopus exstiterat, veniens in Angliam, Edwardo regi aliquam diu adhærabat, ejusque curiam cum magna ipsius Regis gratia sequebatur. Erat autem vir grandævus et honorabilis, cunctisque Regni primatibus pro reverentia sui amabatur. Dum igitur versaretur in Regali curia, fama Elyensis Religionis delectatus, locum ipsum visitare decrevit, volens ibi reliquum vitæ tempus transigere, si fratrum gratia cum sua voluntate concordaret. Quo perveniens, loci amœnitate et fratrum devotione detinetur, et in plenam fraternitatem receptus, omnia Episcopalia apud eos eorum petitione faciebat, hoc enim solum omnes Episcopi huc se conferentes sibi retinuerunt, ut relicta cura Episcopatuum, solum Episcopale officium exercerent. Duravit autem piissimus vir iste apud hanc ecclesiam a temporibus Wlfrici Abbatis, qui eum susceperat, usque ad tempora Turstani Abbatis, sub quo defunctus Episcopalia ornamenta, hic dum viveret, concessa nobis dereliquit, et tandem de veteri sepultura a nobis translatur in pace requiescit."

reads somewhat strangely when we recall his earlier years, though it must not be forgotten that Adam of Bremen's account of his proceedings and character is likely to have been coloured by natural jealousy for the prerogatives of the see of Bremen. Osmund was buried in the monastery church at Ely, but after the cathedral was built his remains were trans-ferred to it, and were eventually deposited in the south wall of Bishop West's Chapel where the inscription may still be read, " Osmundus e Suedia, obiit Anno Domini MLXVII."

Osmund has been identified with Asmund Kareson, the famous northern rune-writer, of whose work something like forty examples are known to exist. Asmund apparently began his work about the year 1025, and continued it for something like thirty years, for on one of the stones he mentions King Emund. [407] His special devotion to the Blessed Virgin Mary is very characteristic of his inscriptions, while the fact that in one point they seem to show the influence of English rune inscriptions makes it very probable that their author had some connection with England. That Uppland at this time was still largely heathen makes it probable that he was a cleric, while the period assigned to the rune-stones is that at which we know Osmund to have lived. It seems, however, a little strange to think of a court-bishop as a rune-master, so that if Asmund and Osmund are identical we must suppose that he set off on his travels early in the reign of Emund and that though wide, they were not lengthy in regard to time. [408]

There was yet another relative of Sigfrid, who was of English birth [409] and who played a prominent part in the

---

[407] This is the Jarsta stone in Valbo parish, raised by the brothers Tjudger, Gudleif and Karl to the memory of their father Tjudmund. The inscription " God and His Mother help his soul " is very charac-teristic of Asmund's runestones. See O. von Friesen: " Upplands Runstenar," p. 36.

[408] Fredrik Sander was perhaps the first to identify Osmund and Asmund. Von Friesen seems to think the identification possible; see " Upplands Runstenar," p. 38.

[409] Rhyzelius: " Epis.," I., p. 207, thinks that he was not an English-man but a Goth who had gone to England to study there. The " Vita Sancti Eskilli, S.R.S.," II., i., p. 395, however, has the statement " Sanctus Eskillus . . . spretis parentibus et patria, a Britannia (ubi ori-undus exstitit) ad regnum Sveciæ perrexit "; while Ailnoth in his " Historia Vitæ S. Canuti, S.R.D.," III., p. 330, also speaks of his coming

Eskil -(relative of Sigfrid)

conversion of Sweden. This was Eskil, who did so much for
the evangelization of the province of Södermanland, and
whose name is perpetuated in the well-known town of
Eskilstuna, the Sheffield of Sweden.

In all probability Eskil was invited over from England by
Sigfrid some time during the reign of Anund Jakob, and was
then consecrated bishop by him. [410] He is also spoken of as
having acted for a time as chaplain to Sigfrid. Though often
reckoned as the founder of the see of Strängnäs he would
appear to have been, like his uncle, a missionary bishop, who
made the church that he built at Fors, near the southern
shores of Lake Mälar, the centre from which he made his
evangelistic journeys into the surrounding territories, and
which remained as such for many years. This town, or Tuna,
which adjoined it, was probably an important trading centre,
for it seems to have been a usual practice for Christian
missionaries to settle in such a place, if it was not specially
associated with the observance of heathen rites, and from it
carry on their evangelistic work. Such a commercial centre
would have more than one advantage ; there would be greater
opportunities of reaching a large number of hearers than in
most places ; those hearers, coming as they would from many
parts, would be able to carry back to their own districts what
they had heard of the new Faith, and so prepare the way for
the visits of the missionary ; and in a large commercial town
visited by merchants from other lands, some of whom might
be Christians, there would probably be less bigoted adherence
to the old heathen beliefs and customs, more tolerant views,
and a more ready disposition to listen to the claims of the
Gospel, than there would be in a place where age-long

ie before c. 1052

from England. The latter is the earliest historical writing that mentions
Eskil. Cp. the expression in the Officium S. Eskilli in the Skara Breviary,
"S.R.S.," II., i., p. 402, "O proles Britanniæ," and the Strängnäs
Breviary :—

> "Laudant Sudhermanniæ
> Pueri parentem,
> In prole Britanniæ
> Lapsos erigentem."

[410] "Legenda S. Eskilli, S.R.S.," II., i., p. 392.

customs had been unaffected by contact with outside influences.

For a considerable time Eskil would appear to have carried on his labours unostentatiously and uninterrupted by the changes that took place in the occupancy of the Swedish throne. Anund Jakob, as we have seen, had been succeeded by his half-brother Emund, and the latter, who was probably the last of the line of kings who traced their descent directly from Odin, had for his successor the jarl Stenkil, [411] whom we have already met befriending Bishop Adalvard at the court of King Emund. Stenkil was a zealous Christian, and Bishop Adalvard [412] seems to have hailed his accession as affording the opportunity for the destruction of the idols in the Uppsala temple and the forcible imposition of Christianity on the Swedes. In this proposal he was supported by the Danish bishop, Egino of Skåne, the first bishop of the united sees of Dalby and Lund, [413] who seems some time previously when on a visit to Sweden to have destroyed an image of Freyr at some place in Västergötland [414]; but Stenkil's zeal was tempered with discretion, and he refused to entertain the plan, for he was able to estimate more accurately than the two prelates what would be the probable result if he were to put it into action. It would mean, he told them, for him the loss of his kingdom, for them a martyr's death, and for the country a complete relapse into heathenism, and later events were to show how accurately on the whole the king had judged the temper of his Swedish subjects. The two bishops, however, seem to have found a field for their iconoclastic fervour in Götaland, which was not yet entirely christianized, and we are told that they journeyed through all the towns of

[411] The West Gothic Lawbook places Håkon the Red between Emund and Stenkil, but this is a mistake. See Adam Br., III., Schol. 85. His love for the West Goths is strongly emphasized. "Han aelskaeđi waestgötae umfram allae þe maen, i hans riki waru. . . . Ok e gladdus waestgötaer af hanum, maeđaen hans lifdaghaer waru."

[412] This was Bishop Adalvard the Younger, who had been consecrated bishop for Sigtuna, and afterwards endeavoured to succeed the elder Adalvard at Skara, in consequence of which he was recalled to Bremen. Adam Br., III., c. 70, Schol. 94; IV., Schol. 131.

[413] Adam Br., IV., cc. 8, 9.

[414] Adam Br., IV., c. 9.

the Goths, broke down the images of the gods and won over to Christianity many thousands of the heathen. [415]

After the death of Stenkil, which happened about the year 1066, [416] there was a period of great confusion, and it is difficult to reconcile the accounts of the different chroniclers. Apparently a sanguinary struggle for the crown took place, during which two claimants, both bearing the name of Erik, were killed. [417] It is not at all unlikely, as Schück suggests, [418] that one may have been the nominee of the heathen party, the other of the Christians. Hallsten, son of Stenkil, was then king for a short time, but was driven from the throne, which was then occupied by a certain Anund from Russia, who in his turn was displaced by Håkon the Red. [419] The latter, who was possibly a great-grandson of Erik Segersäll, reigned for a period of thirteen years, [420] and then we find Inge, another son of Stenkil in possession of the throne, [421] though at least for part of his reign only as co-ruler with his brother Hallsten, [422] of whom the chronicle speaks highly. [423]

Inge's enthusiasm for the conversion of his Swedish subjects led him to revive the project of Adalvard. He not only abolished the sacrifices at Uppsala, but seems to have planned

[415] Adam Br., IV., c. 29.
[416] Hervarar Saga, c. 20. "þà vard han sottdaudur i Sviþiod, naer þui er Haralldur Kongr fiell a Einglandi." Cp. Saga of Magnus Barefoot, c. 13.
[417] Adam Br., III., c. 52.
[418] "S.F.H.," I., p. 284.
[419] Adam Br., III., Schol. 85. "Duobus Hericis in prœlio interfectis, Halzstein, filius Stenkel regis, in regnum levatus est. Quo mox pulso, accersitus est Amunder a Ruzzia, et illo nichilominus amoto, Sueones quendam elegerunt Haquinum." The Saga of Magnus Barefoot, c. 13, says that Håkon succeeded Stenkil. Geijer: "History of Sweden," E.T., p. 41, note 1, thinks that Håkon was probably never acknowledged by the Swedes, but the runestone at Hofgård in Uppland inscribed at his command to the memory of his son, would seem to show the contrary. For a good account of the succession at this time, see Schück: "Den äldsta kristna konungalängden i Sverige," pp. 21–9.
[420] "U.Ä.B.," p. 30. "þraettan wintaer war han konongaer."
[421] "U.Ä.B.," p. 32. "Saetti war Ingi konongaer. Han styrði Sweriki maeð draengskap. . . ."
[422] Hervarar Saga, c. 20.
[423] "U.Ä.B.," p. 33. "Syundi war Hallsten konongaer, broðer Ingae konongs, hofsambaer ok godlyndaer. Hwart mal, fore han kom, þa war han bötaendi at. Fore þy uslaeðis Sweriki af hans frafallum ok döðae."

the destruction of the temple there, [424] while he also gave the order that all persons should submit themselves for baptism. The result showed how correct had been his father's estimate of the danger of employing force to secure conversions, for his Swedish subjects, indignant at this interference with their liberties, rose in rebellion. They considered that the king would break the law of the land if he destroyed those things that Stenkil had allowed to remain undisturbed. [425] A " thing " was held, and Inge was presented with the alternatives of maintaining the old laws and customs or of giving up his kingship. Inge refused to come to terms with his subjects and a riot ensued, in the course of which he was stoned and driven from the assembly. After his departure his brother-in-law Sven, afterwards known as Blot-Sven, [426] or Sven the Sacrificer, told the Swedes that he would offer the blood sacrifice for them if they would confer on him the kingship, and when they had agreed to his terms, a horse was brought forward and slaughtered, and the accustomed rites were carried out. [427] King Inge took refuge in Västergötland and for three years Blot-Sven ruled in Sweden proper. [428]

[424] Westman, p. 4, note 2, conjectures that he actually destroyed it. He thinks this is implied by the account of his proceedings given in the Hervarar Saga. But though he is said to have put a stop to the sacrifices (hann eiddi blótum) it does not necessarily follow that the temple was destroyed.

[425] Hervarar Saga, c. 20.

[426] In the " Legenda S. Eskilli, S.R.S.," II., i., p. 393, he is called Blodhsven, and the author adds " merito sic vocatum, quia permisit eos bibere sanguinem animalium simulachris libatum, et vesci idoloticis." Cp. " Minsta Rimchrönikon," ll. 534–7 :—

> " Djurabloden med samma kost
> Lät jag them dricka, som äplemost,
> Ty wedernamn jag af almogen fick,
> At jag kallas Blodsven för samma dickt."

But it is practically certain that the additional name is derived from blota, to sacrifice to idols.

[427] Hervarar Saga, c. 20. " Var Sveinn þá til kongs tekinn yfir alla Svíþióð, var framleidt hross eit á þingit ok höggvid í sundr, ok skipt til áts, enn ríódudu blodinu blót-trie." The " Legenda S. Eskilli," p. 393, speaks of the slaughter and sacrifice of sheep and oxen at the assembly at Strängnäs, " immolatis bobus et ovibus."

[428] Hervarar Saga, c. 20. " Blót Sveinn var þria vetr kongr yfir Svium." This was probably either from 1076 to 1079 or from 1079 to 1082. Gams: " Series Episcoporum," p. 339, assigns Eskil's martyrdom to the year 1129, a most improbable date.

Eskil

It was during this time of heathen triumph that St. Eskil suffered martyrdom. King Inge had supported his missionary work strongly, [429] and we read of many baptisms taking place at a well west of Strängnäs, afterwards called by the bishop's name, [430] and of his converts in their enthusiasm destroying the heathen images and altars, and hewing down the groves, [431] a course of action no doubt approved of by the king. As already mentioned, Eskil seems to have made the town of Fors the centre from which he carried out his missionary journeys. Some miles away, on a spit of land jutting out into Lake Mälar, was the town of Strängnäs, where the men of Södermanland were accustomed to hold their principal sacrifice. Eskil, hearing that Blot-Sven was sacrificing there, hastened with his clergy and a few other followers to the gathering, and tried to restrain the people from countenancing the heathen ceremonies. [432] His action would seem to imply, either that a number of his converts, frightened by the fate that had overtaken King Inge, had relapsed into heathenism and needed to be made to comprehend what such a denial of their faith involved, or else that the recent pagan triumph demanded from him a stronger policy than the one that he had hitherto adopted.

But his exhortations to the people failed of their purpose, and the saint then prayed that God would by some sign convince their stony hearts that He alone is God. A terrible storm of thunder, lightning, snow, hail and rain followed; the sacrificial altars were overthrown and the victims destroyed, but Eskil himself remained scatheless. [433] Anger, however, rather than awe took possession of the assembled multitude at this striking interposition in answer to the bishop's prayer. A certain soothsayer, named Spabodde,

[429] En kort Berättelse om S. Eskil, S.R.S.," II., i., p. 397.
[430] See the letter of Archbishop Laurentius Petri to Olaus Nicolai, Bishop of Strängnäs, about the offerings brought to this well. "S.R.S.," II., i., p. 404.
[431] "Legenda S. Eskilli," p. 393.
[432] "Legenda S. Eskilli," p. 393. Cp. pp. 396, 398.
[433] "Legenda S. Eskilli," p. 394. "Fragore magno intonuit Dominus, grando, nix et pluvia descendentes, aras immolantium et hostias destruxerunt, super Episcopum vero nec una gutta pluviæ venit." Cp. p. 398.

Eskil a martyr

struck Eskil on the head with a stone; another pagan protagonist cleft his skull with an axe; and then, still breathing,
he was carried by the order of the king to a hill, afterwards to
become the site of a Dominican monastery, [434] and there
stoned to death. [435]

Some faithful followers, whom the chronicler compares
with the seven thousand in Israel who had not bowed the knee
to Baal, [436] carried off his body with the intention of taking it
to Fors for burial, but when they had gone a certain distance
the threatening appearance of the sky and the curious
heaviness of the body compelled them to halt and remain for
the night. [437] The next day, instead of completing their
journey, they decided to bury the body of the saint there.
Later on a church was built, and the town that grew up
around it perpetuated in its name the memory of the martyred
bishop. In this last statement the legend would seem to be in
error, for, as we have already noticed, Tuna seems to have
been an important trading centre before the time of the
martyrdom, and there was in all likelihood a church there in
the bishop's lifetime. [438] We should hardly gather, too, from
the legend that Fors and Tuna were adjoining places, though
the later Swedish relation speaks of them as identical. [439] In
any case, some time elapsed before Tuna became known as
Eskilstuna, for in the early part of the twelfth century, when
we find it as the see city of an independent diocese, it is still
named simply Tuna, and it was not till long after this became
merged in that of Strängnäs that the town got the name of the

[434] Anjou: "Kyrkoreformationens Historia," I., p. 37; "Scandia,"
IV., p. 106. The monastery, like those at Skara, Skeninge and Åbo, was
dedicated to St. Olav.
[435] "Legenda S. Eskilli," p. 394; Cp. "S.R.D.," III., No. 88, p. 331.
[436] 1 Kings xix. v. 18.
[437] "Legenda S. Eskilli," p. 394. "Venientibus autem eis ad locum,
qui dicitur Eskilstuna, tanta densitate nebula ærem obscuravit, quod
ulterius ire non potuerunt, et ita ponderosum effectum est corpus ejus,
quod illud movere nullatenus potuerunt."
[438] Archæological investigations seem to show that there was a well-
organized Christian community at Tuna about the middle of the eleventh
century. See Lindqvist: "Den helige Eskils biskopsdöme, pp. 13f.
Messenius thinks that Cluniac monks settled there in the time of Eskil,
but this seems extremely doubtful.
[439] Relatio Svecica, "S.R.S.," II., i., p. 397. "Fors eller Eskielztuna."

saint. [440] It was also the seat of an important monastery of the Order of the Knights Hospitallers of St. John, founded some time before 1185, [441] and until the arrival of the Friars the only religious house in Sweden that did not belong to the Cistercian Order. For a long time its parish church contained some relics of the saint; others were preserved in the cathedrals of Uppsala and Strängnäs; and others again in the Danish Franciscan monasteries of Copenhagen and Roskilde.

It seems almost certain that St. Eskil was never formally canonized, but that, as in the case of St. Sigfrid, his sanctity gradually became recognized throughout the whole of Sweden, and even beyond its bounds. He was looked upon as the patron saint of the see of Strängnäs, and there were two diocesan festivals held in his honour, one commemorating his death on June 11th, [442] the other commemorating his translation on October 6th. In the dioceses of Uppsala, Linköping and Åbo, June 12th was appointed as the day of his commemoration, while his translation was observed in Linköping and Västerås on October 6th, and in Skara on October 8th. With regard to the rank of these festivals, as might be expected the two observances in Strängnäs were both " totum duplex," and the octave of the translation was also observed as a

---

[440] The exact date when the union of the two dioceses took place is unknown. It must have been at some time between 1120, when Eskilstuna is named in a document as an independent see, and 1164 when the Papal bull which made Uppsala the seat of an archbishopric placed under it four suffragan sees of which Eskilstuna was not one, having evidently been merged with Strängnäs before that date. After the district around Lake Mälar had been thoroughly evangelized, fewer centres would be needed. There is a letter of Pope Gregory IX. to the Knights Hospitallers in Denmark written in 1231 in which he refers to the town as Tuna (" ecclesiam beati Eskilli Martyris et pontificis de Tunæ "). Sv. Dip., No. 839; Celse: " Bullarium," p. 63 ; Potthast, No. 8797. Dated September 6th, 1231, Rieti.

[441] Hildebrand : " S.M.," III., p. 57 ; Westman, p. 181.

[442] In the Vallentuna Calendar June 11th is assigned to both Eskil and Barnabas. In the Strängnäs Calendar the latter has June 12th instead of the 11th. In the English Martyrology of John Wilson, Eskil is assigned to April 10th, which date is also given in Alford : " Fides Regia Anglicana," III. Wilson quotes from Johannes Magni, but the latter gives no date. In the Martyrologium Usuardi, Auctaria Greven et Molan, Eskil is only given under October 6th, the day of his translation.

" simplex " ; in Linköping the death-day of the martyr was only a " simplex," but the translation was " duplex " as it was also in Västerås, which had no commemoration at all of the death-day; in Uppsala the feast was " semi-duplex " and in Åbo " duplex." [443]

If, as in the case of Sigfrid, we judge of the spread of his cult by taking note of the letters and documents that bear his name in their dating, we find that not only is it considerably later before we find one dated St. Eskil's Day, [444] but that the festival does not seem to have become used as generally as that of St. Sigfrid for this purpose. For a long time " in crastino beati barnabe apostoli," with slight variations seems to have been the usual style of date for June 12th. [445] As late as 1402 we have Bengt, priest of Algutstorp, selling some land and dating the document " in die beatorum martirum Cirini Naboris et Nazarii," [446] and even later documents of June 12th do not always bear the name of Eskil. [447] On the other hand, we sometimes find days other than June 12th dated with reference to the saint, as " in profesto beati eskylli episcopi et martiris," [448] " in crastino beati Eskilli martiris,"[449] and even " feria secunda octavas sancti eskilli episcopi et martiris." [450]

We do not find the name of Eskil in the Lund Calendar, which was very sparing in its commemoration of Swedish saints, but the Danish Franciscans possessed relics of him in

[443] This was also the case in the Finnish Calendars of Kangasala and Vesilahti. The translation did not occur in either of these Calendars or in that of Åbo.

[444] The first thus dated seems to be a bequest to Skara Cathedral by Helge, priest of Langhem, Sv. Dip., No. 2855. The date runs "Anno domini Millesimo. CCCºXXXIº. in die beati eskilli episcopi et martiris." There is a document issued by Bishop Styrbjörn of Strängnäs relating to two churches on Sela island, which is a few years earlier but is dated the day of the translation—"Datum Anno domini. MºCCCºXXVIIº. jn translacione beati eskilli episcopi et martyris." Sv. Dip., No. 2634.

[445] E.g., Sv. Dip., Nos. 2563, 2564, 2670, 3428, 3494. Occasionally we have other datings, as No. 1052, "secundo ydus junii"; No. 2194, "tercia feria proxima ante botolphi abbatis"; and No. 1667, "feria sexta infra octavas pentechostes."

[446] Sv. Dip., II., No. 187.

[447] E.g., Sv. Dip., II., Nos. 602, 1068.

[448] Sv. Dip., No. 3956. Fröberga, 1345.

[449] Åbo, D.S., No. 496. Söderköping, 1441.

[450] Sv. Dip., II., No. 844; Åbo, D.S., No. 315. Åbo, 1407.

their houses at Copenhagen and Roskilde,[451] and he became
venerated in Norway and eventually in Poland,[452] as well as
in the country of his adoption. One rather curious witness to
the honour in which his name was held in Södermanland was
that by the law of that province anyone who broke the peace
in Eskilstuna at the time of St. Eskil's Mass and slew a
member of the community, had not only to pay to the king a
fine of twenty marks, but also a similar sum to the Bishop of
Strängnäs.[453] In the district of Rekarne in the diocese there
was a special modification of the payment of Peter's Pence.
Each inhabitant had to pay four pennies yearly, of which two
were paid to the cathedral, and of these the Papal Chancery
had a fourth part; that is, a halfpenny. One penny went to
Eskilstuna church for the sake of St. Eskil, and the fourth
penny was divided between the Johannites in Eskilstuna and
St. Olav. In the remaining parts of Södermanland the
inhabitants paid only three pennies a year; again the
cathedral received two and the Papal Chancery a quarter of
this, but the remaining penny was divided—one half to
St. Olav, and one-sixth each to the Johannites, St. Eskil and
St. Botvid.[454] Later on the arrangement was altered, and it
was no longer ordered that a special portion of the tax should
be paid to St. Eskil. We may notice too that a synod held at
Arboga in 1396 decreed his invocation in the mass " pro statu
regni " in the diocese of Skara.[455]

[451] " S.R.D.," VIII., No. 215, pp. 284, 290 ; No. 216, p. 309.
[452] In the Norwegian Missal the day of his translation only was
observed, and the festal rank was a mere commemoration. " Oct. ii.
nones. Eskilli epi. & mar. cō." In Poland we have the death day only,
but observed as a duplex on June 22nd instead of the 12th. Officia
Propria P.S.
[453] " S.R.S.," II., i., p. 390. Cp. also the Law of Uppland in Schlyter :
" Corpus Juris Sveo-Gotorum Antiqui," III., p. 84.
[454] See " S.R.S.," II., i., 390 ; Lindqvist : " Den helige Eskils biskopsdöme," pp. 7–9 ; Brilioth : " Den påvliga beskattningen af Sverige,"
pp. 45, 46. The last-named quotes from the Liber Ecclesiæ Strengen-
ensis, " Nota quod quilibet inhabitans in provinciis østerrek et waesterrek
solvit pro censu Romano quatuor denarios annuatim, et sic consuevit
dividi ab antiquo, quod ecclesia cathedralis levavit dimidietatem, de qua
camere Romane quarta pars debebatur, sed de medietate residua ecclesia
eskilstuna nomine sancti eskilli levavit dimidium, etc."
[455] Gummerus : " Synodalstatuter," p. 28. His name in this connection comes next to that of St. Sigfrid, and before those of SS. Henry,
Helena, Birgitta, David and Olav.

David [margin annotation]

About the same time that Eskil suffered martyrdom, or a little later, death brought to a close the earthly labours of yet another English missionary bishop in Sweden. This was David, the Apostle of Västmanland, sometimes accounted the founder of the first monastery in Sweden as well as the first bishop of Västerås.

Pre-Norman Ch. in Engd [margin annotation]

As in the case of St. Eskil we know very few details of the life of the saint. He is said to have been the son of pious parents living in England and to have been given by them a liberal education.[456] Eventually he became a monk of the Cluniac order, and as such was noted for his excellent life and great austerities. Indeed " such rich treasures of grace and virtue were to be seen in him that he shone in the temple of God as the morning star shines amid the mists." When he

O. gives no date for this martyrdom. If Stomberg (or wipro) is right it must have been after 1020. [margin annotation]

heard of the martyrdom of the nephews of Sigfrid at Växjö, the desire that he too might win the martyr's crown became so strong that he left England, and after crossing the North Sea made his way to Växjö, where Sigfrid was at the time working.[457] When this was it is not easy to say, for though David presumably set out very shortly after he had heard of the death of the martyrs, it may have been many years before the report of this reached England. On the whole it is perhaps most likely that he reached Sweden shortly before, or shortly after, the death of Olov Skötkonung.[458]

At first he worked in southern Sweden, preaching the Gospel with great zeal, but presently, on the advice of Sigfrid, he fixed his seat in Västmanland,[459] choosing as his headquarters Munktorp, a place in Snävringe district, in the

---

[456] " Historia S. Davidis," Lectiones 1, 2. " Hic itaque David in Anglia oriundus parentes habuit nobiles, non tam ingenuitate sanguinis, sed et fidei catholicæ sinceritate præclaros. Hi igitur devotione assidui et christianæ fidei zelatores præcipui filium suum, sanctum David imbuendum liberalibus studiis tradiderunt."

[457] Stomberg: "H.S.," p. 136, rather strangely says that David was probably the first English missionary to come to Sweden, and that the date of his arrival was some time after 1020. Both Gotebald and Sigfrid must have worked in Sweden many years previously to that date.

[458] Rameen, c. iv., p. 9. The "Chronicon Episcoporum Arosiensium, S.R.S.," III., ii., p. 121, says of David "En Engeländare kom först inn i Swerige i Olof Skott Konungs sista regements åhr."

[459] " Chronicon Episcoporum Arosiensium, S.R.S.," III., ii., p. 121. He was also to work in Bergslagen and Dalarne.

neighbourhood of Västerås, where the "things" of the province were held as well as the principal sacrifices, and from there, in the manner of Sigfrid and Eskil, he travelled round to the towns and farmsteads, preaching the Gospel and baptizing converts.   Near the town of Sandsta is a well where he is said to have baptized, and other places in the neighbourhood—as the island of Biskopshamn in the lake, and Dåvö—appear to have derived their names from their association with him.   On Biskopshamn he built a little wooden chapel, and he also lived for a time at Dåvö, which thus acquired its name, an abbreviated form of Davidsö.   His life seems for a time to have been one of almost ceaseless activity.   By day he wandered from one district to another, preaching and baptizing, while his nights were spent in prayer for the success of his work, and it is said that while engaged in prayer he appeared to become changed into a globe of fire.   At Munktorp he is said to have founded, about the year 1030, a Benedictine monastery of which he became the first abbot. [460] If this were indeed so, and certainly David seems to be more commonly referred to as abbot than as bishop, [461] it cannot have lasted long, for when in the next century the Cistercians, at the request of Queen Ulvhild, came to Sweden, its people are said to have known indeed the name of monk, but never to have seen one. [462]   Possibly David had one or more fellow-monks working with him and this gave rise to the legend about his monastic establishment.

David would seem to have met with much success in his

---

[460] Messenius: " Sc. Ill.," IX., c. 29 ; " Historia S. Davidis, S.R.S.," II., i., p. 405.   " In parte Westmanniæ meridionali, et territorio Snavingensi, hodie Snäfringensi, Abbas noster, cum monachis suis, sedes fixit, ecclesiamque hujus regionis primam et primariam condidit, ab eo et comitibus Munketorp appellatam, quam appellationem hactenus retinet."

[461] Even in the " Breviarium Arosiense " he is only styled abbot.   " vii. kal. Julii David abbatis. Totum duplex." In the " Officia Propria P.S.," he is also only styled abbot, though Sigfrid and Eskil are both called bishops.   Gams, however, in the " Series Episcoporum Ecclesiæ Catholicæ," p. 340, has the entry, " Westeræs S. David Anglus ✠ 30. XII., 1082 "; and his name also comes first in the " Chronicon Episcoporum Arosiensium."

[462] " . . . qui monachi quidem nomen audierant, sed monachum antea non viderunt."   " Exordium Cisterciensis Ordinis, S.R.D.," II., p. 643.

work, but whether the privilege of laying down his life for the Faith was granted to him is very doubtful. [463]   As already mentioned he is reckoned the first Bishop of Västerås [464] and the foundation of its cathedral has been attributed to him; but though it is probable enough that he visited Västerås at intervals, as being the chief town of the district, and may even have erected a small church there, he does not seem to have made it his headquarters at any time, and it is better to regard him, like Sigfrid and Eskil, as purely a missionary bishop, and only having the right to the first place in the list of diocesans who occupied the see of Västerås, from that place becoming eventually the see city of the region which for half a century or so had witnessed his evangelistic efforts, and from the fact that he was possibly the first to preach the Gospel there.

A curious story is told of his old age. His sight had become very dim, and one day, mistaking the nature of a ray of sunshine coming through the window of Munktorp Church, he hung his gloves upon it. [465]   They remained miraculously suspended and thereafter David continued to make use of the solar support. One day, however, one of the gloves fell, and David was much distressed, wondering what fault of his had occasioned the loss of privilege. Eventually he went back the way by which he had come and found that he had trampled on some ears of barley. He therefore prayed for forgiveness for his fault, resolved to make amends, and having had a golden spike of barley made, placed it in the church. His

---

[463] Wordsworth : "N.C.S.," p. 82, says "He was martyred, it is supposed, in the year 1082 A.D." Cp. Lindberg : "Die Schwedischen Missalien des Mittelalters," p. 185, "David abb. de Munkatorp soll, vermutlich i J. 1082, den Märtyrertod erlitten haben." But the statement in the "Chronicon Episcoporum Arosiensium" seems to imply a natural death. "Denne Sanctus David blef mycket gammal och åldrig, dödde mätt af lefvande åhr 1082 den 30 Decembris." Nor is he styled martyr in the "Breviarium Arosiense," but only abbot.

[464] Rameen, c. 12, pp. 37–42.

[465] Messenius : "Sc. Ill.," IX., c. 29. "Tempore quodam oculis ejus senio et lachrymis, caligatis, solus in sella orat, existimans esse baculum radios solis per fenestram intrantes, in ipsis suspendit chirothecas. Veniente autem illo ad ecclesiam et mittente quendam pro chirothecis, eas sine omni fulcimento invenit in ære pendere." A similar story is related of St. Etheldreda. See "Acta Sanctorum," XXV., sub die June 23rd.

offering was accepted, and once more the ray of sunshine supported both his gloves. The ultimate fate of the golden spike is uncertain. According to one account it was taken away by Christian II. of Denmark; another makes it used to fashion the chalice that was known as St. David's Cup.[466] We have already said that the mode of David's death is uncertain. Probably he died a natural death from extreme old age and sickness, though it is just possible that, like Eskil, he suffered martyrdom during the heathen reaction under Blot-Sven. The latter, however, may have had good reasons for leaving him unmolested. Possibly owing to his great age he may have been confined to his house and so unable to offer any active opposition to the new king's efforts for the triumph of the old faith; possibly heathen vengeance was sufficiently satisfied by the death of Eskil and required no further victims; possibly David was held in such love and respect as would have made it dangerous to offer him any violence. There was, however, at one time over the altar in the church at Munktorp, so closely connected with the labours of the saint, a representation of three heads—those of Blot-Sven, David and Valfridus—which has been taken to imply that David was a victim of the persecuting zeal of the protagonist of heathenism.[467] But if by Valfridus is meant the Woldred, the story of whose martyrdom is related by Adam of Bremen, he cannot have suffered under Blot-Sven, whose election took place after the time at which Adam wrote.

Like Sigfrid and Eskil, David came to be regarded as a saint without apparently any formal canonization ever taking place, but his cult seems to have been a decidedly limited one —far more so than that of either Sigfrid or Eskil—and indeed to have been of much importance only in the diocese of Västerås. There, as also in the dioceses of Skara, Strängnäs

---

[466] Rameen, c. 6, p. 20.
[467] Rameen, c. 13. The description of the three heads was given to him by Laurentius Croning, who thought that the intention was to show that David suffered martyrdom during the rule of Blot-Sven. He himself seems to have been convinced by this evidence, for he says " In castra itaque eorum transimus, qui statuunt S. Davidem, occiso Svenone Victimario, sub Ingone III., e vita discessisse." Pp. 44, 45.

and Linköping, he was commemorated on June 25th, but in
the Uppsala Missal July 15th is the day assigned to him, as
it is in the English Martyrology. [468]

The earliest reference to the sanctity of David seems to be
the one in a decree issued in 1396 by Archbishop Henry of
Uppsala, [469] in which he granted an indulgence of forty days
to those who visited Åbo cathedral on the occasion of the
" festum reliquiarum " instituted there by Bishop Björn, and
also on certain other occasions visited the cathedral, the
Dominican convent, and the churches of Räntämäki and
St. Karin. Here, and in a similar document issued a little
later by Bishop Björn, [470] he is styled " confessor," which seems
to confirm the opinion that he died a natural death. He never
became such a popular saint as either St. Sigfrid or St. Eskil,
for although his name appears in all the Swedish diocesan
calendars, except that of Åbo, [471] it was only in the diocese of
Västerås that his feast was of high rank. There it was a
" totum duplex," but in Strängnäs and Skara only a " commemoratio " and in Uppsala " tres lectiones." His name is
absent from the Norwegian Missal, though those of Sigfrid,
Eskil and Henry are all found there; and while the festal
rank of the days of these three is " duplex " in the " Missæ
Propriæ Sanctorum Regni Sveciæ Patronum," that of David
has no rank assigned to it and his name is printed in black
instead of in red as are the others. Nor do we find his name
commonly used, as are those of St. Sigfrid and St. Eskil, for
the dating of documents and letters, either those of June 25th

---

[468] Wilson: " The English Martyrologe," sub die July 15th, " In
Suecia the deposition of S. David, Abbot and Confessor, an Englishman
by birth ; died about 1002." July 15th is also given by Ferrarius in his
" Catalogus Universalis," where he calls him " abbas et confessor,
natione Anglus," and by Claudius Castellanus in his " Martyrology." See
" Acta Sanctorum," V. 31, p. 109. This day is also given in the " Officia
Propria P.S.," and at the present day in the Vicariate of Sweden
St. David's Day is July 15th. Alford: " Fides Regia Anglicana," III.,
Index Alphabeticus Sanctorum Angliæ, gives June 15th.
[469] Åbo D.S., No. 279. Dated Sept. 27, 1396. Nyköping.
[470] Åbo D.S., No. 280. Dated Nov. 23, 1396. Åbo.
[471] It is also to be noted that David's name is absent from the Vallen-
tuna Calendar, though it contains the name of his contemporary,
St. Eskil.

Botvid—a Swede—but educated in England

or those of July 15th.[472] Relics of him were possessed by the Franciscan monks at Roskilde, and some were preserved in the church at Munktorp till after the time of the Reformation.[473]

One other name famous in the annals of the conversion of Sweden deserves to be mentioned here, for although Botvid was not an Englishman by birth, yet it was in England that he learned the Christian faith, and gained with it the desire for the conversion of his countrymen that led him to become one of the chief agents in winning them to embrace Christianity. When quite young he had gone to England for trading purposes, and there was received as a guest by a certain priest, who by his manner of life so impressed the youthful Swede that by the desire of the latter he instructed him in the articles of the Christian faith.[474] Eventually he was baptized by his friend, and then after some months' further stay in England returned to Sweden to carry on missionary work there. He met with much success in evangelizing his fellow-countrymen in Södermanland, who were greatly influenced by the Christian virtues he displayed in his life and so were drawn to listen to his teaching, until the grossly ungrateful act of a pretended convert brought his mission to an untimely end. Botvid had purchased a Wendish slave in order that he might liberate him, so that he might return to his own land and there preach the Gospel.[475] He

[472] There does not seem to be a single letter or document in the Diplomatarium Suecanum which bears his name as its date. In the Svenskt Diplomatarium there is one, No. 1324, a document relating to an exchange of land belonging to one of the prebends in Västerås Cathedral, which is dated "næsta thorodaghin æpter sanct Davidz dagh," 1410. For June 25th, Sv. Dip., Nos. 1341, 1726 and 4086, and Sv. Dip., II., Nos. 1072, 1734, 1735, 1969, 1970; and for July 15th, Sv. Dip., Nos. 1434, 2411, 2618, 3432, 3715, 4201, and Sv. Dip., II., Nos. 208, 1077 are all otherwise dated. In the Vadstena Diary though there are entries for June 25th in the years 1420, 1438, 1452 and 1476, it is in no case styled St. David's Day; while the single entry for July 15th—in 1416—has the assignation "Divisio Apostolorum."
[473] "S.R.S.," II., i., pp. 406, 407.
[474] "Vita S. Botvidi, S.R.S.," II., i., p. 378.
[475] "Vita S. Botvidi," p. 379. ". . . ut si posset ad parentes suos et propria reverti, familiam suam christianitati donaret, et quoscunque posset, notos et affines, ad christianitatis cultum et ad notitiam divinæ cognitionis exhortaretur."

had made arrangements for his protégé to sail in a certain vessel which was going to Gottland, from where he would be able to get another sailing to his own land, and Botvid, together with a tenant of his, named Esbern, was accompanying him to the port of sailing. On arriving, the little party found that the vessel had already left, and after vainly rowing about for some time on Lake Mälar in the hope of encountering it, they landed on a small island called Rogö. Botvid and Esbern, tired out by their fruitless search, lay down under a tree and fell asleep. Then the treacherous Wend, possessing himself of the axe which Botvid was accustomed to carry with him, slew both his benefactor and his companion, and taking the boat made his escape without troubling to conceal the bodies of his victims.

As Botvid did not reappear his relatives presently became alarmed and set out in search of him. For a long time their efforts were unsuccessful, but at length they discovered his body, having been guided to the spot, it is said, by a white bird which settled on the prow of their boat and directed their course. [476] A certain Hermond had built a church dedicated to St. Alban at Saby, where in later times a Cistercian convent was to arise, [477] and to this church the remains of Botvid were conveyed and given honourable burial. Nine years later, when many miracles associated with his name had caused local recognition of Botvid's sanctity, they were removed to a wooden church erected on his estate by Björn, the brother of Botvid, and this church when completed was consecrated by the bishops Henry of Uppsala and Gerder of Strängnäs and dedicated to the martyr. The place where it was erected, under the name Botkyrka, has perpetuated his memory to the present time. When Christianity had made further progress in the district the wooden church was replaced by a stone one, and this in its turn was dedicated by Stephen, the first Arch-

---

[476] " Vita S. Botvidi," p. 380. Of the bird it is said " cujus speciem nullus eorum antea viderat."

[477] It is better known by its later name of Juleta. For its history, see Hall: " Bidrag till Cistercienserordens Historia i Sverige," pp. 141f.

bishop of Uppsala, to the honour of the Blessed Virgin, St. Botvid and all saints. [478]

If we use the term " missionary bishop " with a connotation that distinguishes clearly between such bishops and strictly diocesan ones, St. David may be considered as the last of the English missionary bishops who worked in Sweden, but we must not think that he and the other Englishmen whose work has been recorded were the only members of their nation who laboured successfully for the conversion of the Swedes and Goths. In all probability there were many whose names have not come down to us, who worked in various parts of the land with more or less success. In particular the important trading city of Sigtuna—which in the eleventh century took the place of Birka as the chief commercial centre on Lake Mälar—as well as its immediate neighbourhood, would seem to have been christianized either by English missionaries or by Swedes, who, having embraced the teachings of the Gospel while dwelling in England, endeavoured to propagate them when they returned to their own land. King Knud had a number of Swedes in his service, some of whom probably settled in England when their military or other duties came to an end; and though we can hardly accept without some qualification the statement of a modern Swedish writer that following the Norman Conquest a great flight from England to Scandinavia took place, including both bishops and priests who had been deposed by William, [479] yet it seems by no means unlikely that when Norman influence became so strong in England in the time of Edward the Confessor, some members of the Scandinavian nations who were dwelling there may have returned home, and a larger number, including some ecclesiastics, have followed them during the troublous times that followed the victory of William of Normandy at Hastings. The writer just quoted points out how not only the ruins of the churches of St. Peter and St. Olav at Sigtuna show that the original buildings were of a characteristically English or English-Norman type of architecture, but that this same type

---

[478] " Vita S. Botvidi," p. 382.
[479] Cornell : " Sigtuna och Gamla Uppsala," p. 100.

of architecture is shown by several churches in the neighbourhood, among others those of Norrsunda, Skånella and Fären-
tuna, [480] and that the only other part of Sweden apart from
Uppland where we find Anglo-Saxon features in the ecclesiastical architecture is Västergötland. [481]

The first Bishop of Sigtuna was Adalvard the younger, who
was appointed by Stenkil to the see, but who was unable, as
we have seen, to persuade that monarch to allow him to
attempt the destruction of the Uppsala temple. He tried to
succeed Adalvard the elder at Skara, but his attempt to do so
aroused the disapproval of his metropolitan at Bremen, who
recalled him, [482] and with him the German mission may be
said to have ended, although the Archbishops of Bremen
retained their metropolitical rights over Sweden for some time
longer. Archbishop Adalbert's political fall, however, possibly
prevented him from sending a successor to Adalvard at
Sigtuna, [483] and so gave the opportunity for English missionaries to take up the work there that had been begun by
Adalvard, and carry it on with evidently a large measure of
success, although we have no record of their doings.

Another fact that helps to show how largely English
missionaries were responsible for the conversion of Sweden is
the number of English saints that we find commemorated in
the Swedish medieval calendars. Somewhat strangely, as we
have already noted, not one of the English missionaries to

[480] Cornell: " Sigtuna och Gamla Uppsala," p. 103. " The Churches
at Sigtuna, together with some other monuments situated in Central
Sweden, form a definite group in the older medieval Swedish architecture. The distinguishing characteristics of this group are, first, the
use of grey stone as building material, secondly, the design, which does
not occur anywhere else in our country ; .a central square with a tower,
transepts and a choir with an apse."

[481] Cornell, p. 91.

[482] Adam Br., III., c. 70. Adalbert in his letter to William, Bishop of
Roskilde, says, " Nunc autem fraternitatem vestram latere nolo, quid
molestiæ mihi Adalwardus episcopus intulit, quem vobis teste, qui
ordinationi ejus interfuistis, Sictonensis Ecclesiæ consecravi pontificem.
Quem dum barbara gens sibi praeesse noluit, Scariensem ecclesiam
invadere cepit." The West Gothic Lawbook's Bishops' list has confused
the two Adalvards ; see Beckman : " U.Ä.B.," p. 52.

[483] It is uncertain in what year Adalvard was recalled, but it was
probably in either 1067 or 1068. A letter of Archbishop Adalbert of
June 11, 1069, is subscribed with his name ; Hamb. U.B., No. 101. He
died at Bremen. Adam Br., IV., c. 29.

AB - Neglect of English heroes owing to MC

Sweden seems to find a place in any of the English calendars, but this may be largely due to the fact that their labours chiefly occurred in the first eight decades of the eleventh century; that is, in the period preceding and just following the Norman Conquest. The ecclesiastical authorities would be little likely to favour additions to existing calendars of the names of Anglo-Saxon missionary bishops, when the tendency at home was to replace the higher Anglo-Saxon ecclesiastics by Normans; and when eventually the English and Normans had fused into one people, it is highly probable that the names of Sigfrid, Eskil and David had been forgotten, if indeed they had ever been really known in the country of their birth. It seems, however, rather strange that in later times the Birgittines at Syon should not have introduced the cult of any of these Anglo-Swedish saints into England. The " Syon Martyrologium," although it contains three feasts of St. Birgitta—her deposition (July 23rd), translation (May 28th), and canonization (October 7th)—utterly ignores them and also St. Erik, though it has a commemoration of Olav of Norway, but on September 28th instead of July 29th. [484] It seems rather strange too that in the Calendar of the Revised Anglican Prayer Book the commemoration of St. Anskar should have been preferred to that of St. Sigfrid.

The earliest known Swedish calendar, that of Vallentuna, which dates from 1198, [485] contains a large number of English or Celtic saints—Bridget, King Edward the Martyr, Cuthbert, Guthlac, Elphege, George, Wilfred, John of Beverley, Dunstan, Augustine, Bede, Boniface, Botulph, Alban, Etheldreda, Swithin, Germanus, King Oswald, the two Ewalds, Willibrord, King Edmund the Martyr, Columban and St. Thomas of Canterbury. [486] That so many English saints

? ?

---

[484] " The Martiloge in Englysshe after the Use of the chirche of Salisbury and as it is redde in Syon with addicions."

[485] Unfortunately the calendar is not complete for the months of January and February are missing from the MS., a facsimile of which is given in Janse: " Kalendarium Vallentunense." One peculiarity of the Calendar is the inclusion of four Old Testament saints: Amos (March 31), Elisha (May 13), Isaiah (July 5) and David (Dec. 29).

[486] Janse: " Kalendarium Vallentunense." Cp. Lindberg: " Die schwedischen Missalien des Mittelalters," pp. 149f.

were early venerated in Sweden shows how strong must have been the influence of the English missionaries in the development of church life there. It is true that most of these names have been dropped in the later diocesan calendars, but those of George and Thomas of Canterbury appear in all of them; that of Botulph, who seems to have been especially popular, [487] in all except that of Åbo; and those of Bridget, [488] Boniface, [489] Alban, [490] Germanus [491] and King Edmund [492] in one or more of them.

The reaction in which Eskil lost his life seems to have been the last great effort of the heathen party to retain their supremacy in Sweden, and their triumph was not of long duration. For three years Blot-Sven ruled over the Swedes [493] and then Inge recovered his kingdom. Having collected an army and " ridden both day and night " he attacked Sven unexpectedly, early in the morning, and set fire to his palace. Sven endeavoured to escape, but was at once killed, and soon the kingdom was again in the possession of Inge. [494] Warned, however, by his former experience, and perhaps realizing the little worth of forced conversions, he made no further attempt to destroy the Uppsala temple, or to win his subjects to Christianity otherwise than by the peaceful agency of the missionaries. Yet his triumph can be taken as the definite turning point in the struggle between the two religions in Sweden proper. From now onwards the adherents of heathenism were fighting a losing cause, and the ultimate triumph of the Gospel was assured.

[487] In medieval times relics of St. Botulph were preserved in the church of Broddetorp in Västergötland; see Hildebrand: "S.M.," III., pp. 60, 87. He was also popular in Denmark, where six churches and a monastery were dedicated to him; E. Jörgensen: "Helgendyrkelser i Danmark," p. 17.

[488] In those of Uppsala, Linköping, Västerås and Strängnäs.

[489] In Uppsala only.

[490] In Linköping and Strängnäs.

[491] In Linköping, Strängnäs, Västerås and Åbo on July 31st; in Uppsala on August 4th. Germanus was not of British birth, his native town being Auxerre, of which he became bishop, but his mission to Britain against the Pelagians made him famous there.

[492] In Uppsala and Västerås.

[493] Hervarar Saga, c. xx. "Blót-Sveinn var þria vetr kongr yfir Svium."

[494] Hervarar Saga, c. xx.

If we compare the state of affairs after Inge was firmly reseated on his throne with that of a hundred years previously, when the country was overwhelmingly heathen, we cannot but notice the tremendous change that had taken place. The two Gothic provinces were now mainly Christian, and in Västergötland the Church had developed its organization to a fair extent, while in Sweden proper though the great idol temple at Uppsala was still standing its glory had largely departed, and the progress of Christianity in the land was heralding the not-far-distant time when it would not only cease to be the home of the ancient rites, but its very stones would serve to help in the erection of the Christian cathedral that was to take its place as the chief centre of worship for the land. These hundred years had indeed witnessed the triumph of Christianity; and the principal agents in bringing about that triumph had been the English missionaries, Sigfrid, Eskil, David and their companions.

CHAPTER VI

THE ENGLISH DIOCESAN BISHOPS

ALTHOUGH the services rendered by the English Church to the cause of Christianity in Sweden were mainly concerned with the primary missionary work of the evangelization of the country, yet English ecclesiastics were also responsible for a considerable share in what may perhaps be termed the secondary missionary work of the subsequent development and organization of the Church there, and five individuals in particular took a prominent part in this work. One was the agent in the opening up of direct communication between Sweden and the Papacy; a second did much to approximate the discipline of the Swedish Church to that of Western Christendom in general; a third earned for himself the title of the Apostle of Finland, and a fourth established the Church on a firm basis there; while the fifth assisted largely in the formation of a new province of the Western Church with Uppsala as its centre, and then himself, as the first metropolitan of that province, directed its ecclesiastical affairs at a time of very great importance in their development. It is interesting also to note further that in the case of the first " provision " made by any pope to a Swedish diocese, it was an Englishman who was appointed to the see in question.

On account of the long period that elapsed before the efforts of the Christian missionaries began to challenge seriously the sway of heathenism, the Church in Sweden was slow in developing its organization. When once, however, it commenced to extend the sphere of its influence with some rapidity, it was not long before it began also to take an organic form corresponding to that obtaining elsewhere in western Europe. The development of this organization, however, was a very gradual one. Even when certain places began to have a regular succession of bishops the limits of the various dioceses were probably for some considerable time very ill-defined, while not until the thirteenth century do we find properly constituted cathedral chapters set up,[495] although it is possible that after the introduction of monasticism the bishops in certain cases may have had an informal kind of chapter composed of a number of monks from a neighbouring monastery.[496] Heathenism, too, though the revolt against King Inge I. was the last serious anti-Christian reaction, was far from being dead, and so for some time the work of the diocesan bishops probably included, to a greater or lesser extent, missionary efforts for the extension of Christianity, as well as the ordinary episcopal functions.[497]

Skara, as we have seen, had, as the residence of Olov Skötkonung, become the seat of a bishopric about the year 1020, though there seems to be some doubt as to whether the first few bishops actually resided in Skara itself or at Husaby[498]; in any case it would seem to have been for some time the only bishopric proper in the country, for not until about sixty years later did the East Goths have their own bishop with his episcopal seat at Linköping.[499] The sees of

---

[495] In 1220 Honorius III. authorized Bishop Bengt of Skara to institute a chapter in accordance with the rules of the Augustinian Order, but if he should not find this possible he was to appoint secular canons. Sv. Dip., No. 194; Celse: "Bullarium," p. 58; Reg. Honorius III., No. 2757; Potthast, No. 6390. Dated Nov. 4, 1220, Lateran. There are traces of earlier chapters at Uppsala and Linköping, but when the papal legate, William of Sabina, visited Sweden in 1248, the cathedrals of Strängnäs, Växjö and Västerås were still without chapters. See Lindqvist: "De svenska domkapitlen," pp. 19–50.

[496] Reuterdahl: "S.K.H.," II., i., p. 156. He thinks that the Bishop of Strängnäs may have had some monks for this purpose from the neighbouring monastery of Juleta.

[497] It has already been pointed out that Honorius III. when appointing Egidius to the see of Västerås stated that one of his chief duties would be to extirpate heathenism in his diocese.

[498] In the Bishops' List in the West Gothic Lawbook it is said of the third bishop, Asmund (Osmund) "Han satti fyrst staf oc stol i Skarum." "U.Ä.B.," p. 51. But this list is a very unreliable source in regard to the earlier bishops named in it. As already pointed out, it omits Thurgot, the first bishop, and has other errors and omissions.

[499] The times assigned to the first two bishops—Herbert and Richard—in the "Chronicon Rhythmicum Episcoporum Lincopensium" are evidently erroneous; while Gislo, the third bishop, is also wrongly said to have been contemporary with St. Sigfrid. He attended a synod held at Lund in 1139, and in 1145 took part in the dedication of the cathedral ("Necrologium Lundense, S.R.D.," III., p. 456), but how long he had then been ruling his see is unknown.

Strängnäs [500] and Västerås [501] probably date from a little later time than that of Linköping, while Växjö, which from the long residence there of St. Sigfrid we should have expected to have become one of the earliest settled sees, after a short independent existence became merged first in that of Skara, afterwards in that of Linköping, [502] and only recovered its independence towards the end of the twelfth century. [503] Birka, the cradle of Christianity in Sweden, with its memories of Anskar, Herigar and Unni, was apparently destroyed at some time during the eleventh century, [504] and its place as the commercial capital of the country was taken by Sigtuna, which when Christianity had made more progress among the Swedes became for a time the seat of a bishop. But Uppsala was not far away and had been for so long the national centre

[500] St. Eskil, though sometimes reckoned the first Bishop of Strängnäs, ought not rightly to be counted as such. As we have seen, he was really a missionary bishop with his centre at Fors. We hear of Bishop Gerder of Strängnäs joining with Henry of Uppsala to consecrate the church of St. Botvid at Botkyrka, probably about 1150. Who was Bishop of Strängnäs when it is first mentioned as the seat of a bishopric, about 1120, is unknown.

[501] St. David, placed first in the "Chronicon Episcoporum Arosiensium," is also better considered as a missionary bishop, and the same may be said of Osmund, who comes second, and whose record is very inaccurately given. Henry, the third bishop, is said to have been confirmed in his office by Pope Paschal II. (1099–1118).

[502] "Chronicon Episcoporum Wexionensium, S.R.S.," III., ii., p. 129. "Quartus Johannes episcopus. Postea translata est sedes potestate non justicia ad Skarensem ecclesiam et deinde ad Lincopensem ecclesiam."

[503] From a Danish source—"S.R.D.," I., No. 20, Chronologia auctore Cornelio Hamsfortio Cimbro—we know of a Baldwin who was Bishop of Växjö in 1170; but the circumstances in which he is mentioned make it possible that the see of Växjö was at this time suffragan to Lund and not to Uppsala. He is not mentioned in any Swedish chronicle, and it is not easy to harmonize the fact of there being an occupant of the see of Växjö in 1170 with the statement in the Chronicle as to how the people of that town got a bishop of their own again: "In tempore hujus (i.e. Kol, Bishop of Linköping) populus dolens de amisso pastore obtulerunt pecuniam regi Karolo ut sibi dignum pastorem in salutem animarum suarum provideret qui precibus eorum annuens monachum quendam ex Cystersiensi ordine cognatum suum Stenarum nomine virum utique providum et honestum eis in salutem animarum prefecit." "S.R.S.," III., ii., p. 129. There is the further difficulty that Kol did not become Bishop of Linköping till after the death of Karl Sverkersson. Possibly Växjö was made a see and placed under Lund during the time of the civil war that followed the defeat and death of Karl Sverkersson in 1167; then after the final triumph of Knut Eriksson became suffragan to Uppsala.

[504] See Note 18.

of worship that it was but fitting that, when Christianity had superseded the worship of Odin and Thor as the national religion, the old pagan stronghold should come to occupy a position of outstanding importance in the new order of things, and first take the place of Sigtuna as the seat of the bishop of the Uppland province—the chief of the provinces of Sweden proper—and then eventually come to be again the ecclesiastical capital of the whole land, when from being a simple bishopric it was raised by the Pope to the rank of a metropolitical see.[505] Eskilstuna, like Sigtuna, was only for a short time a see city, but in this case it was not removal but absorption that caused it to lose its status, for the bishopric to which it gave its name was united with that of Strängnäs,[506] a union that had a special appropriateness in view of the association of both towns with the martyrdom of St. Eskil. Finland, first the scene of Christian missionary enterprise about 1157, had the original seat of its bishop at Nousis, from where it was transferred, first to Räntämäki, and finally to Åbo. With this last change the diocesan arrangements of the Church of Sweden were complete for the time, and the number of sees remained at seven—Uppsala, Linköping, Skara, Strängnäs, Västerås, Växjö and Åbo—until after the commencement of the Reformation.

When we study the lists of the bishops of these sees, we notice how many of the earlier names are those of foreigners. For instance, Benedictus Germundi, the son of an Uppland lagman, though ninth in the list of the bishops of Västerås, was the first native Swede to fill the office,[507] while most of the early bishops of Skara were foreigners. It was only natural, of course, that in a land where the struggle with

[505] In 1164. See Chapter IX. for the account of the establishment of the Archbishopric by Pope Alexander III.

[506] Exactly when the union of the two sees took place is unknown, but the Bishop of Strängnäs was specially confirmed in the possession of the district of Närke, which contained the town of Eskilstuna by a Protective Letter issued by Pope Alexander III. Sv. Dip., No. 58; Celse: "Bullarium," p. 41; Örnhjälm: "H.E.," IV., v., p. 538; P.L. 200, Alexander III., E. and P., No. 973; Jaffé, No. 12111. Dated Sept. 7, 1171–2, Tusculanum.

[507] "Chronicon Episcoporum Arosiensium, S.R.S.," III., ii., p. 122.

heathenism was still going on high offices in the Church should be at first held mainly by men of foreign birth, for the converts—even if for the most part of higher rank, as seems to have been the case at first in Sweden—in general lacked the opportunity of acquiring the knowledge and training necessary for the successful holding of such positions. Only as centres of learning, such as monastic schools, were founded in the country, or opportunities were afforded of pursuing a course of study at some university or other similar institution in one of the western lands where Christianity had been for some time firmly established, could it be expected that Sweden would come to possess an entirely native-born episcopate. When, however, with the coming of the Cistercians and other developments, the difficulty of obtaining the necessary training and education disappeared, the appointment of foreigners to high positions in the Swedish Church became largely a thing of the past, and although the Popes exercised their power of " provision " in Sweden as in other western lands, they seem as a rule to have appointed Swedes, and not foreigners, to vacant benefices, and to have exercised a discretion and moderation that made the practice a very different thing from what it was in England where it was much abused. [508]

With regard to the nationality of these foreign bishops who in early times filled the various Swedish sees, some were Danes, [509] some were Germans, [510] while of some we cannot now name the country of their birth; but in addition to the purely missionary bishops there would appear to be at least eight who were of English birth. Of these the see of Skara claims three—Rodolvard, Rikulf and Edward—who, strangely

[508] It was this abuse, for particulars of which see Stephens: " History of the English Church," II., pp. 232, 239–42, which caused the passing of the Statutes of Provisors in 1351, by which it was enacted that all persons receiving Papal provisions should be liable to imprisonment, and that all preferments to which the Pope nominated should be forfeit for that turn to the king. See further Ollard and Crosse, Art. " Provisors."

[509] Among the early bishops of Västerås Henricus Pauli and Petrus Olavi were Danes. In later times the notorious Johannes Jerechini, who was for a time Archbishop of Uppsala, was also a Dane.

[510] E.g. Goteschalk, who succeeded Thurgot as Bishop of Skara.

enough, occupied it in succession; while two others—Ilianus and Egidius—were successively bishops of Västerås, the see that claimed their fellow-countryman St. David as its founder. Henry, the fourth Bishop of Uppsala, is better known as the Apostle of Finland, where he laboured as a missionary bishop, much as Sigfrid had done in Sweden, though for a very much shorter length of time; Thomas of Finland may be looked upon as both a missionary and a diocesan bishop; while Stephen, who became the first Archbishop of Uppsala, had previously been a monk in the Cistercian monastery of Alvastra.

Of certain of these bishops we know very little beyond their names, and in one case the little that we do know is decidedly discreditable to the prelate in question. This was Edward, the third English Bishop of Skara, who succeeded Rikulf in the administration of that diocese about the year 1102. Of him we are told that he had a wife and children, whom he left behind in England, and that when he had acquired sufficient wealth from the revenues of his see, he stole away secretly with it and returned to his native land and family.[511] Whether he was consecrated before or after arriving in Sweden is not related, but it seems extremely improbable that a married man would have been able to secure consecration in England at this time. In Sweden, on the contrary, for long after this it was a quite usual thing for the clergy to marry; at a later time they even claimed to have been given a dispensation to do so by Nicholas Breakspear, Cardinal of Albano, when as Papal legate he visited the country in 1152[512]; and it was not

[511] "U.Ä.B.," p. 53. "Niundi war Haerwardaer biskupaer ok aenskaer. Han atti baði kono börn i Aenglandi ok lopp fra þem ok hit til lanz ok war haer biskupaer ok ökte hwarti staf aellaer stol. Han sankaeði gul oc sylwaer ok stals swa haeðaen ok attaer i Aengland til sinnaer kono oc til sinnae barnæ."

[512] When Archbishop Andreas of Lund informed Pope Innocent III. of this claim the latter replied, "De presbyteris autem Svethiæ non possumus dare responsum, nisi viderimus privilegium quod prætendunt." Sv. Dip., No. 150; Celse: "Bullarium," p. 52; P.L. 216, Reg. Innocent III., Book XVI., No. 118; Potthast, No. 4820. Dated Oct. 3, 1213, Segni. No documentary evidence, however, seems to have been produced in substantiation of the claim, and it is worthy of note that the Norwegian clergy made a similar claim and were equally unable to substantiate it. See the letter of Gregory IX. to Sigurd, Archbishop of Throndhjem. Dip. Norv., I., No. 19; Regesta Norvegica, No. 449; Potthast, No. 10352. Dated May 16, 1237. Viterbo.

Rodolvard Engl Bp of Skara. begins first
direct intercourse betw. P? & Swedish Ch

130 THE ENGLISH MISSIONARIES IN SWEDEN AND FINLAND

until the visit of another legate, William of Sabina, that at the Council of Skeninge, held in 1248, the rule of clerical celibacy was definitely adopted by the Swedish Church,[513] and even then it was by no means easy to enforce.[514] Probably, therefore, the fact of Edward's possession of a wife and family, if it were known at the time, would prove no serious impediment to his obtaining the conferment of episcopal orders if he were consecrated in Sweden,[515] and it is hardly likely that he went for them to the Archbishop of Bremen.

Of his predecessor Rikulf we know even less, for no reference is made in the chronicle to his character or work. It is simply related of him that he was the eighth Bishop of Skara, was an Englishman by birth, and was buried in his see city.[516] Rodolvard, however, the first of the trio, was in all probability the bishop who played such an important part in the first direct communications that took place between Sweden and the Papacy, though if the old chronicler had good reasons for styling him, as he does, "the worst of all thanes,"[517] he does not seem to have deserved to have been entrusted with the important mission of going as the representative of the Swedish Church to Rome in response to an invitation sent to King Inge by Pope Gregory VII.

Of all the pontiffs who have occupied the chair of St. Peter none is more outstanding than Gregory VII., better known

[513] Sv. Dip., No. 359; Sv. Tr., No. 90; Celse: "Bullarium," p. 70; Von Troil, II., p. 307; Hjärne: "Medeltidens Statsskick," p. 296. Cp. Donner: "Kardinal Wilhelm von Sabina," pp. 371f.

[514] This is shown by the reference to the matter at the Council of Telje, held in 1279. Sv. Dip., No. 692. "Sane nobis dolor est cordi et rubor ori quod cum multa et diversa sanctorum patrum statuta, super vita honesta et moribus clericorum emanaverint, adeo tamen incontinencie morbus clericos hujus provincie multipliciter et dampnabiliter infecerat, quod pauci vel nulli ab hoc morbo reperiuntur immunes, fecerat hoc turpis questus in magnum scandalum et obprobrium cleri introductus. . . ."

[515] For the method of appointment of bishops in Sweden before it was included in the province of Lund, see Fryxell: "Om Svenska Biskopsval," pp. 1–9.

[516] "U.Ä.B.," p. 53. "Attundi war Rikulwaer biskupaer. Han war aenskaer at aedlum, ok i Skarum liggaer han." Cp. "Chronicon Rhythmicum Episcoporum Scarensium, S.R.S.," III., ii., p. 116. Beckman thinks it is doubtful whether it were he or Rodolvard who was the messenger to Pope Gregory VII.; the general consensus of opinion favours the latter.

[517] "U.Ä.B.," p. 52. "Aldrae þaeghnae waerstaer."

perhaps by his name Hildebrand. It is true that his importance has been exaggerated; that his fame has unduly eclipsed
that of the first great reforming Pope, Leo IX.; that as in
later times Innocent III. came to be credited with ecclesiastical developments that were really due to Alexander III.,
so Gregory has been pictured as the real dictator of the Papal
policy from the time when, as the monk Hildebrand, he
accompanied Leo to Rome until he himself assumed the
tiara.[518] But Leo " needed no Hildebrand, with the warning
of an older prophet, to guide his steps; he knew a bishop's
duty and the needs of the Church," [519] and although under his
successors Hildebrand's influence undoubtedly increased, he
did not perhaps become the most influential person at the
Papal court till the time of his immediate predecessor,
Alexander II., and even then the policy of the two men was
not always identical. When, however, in 1073, he was at last
elected Bishop of Rome so thoroughly did he attempt to put
his ideals into practice, and so greatly did he intensify the
reform movement, that we can understand how such terms as
" the Gregorian renaissance " and " sæculum Hildebrandi-
cum " have come into common use.

Henry III. of Germany had brought to a close the degradation of the Papacy when in 1046 he caused the Synod of Sutri
to be held, with the ultimate consequences that the three rival
Popes—Benedict IX., Sylvester III. and Gregory VI.—were
deposed, and the Emperor's nominee, Suidgar of Bamberg,
came to fill the apostolic chair as Clement II. Leo IX., not

---

[518] E.g. Gregorovius: "History of the City of Rome," IV., p. 77.
"Behind Leo stood Hildebrand . . . henceforward during the reign of
six popes the all-powerful minister "; Flick: "Rise of the Mediæval
Church," pp. 445, 446. "For twenty-five years Hildebrand had been the
power behind the papal throne. He had largely moulded the policy of
eight (!) successive popes . . . he had become the greatest statesman and
the shrewdest churchman in Europe." Cp. further, Lavisse et
Rambaud : "Histoire Générale," I., p. 569, II., p. 70.

[519] Whitney, in "Camb. Med. Hist.," V., p. 25. Cp. Fliche: "La
Réforme Grégorienne," I., p. 366. "On a pendant longtemps
attribué à Hildebrand l'idée même de la réforme à laquelle il a laissé son
nom, comme on a fait de lui l'inspirateur de toute la politique ponti-
ficale de 1048 à 1073. Il n'a été en réalité ni l'un ni l'autre." See
further, Whitney: "Hildebrandine Essays," p. 23 ; Fisher: "History
of Europe," I., pp. 198, 199.

only by his reforming zeal, but by travelling incessantly through Italy, France and Germany, to hold synods, make appointments, and manage the affairs of the Church in general, had laid firmly and well the foundation of the greatness of the medieval Papacy; Nicholas II. by his decree of 1059 had given to the College of Cardinals an overwhelming preponderance in regard to Papal elections[520]; and the reform movement, partially, at least, emanating from Cluny,[521] and having as its three chief aims the abolition of simony, the enforcement of clerical celibacy, and the freeing of ecclesiastics from undue lay interference, had become thoroughly identified with Papal policy. But in connection with the last of these reforms there was the question of lay investiture. This long-exercised privilege seemed to Gregory an abuse which must not be tolerated; the Emperor naturally was unprepared to surrender what he considered to be his lawful prerogative; and so there commenced, with Henry IV. and Gregory VII. as the respective protagonists, the struggle between Empire and Papacy that was to dominate European politics for nearly two centuries.[522]

The struggle was not, however, solely concerned with the investiture question; the real matter at issue was the relation of the Pope and the Emperor to each other. That both were

[520] The decree has come down to us in two forms, one more favourable to the Emperor, the other to the Church. See Fliche: "La Réforme Grégorienne," pp. 313–34, where both forms are given; Whitney: "Hildebrandine Essays," p. 18.

[521] Fliche thinks that the influence of Cluny on the reform movement has been exaggerated: "Cluny, peut on dire, réalise l'unité de l'Église régulière, mais sa mission s'est bornée là. Le mouvement clunisien est exclusivement monastique et il ne pénétrera guère l'Église séculière" (p. 41). This judgment does not seem to allow sufficiently for the influence of Cluny on Leo. IX. and Hildebrand. Cp. Belloc: "Europe and the Faith," p. 248. "As much as one man could, he, the heir of Cluny, had remade Europe."

[522] For the Investiture Struggle, see "Camb. Med. Hist.," V., c. 2; Lavisse et Rambaud: "Histoire Générale," II., pp. 68–115. Note the remarks of Previté-Orton, p. 6, with regard to the triumph of the Papacy. "Why the Papacy vanquished its rival is not hard to say. The Empire rested on dreams of the past, and met present needs unsatisfactorily: the forces it could command were inadequate to prolonged exertion. The Papacy, on the other hand, drew strength from the immense reservoir of its spiritual authority, the keys of Heaven and Hell. The typical medieval, living in a disastrous present, was all the more anxious concerning the life beyond the grave."

necessary for the government of Europe was generally admitted, but how was that government rightly to be shared between them? Was the Pope not only the head of the Church, but also the supreme ruler of the world, while to the Emperor merely fell the duty of enforcing his commands? Or was he little more than a kind of chaplain to the Emperor, who ruled the world both by Divine appointment and as the successor of the Roman Augusti? Or was the Pope supreme in ecclesiastical affairs and the Emperor equally supreme in civil ones? There are many outstanding movements associated with the Middle Ages—the rise of feudalism and its subsequent decay; the growth of national monarchies; the Crusades; the various monastic revivals—but the most characteristic of all is the struggle for supremacy between the Empire and Papacy; a struggle that after enduring for two and a half centuries resulted in the triumph of the latter—a triumph, however, without the necessary elements of permanence, and consequently followed in due course by a decline and fall.

Whether Gregory's ultimate aims were all included in his programme when he assumed office is doubtful, but they presently became clear enough. " His ideal was to reform the world by establishing a sort of universal monarchy for the Papacy. He saw all round him that kings and princes were powerless for good, but mighty for evil. He saw churchmen leading greedy and corrupt lives for want of higher direction and control. Looking at a world distraught by feudal anarchy, his ambition was to restore ' the peace of God,' civilization and order, by submitting the Church to the Papacy and the world to the Church." [523] But although he brought to his task indomitable courage, tireless perseverance and consummate ability, he soon met with disappointment and worse.

Certainly he centralized the power of the Church in the person of the Pope to a degree unknown before. All bishops had to take an oath of allegiance to him; all clergy had a

[523] Tout: "The Empire and the Papacy," p. 126. Cp. Fisher: "History of Europe," I., pp. 199–200.

free right of appeal to him; all questions could be rightly decided by him, either in person or through his legates; he alone could make new laws, found new churches, and divide or unite bishoprics; no book could be held canonical without his consent; he could be judged by no one; he alone was by right called universal; he could release subjects from their allegiance to a prince if he ruled unjustly; and he could even depose the Emperor.[524] But the individual claims that Gregory put forward for the acknowledgment of his suzerainty, although for the most part founded on past concessions of some kind or other, did not fare any too well. The Normans of southern Italy had, it is true, become the vassals of the Papacy in the time of Nicholas II.[525]; but although it was owing to Hildebrand's intervention that Alexander II. had so strongly supported the English expedition of William of Normandy, that ruler, while promising to see that Peter's Pence were promptly paid, utterly refused to hold his kingdom as a fief of the Pope[526]; in Spain his legates were ill-treated; while the letters that he wrote to Svend of Denmark in 1075, first asserting his universal rule over kings, princes and all Christians, and then claiming suzerainty over Denmark,[527] seem to have been ignored. The same year the investiture contest broke out, and Gregory found himself engaged in a desperate struggle with the Emperor. A synod of German bishops, held at Worms, and presided over by the Archbishop of Mainz, after making terrible charges against him, declared him deposed, while after his excommunication

[524] Gregory's claims are set out in the twenty-seven articles of the "Dictatus Papæ." They are conveniently given in Thatcher and Schwill: "Europe in the Middle Ages," pp. 261, 262; and in Ogg: "Source Book of Medieval History," pp. 262-4.
[525] Chalandon: "Histoire de la Domination Normande en Italie," I., pp. 167-72. The text of the oath taken by Robert Guiscard is given in Fabre: "Liber Censuum," I., pp. 421-2.
[526] For the relations of William I. with the Papacy see Mann: "P.M.A.," VII., c. 9; Brooke: "The English Church and the Papacy," c. 9; Fliche: "La Réforme Grégorienne," II., pp. 345-9, 356.
[527] P.L. 148, Gregory VII., Book II., Ep. 51 and 75. Jaffé Nos. 4928, 4956. Cp. Fliche: "La Réforme Grégorienne," II., pp. 322, 342, 343, 346, 352. For Gregory's claims to suzerainty over other lands—Hungary, Russia, etc.—see Fliche, II., c. 6, and Macdonald: "Hildebrand," cc. 9, 11, 13.

of the Emperor a like sentence was passed on him by the Bishop of Utrecht. [528]

Undaunted, however, by misrepresentation and opposition he pursued his unyielding way, and perhaps felt, when he heard of the spread of the Gospel in Sweden, that from the ruler of that northern land he might get a kindlier response to his claims. But first it was necessary to have further information, and so we find him, probably in 1080, [529] addressing a letter to Inge, " the glorious king of the Swedes," in which he says that he has heard to his great joy that Christian missionaries sent by the Gallican Church have come to his realms. [530] He then proceeds to point out that their teachings had their original source in the treasures of the holy Roman Church, and requests Inge to send to Rome either a bishop or some other suitable ecclesiastic, so that he may be informed about the customs and character of the Swedes, and the apostolic mandates may be taken back to Sweden by the messenger. Meanwhile he urges the king to govern his realm righteously, so that he may finally merit to hear the words, " Come, ye blessed of My Father, receive the kingdom prepared for you from the foundation of the world."

The letter shows that the Pope was not very well informed as to the actual state of affairs in Sweden at the time when he wrote. He addresses Inge as the " glorious king of the Swedes," whereas it seems probable that the heathen reaction had already taken place, which caused Inge to take refuge in Västergötland and transferred the rule of the Swedes to his

[528] Mann: " P.M.A.," VII., p. 102 ; Fliche, II., p. 291 ; Macdonald: " Hildebrand," pp. 160–9. William of Utrecht died soon after pronouncing the excommunication, and is said to have despaired of his salvation on account of his contempt of the Pope. Gregory's excommunication of Henry is given in the " Liber Pontificalis," II., p. 283, and an English translation in Ogg: " Source Book of Medieval History," pp. 272, 273.
[529] This is the usually accepted date. Örnhjälm: " H.E.," III., xxi., p. 322, assigns the date 1074 to the letter and thinks it was addressed to Håkon the Red. Celse: " Bullarium," p. 23, follows him in this.
[530] Sv. Dip., No. 24 ; Sv. Tr., No. 27 ; Celse: " Bullarium," p. 23 ; Johannes Magni: " Hist. Met., S.R.S.," III., i., p. 18 ; Örnhjälm: " H.E.," III., xxi., p. 322 ; Hamb. U.B., No. 112 ; P.L. 148, Reg. Gregory VII., Book VIII., No. 11 ; Jaffé, No. 5185. Dated Oct. 4th, Rome, no year given.

brother-in-law, Blot-Sven. The reference to the Gallican Church is also very obscure.[531] It may possibly refer to the fact that St. Anskar had originally been a monk in the monastery at Corbie, and so could be looked upon as a Gallican missionary; another possibility is that Gallican missionaries had been working in Sweden of whom no records have come down to us[532]; more probably, however, Gregory's informant—of whose identity we are unfortunately completely ignorant—had unwittingly misled him in regard to the ecclesiastical position in the northern land and had attributed to the work of French missionaries what was really due to that of English ones, a mistake which may have been partly caused by the connection between England and France that had been brought about by the recent conquest of the former by William of Normandy.[533]

It was in answer to the request of Gregory that Rodolvard was sent to Rome to supply the Pope with the desired information. Rhyzelius' account of the matter does not seem to accord well with certain facts as we know them. According to him Rodolvard was appointed to his see by Håkon the Red and consecrated by the Archbishop of Bremen in 1077, but during the rule of Blot-Sven was driven out of the land and then went to Rome. When he returned from there in 1080 he brought a letter from Gregory to Inge and his brother Hallsten, and in the following year wrote a noteworthy letter to the Pope describing the state of the Church in Sweden.[534] It is true that Gregory's letter to the two kings mentions the

---

[531] "Gallicana siquidem Ecclesia non vos alienis documentis instruxit, sed quod de thesauris matris suæ S. Romanæ Ecclesiæ accepit, salubri vobis eruditione contradidit."

[532] This is the opinion of Schmid: "Sveriges Kristnande," pp. 71–4. He further suggests that they may have come to Sweden by way of Norway, and that they were possibly Cluniac monks.

[533] Bull: "Folk og Kirke i Middelalden," p. 105, says in regard to the reference, "De hamburg-bremenske erkebisper har ialfald forsökt at bringe sin myndighet til anvendelse i Norge. Og som mottraek har så kong Harald Hårdråde sökt forbindelse med franske og engelske biskoper og derigjennem tratt den katolske centralutvikling naermere. Saerlig den franske kirke stod ved denne tid kurien og den der herskende kluniacensiske åndsretning naer, som det bl. a. fremgår av et brev av okt. 1080 på Gregor VII til den svenske kong Inge."

[534] Rhyzelius: "Epis.," I., p. 166.

Letters of Gregory 1081 (? 1080)

visit to Rome of a bishop " R, " who presumably is Rodolvard, [535] but the letter [536] almost certainly belongs to the year
1081 not 1080, and it is far more probable that Rodolvard
was sent in answer to the request in Gregory's first letter than
that he was expelled from the country and in the course of
his wanderings visited Rome. Västergötland apparently
afforded a safe shelter to King Inge from the tyranny of the
usurper, so there seems no reason why it should not have
afforded an equally safe shelter to its bishop, unless indeed he
had filled his office in such a way as to cause great discontent
and justify the epithet applied to him in the Chronicle of
" the worst of all thanes." At the same time it seems probable
enough that Pope Gregory's second letter was actually brought
by Rodolvard and not by some other messenger.

From the letter we gather that Gregory was now much
better acquainted with Swedish affairs than when he had
written a year previously. He knows that Inge is not sole
king, but is joint ruler with his brother Hallsten, [537] and the
fact that he addresses them as " kings of the Visigoths " may
well imply that Rodolvard had given him an account of the
heathen uprising that caused Inge for the time to lose the rule
of Svealand and possibly that of Östergötland also. It has,
however, been suggested that the Pope may have given the
title " kings of the Visigoths " as one of honour on account of
the fame of the Gothic nation. [538] It certainly seems somewhat

[535] It is, of course, just possible that the "R" may refer to neither
Rodolvard or Rikulf, but be the initial of some unknown court bishop.
[536] Sv. Dip., No. 25; Sv. Tr., No. 28; Celse: "Bullarium," p. 23;
Johannes Magni: "Hist. Met., S.R.S.," III., ii., pp. 18, 19; Örnhjälm:
"H.E.," III., xxii., p. 331; Hjärne: "Medeltidens Statsskick," p. 277;
Hamb. U.B., No. 113; P.L. Reg. Gregory VII., Book IX., No. 14;
Jaffé, No. 5221. Undated.
[537] The Pope merely gives the kings' initials, I and A. I = Inge, A
= Alstan = Hallsten, is the usual interpretation; but it is just possible
that A = Aquinus = Håkon the Red, and that Hallsten did not become
joint ruler with his brother until somewhat later. A less probable con-
jecture than either Hallsten or Håkon is that A is the Anund from
Russia mentioned by Adam of Bremen (III., c. 52, Schol. 85).
[538] Tunberg: "Äldre Medeltiden," p. 31; Schück: "Den äldsta
konungalängden i Sverige," p. 29. The title "King of the Swedes and
Goths" seems to have been first used by Pope Alexander III. in his letter
of August 8, 1164. See Kjellberg: "Den äldsta svenska konungatiteln," p. 9.

strange that if the Pope knew of the heathen reaction and the martyrdom of St. Eskil he should not allude to either.

The letter itself is but little longer than his previous one. Gregory expresses to the joint rulers his joy that their subjects have been brought, through the mercy of God, from the errors of heathenism to the truth of the Gospel, from darkness into light, from death unto life; and in virtue of the authority of the holy Roman Church he urges his very dear sons that they should recognize how transitory are the things of this life, and should take care to ensure the preservation of concord and the payment of respect to the clergy and especially the bishops; also that pity should be shown to the poor and afflicted, and that tithes should be paid for the support of the clergy, the churches and the poor. Finally, because their conversion to the Christian faith has taken place recently, their subjects are not yet sufficiently instructed in its doctrines; they should therefore send clergy frequently to Rome, that there they may be more fully taught the customs of the Church, and so be able to show their fellow-country the things that ought to be done. [539]

Whether Gregory intended by the last request to pave the way for a demand that the Swedish kings should hold their realm from him as overlord, by causing any clergy who might be sent to become familiarized with the idea of the supreme temporal, as well as spiritual, authority of the Roman pontiff; or whether the account of Sweden given to him by the Bishop of Skara showed him that to make any such claim would be

---

[539] " Quia vero, noviter ad Christum conversos, nondum christianæ fidei et religionis doctrinam sufficienter vos sumpsisse putamus, volumus, ut frequenter ad hanc sedem clericos vestros mittatis, talesque personas provideatis ad nos destinare, quæ et S. Rom. Ecclesiæ moribus plenius instrui et instructæ valeant ad vos docte et salubriter, quæ sunt agenda, referre."

It is interesting to note that a few years previously Gregory had written in a somewhat similar strain to Olav Kyrre, King of Norway, asking him to send some high-born Norwegian youths to Rome for the purpose of instruction, as owing to the difficulties of distance and language he could not well send foreigners to Norway. Dip. Norv., VI., No. 1; Johannes Magni: "Hist. Met., S.R.S.," III., ii., p. 20; Örnhjälm: "H.E.," III., xxi., p. 320; P.L. 148, Reg. Gregory VII., Book VII., No. 13; Regesta Norvegica, No. 31; Jaffé, No. 5096. Dated Dec. 15, 1078. Rome.

useless, and he merely wished to ensure that the ecclesiastical standards of doctrine and discipline should be the same in Sweden as elsewhere, cannot be said. But as far as is known, no priests were sent from Sweden to Rome in consequence of his exhortation, nor does he seem to have sent any further letters there. This, however, is hardly surprising, for not only was there now an anti-Pope, Clement III., whose activities had to be combated, but open war had broken out between him and the Emperor—a war mainly fought in Italy. It was no time for adherents of Gregory to be paying visits to Rome, while the violence of the struggle necessitated the concentra- tion of all his energies to enable him to hold his own, so that scant leisure would he have for arranging for instruction to be given to the clergy of a little-known northern land, even before the eventual exile during which he died at Salerno.

But although Gregory's letter was apparently unproductive of any immediate results its importance must not be under- rated, for together with his previous letter it marked the beginning of a very important change in the Papal policy with regard to the Church in Sweden. Hitherto the Pope had been content, as we have seen, to leave the supervision of eccle- siastical affairs there to the archbishops of the Hamburg- Bremen see, with the result that the development of the National Church was proceeding in such a way that there was a danger that organized Christianity in the northern kingdom would differ very considerably in its discipline from the ideals that were now in favour at Rome and had already been largely imposed on Western Christendom as a whole.

Although the Christianization of Sweden had made great headway, the Romanization of its Church had hardly yet begun, and if the Papal Curia wished the organization and discipline of the latter to approximate closely to what was found in the Churches of lands like France and England, and at the same time to make the prevailing centralizing policy as effective in Sweden as elsewhere, it seemed necessary that more immediate relations should be established between the Papacy on the one hand and Church and State in the realms of the Swedes and Goths on the other.   To Gregory then

L

belongs the credit of having been the first Pope to attempt to bring about such relations; and although his own efforts accomplished little, yet they created a precedent, which after a considerable lapse of time was acted upon by his successors, who devoted much attention to affairs in Sweden, with the result that the Romanization of the Church there commenced in earnest. The process met with considerable opposition from both people and clergy but it was eventually carried through to a successful conclusion by the middle of the thirteenth century.

The two English bishops of Västerås, Ilianus and Egidius, are best mentioned here, although they belong to a considerably later time, when this process of Romanization had already made good progress; and just as the Englishman Rodolvard has great interest for us on account of the part he played in the first attempt at commencing the process, so his fellow-countryman, Egidius, is also of interest in connection with one particular development of it.

Ilianus, who preceded him, is said to have been an able, rich and generous man, who built the castle at Västerås, which even at the time of the Reformation still went by the name of St. Ilian's House. He also purchased from their respective owners a number of farms and homesteads lying to the north of Västerås, on both sides of the Svart Å, and formed them into a parish with the name of St. Ilian. After ruling his diocese successfully for about nine years, and accomplishing " an immeasurable amount of good," the bishop died at his castle and was buried in the chapel which he himself had built. [540]

The early missionary bishops had, for the most part, already been consecrated when they came to Sweden, and for carrying on their work of evangelization, as well as for exercising the episcopal functions in connection with it, had been dependent on the goodwill of the king and people. Thurgot of Skara had been consecrated, as we know, by Archbishop Unwan at the request of Olov Skötkonung, while Archbishop Adalbert

---

[540] " Chronicon Episcoporum Arosiensium, S.R.S.," III., ii., p. 123.

sent several bishops to work in Sweden. [541] As the different
see cities came to have an orderly succession of bishops and
their dioceses gradually acquired fairly definite limits, the
usual mode of procedure when a fresh bishop was required
seems to have been for him to be chosen by the king and
people, including the clergy, and then consecrated to his
office. [542] The West Gothic Law-book is naturally the only
one of the provincial law codes that contains any regulations
in regard to the matter, as the other codes were reduced to
writing after the Papal legate, William of Sabina, had decreed
that in all cases the bishop must be elected by the cathedral
chapter, and that in those cases where no chapter existed one
must be formed, although there seems to have been considerable delay in carrying out this injunction. [543]

The regulations in the West Gothic Law-book were as
follows. When a bishop was required the king had to ask the
people on whom they wished the office to be conferred. The
man chosen had to be the son of a bonde, and after his election the king placed the pastoral staff in his hand and the ring
on his finger, and he was then taken to the church and placed
in the bishop's seat. [544] These ceremonies made him fully

[541] Adam Br., III., c. 70, Schol. 94.

[542] See Fryxell: "Om svenska biskopsval under medeltiden," pp. 24–52.

[543] It is uncertain whether this order was made by William at the
Council of Skeninge or on some other occasion. It was confirmed by
Pope Alexander IV. in 1250. Sv. Dip., No. 382; Sv. Tr., No. 92.
Celse: "Bullarium," p. 74; Hjärne: "Medeltidens Statsskick," p. 301;
Reg. Innocent IV., No. 4949; Potthast, No. 14136. Dated Dec. 7, 1250,
Lyons (Celse, Dec. 6). At the time of the visit of William three
cathedrals lacked chapters—those of Strängnäs, Växjö and Västerås.
The first reference to the chapter of Strängnäs is found in a letter of
William, Prior of the Augustinian Order at Paris, saying that Ysarn,
Canon of Strängnäs, has received a number of relics of saints, which
have been found at Cologne, and will bring them back with him to
Sweden. (Sv. Dip., No. 973. Dated August 16, 1288, Paris.) The date
of the founding of the chapter at Växjö is unknown, but would seem
from a letter of Archbishop Jakob, dated Feb. 15, 1280 (Sv. Dip.
No. 1716) to have been prior to that year. The chapter at Västerås was
apparently the last to be formed. See Lundqvist: "De svenska domkapitlen," p. 39.

[544] "U.Ä.B.," p. 84. "Aen biskup skal takae, þa skal konongaer allae
landae at spyriae, hwarn þer williae hawe. Han skal bondaesun waerae.
þa skal konongaer hanum staf i hand saeliae oc gullfingrini. Siðaen
skal han i kirkiu leðae ok i biskupsstol saetiae. þa aer han fulkomen til
walz utaen vixl."

142 THE ENGLISH MISSIONARIES IN SWEDEN AND FINLAND

installed in his office except as regards consecration, which
may have at first been performed by the Archbishop of
Bremen, later on by the Archbishop of Lund, and then, after
Sweden had in 1164 been made a separate province, by the
Archbishop of Uppsala.

Egidius.

But in the case of Egidius, the successor of Ilianus, we have
a distinct departure from this custom; we have, in fact, a
foreshadowing of the Papal right of " provision," which was
to be exercised fairly extensively, if at the same time sym-
pathetically, at a later period, and so we can look upon his
appointment as an important link in the chain that was being
forged to bind the Swedish Church closely to the Roman see.
The letter of Pope Lucius III. to King Knut,[545] the only
account that we have of the matter, shows that it was not a
typical case of " provision." The Pope says that in response
to the king's request, and in accordance with his promise, he
sends to him his beloved son Egidius, whom he has made
Bishop of Västerås in place of the deceased Ilianus, so that he
may root out paganism and establish Christianity. He gives
high praise to the character and abilities of Egidius, and
exhorts the king to see that due honour is paid to him, and
thus show how sincere is his own attachment to the apostolic
chair.

It will be noticed that although this is the first case of the
appointment by the Pope of a bishop to a Swedish see, it is
not an actual " provision " in the ordinary sense, since Lucius
was acting at the king's request; possibly Knut may even
have nominated Egidius for the vacant office, though this
seems hardly likely; but at least the Pope's action paved the
way for the later " provisions," though it was not until 1225
that we get the first of these, when Honorius III. addressed a
" mandatum de providendo " to the Archbishop of Uppsala,
requesting him to provide a suitable benefice for a certain
deacon " I ", who had studied for a long time at Paris, and

---

[545] Sv. Dip., No. 94; Celse: "Bullarium," p. 43; P.L. 201,
Lucius III., E. and P., No. 12; Jaffé, No. 14544. Dated Dec. 30, 1181,
Lateran. Cp. "Chronicon Episcoporum Arosiensium, S.R.S.," III., ii.,
p. 122.

had worked in foreign lands for two years. [546]   After that
there seem to have been no further " provisions " in Sweden
till about eight years later when two were made by Pope
Clement V., [547] and although afterwards the practice became
frequent enough, Sweden seems to have suffered far less than
England did from its abuse. [548]   Indeed, with regard to the
bishoprics the Pope seems often to have " provided " the ecclesiastic who had been chosen by the cathedral chapter to fill
the vacant see, so that his action was really one of confirmation rather than provision.   There does not seem to have been
a single case of a non-resident Italian bishop being appointed
to a Swedish see, [549] though there are several instances of
resident foreigners occupying one or other of these. [550]

Egidius ruled the see of Västerås for a period of over thirty
years, but we know very little about him, save that he is said
to have been a good bishop and that he built a beautiful
church which became the church of the parish formed by his
predecessor. [551]   It would be interesting to know how far he
was successful in eradicating the heathenism that still lingered
in his diocese—presumably in the more remote portions of it
—a task for which Pope Lucius had evidently deemed him

[546] Sv. Dip., No. 236 ; Reg. Honorius III., No. 5596 ; Potthast,
No. 7460. Dated Aug. 12, 1225. Rieti.

[547] Brilioth : " Den påfliga beskattningen af Sverige," p. 354. In this
work he gives (pp. 353–85) a list of the known provisions to Swedish
benefices from 1309 to 1371 ; and in his further work, " Svenska kyrka,
kungadöme och påvemakt, 1363–1414," a list of those that took place
during the Great Schism (pp. 368–76).

[548] For instance, Cardinal Otho, legate of Gregory IX., demanded in
1240 from the Archbishop of Canterbury and the Bishops of Lincoln
and Salisbury that provision should be made for three hundred Italian
clerks before any preferment was bestowed on Englishmen (Stephens :
" Hist. of the English Church," II., p. 232), but not a single provision did
Gregory require to be made in Sweden. See also Note 508.

[549] Just before Sweden broke with the Papacy Adrian VI. bestowed the
see of Skara on Francesco de Potenza, who had been papal legate in the
North. Gustavus Vasa resolutely refused to acknowledge the appointment, and Clement VII., the successor of Adrian, agreed to withdraw it,
and eventually gave to Francesco the see of Nazareth, which had been
removed to Barletta in Italy during the time of the Crusades ; see
Martin : " Gustave Vasa et la Réforme en Suède," pp. 234, 297–99.

[550] E.g. Petrus Ingevasti and Olavus Helgonis of Västerås were Danes ;
Arnold of Strängnäs and Rodolf of Skara were Germans.

[551] " Chronicon Episcoporum Arosiensium, S.R.S.," III., ii., p. 122.

well fitted, but unfortunately the chronicle makes no mention of his activities in this direction. On his death, which took place in the spring of 1213, he was buried by the altar in the church that he had built, and with him there ends the list of the English bishops who worked in Sweden proper.

CHAPTER VII

THE COMING OF THE MONKS

ALTHOUGH it was a monk who first preached Christianity in Sweden, and although later on other monks had also worked as missionaries among the Swedes and Goths, no attempt seems to have been made during the struggle between Christianity and heathenism to found any religious house, with the possible exception of that of Munktorp by St. David, [552] a fact which was no doubt a contributory cause to the slowness of the conversion of the country. Well over three hundred years had elapsed since the time when Anskar appeared at the court of King Björn when the first permanent monastery was founded, and this event, like many other important ecclesiastical ones, happened while Sverker I., who was first chosen as king by the people of Östergötland about 1133, was ruling. Before the coming of the monks in the time of that monarch there had been important happenings in the ecclesiastical realm, as well as in the state, that were to influence greatly the future development of the Church in Sweden; but it will be better to omit any reference to them here, and consider them later with regard to their bearing on the visit of the Papal legate, Nicholas Breakspear, in 1152.

The English missionaries, as we have already seen, had been chiefly responsible for the christianization of Sweden; English monks were now to take an important share in the successful establishment of monasticism there. This, as in other lands, was an event of great ecclesiastical and social importance. In an age when the constant occurrence of war—public or private—and the frequent visits of pestilence made life uncertain for all; and when, too, the lot of the peasantry was in general one of heavy toil and bitter poverty—though

---

[552] " Historia Sancti Davidis, S.R.S.," II., i., p. 405.

this was far less the case in Sweden than in most lands—the monk, when true to his ideals, showed by his manner of living that in his estimation the things of the present life were as nought compared with those of the life to come. He was thus a constant reminder to nobles and peasants alike that they too should set their affections on things above, and should not fail to repent them of their sins, lest in that life beyond the grave their portion should be one of endless woe instead of eternal happiness. But the influence of the monks did not end here. They helped largely to develop the life of the Church and increase its privileges; they made Papal authority a far greater reality; their cloisters were the homes of learning and supplied suitable men to fill high positions in the Church; while becoming wealthy—almost unavoidably, through the gifts showered upon them by those who hoped thus to gain the favour of heaven—they were enabled to do much in the way of encouraging agriculture, entertaining travellers, and ministering to the wants of the sick and needy.

St. Sigfrid and his companions and successors, in spite of their remarkable achievements, are somewhat shadowy personages; but at least it is possible, unless we are unduly critical of our sources, to connect certain events with them. In the case of the early monks, however, while we know that many of them were of English nationality—and indeed, for the most part, they were either Germans or Englishmen [553]—we cannot definitely claim any individuals as our fellow-countrymen, with the exception of Stephen, one of the original monks at Alvastra, who became the first Archbishop of Uppsala. All that can be done then is to give an account of the introduction of monasticism into Sweden and its subsequent spread there, and to keep in mind that it is a story in the early part of which the characters were largely men of English birth.

It was monks of the Cistercian Order—the most important of the new Orders that sprang from the monastic revival,

---

[553] "Quia propter paucitatem Clericorum vix aliquis de terra illa convertebatur, Dominus fideli suo de partibus Germaniæ et Angliæ literatas et discretas personas mittebat, per quas disciplina Monasticæ Religionis in regno illo fundata crescebat, et fructificabat competenter in populis." "S.R.D.," II., No. 72, p. 643.

Cistercians
c. 1143

which accompanied the reformation of the Papacy that followed the period of degradation in the ninth, tenth and eleventh centuries—who now came to Sweden. The Order had been founded by Robert of Molême, and had first established itself at Citeaux, from which place it took its name, in 1098. It owed its early success very largely to the organizing capacity of the Englishman, Stephen Harding, and the renown for sanctity gained by Bernard, the first abbot of the daughter house of Clairvaux, and in 1119 its constitution was approved by Pope Calixtus II. His successors showed it great favour, for its aims accorded well with the reforming tendencies that now held sway at Rome, and recognizing the important position it had so speedily acquired they sought to enlist its influence to extend their own power, at the same time conferring on it special privileges in order to equip it more fully for the work it was to do for the Church in western Europe. We can understand then how the establishment of the Order in Sweden would be likely to play a considerable part in increasing the Papal power there, especially when the rapid spread that had characterized it in other lands was again in evidence, so that before many years elapsed there were not only several monasteries in various parts of the country, but a number of nunneries also.

According to the old legend [554] St. Bernard of Clairvaux, at the request of Queen Ulvhild, wife of Sverker I., sent a party of monks to Sweden, probably in 1143 or 1144, [555] and they founded their first monastery at Alvastra, [556] at the foot of the Omberg, on land which had been the dowry of the queen. King Sverker did much to ensure the success of the founda-

---

[554] "Narratiuncula de fundatione Monasterii Vitæ, S.R.D.," IV., No. 120, pp. 548f.

[555] "S.R.S.," I., i., p. 51. "CIƆCXLIV. Conventus missus est in Alvastrum." "S.R.S.," I., i., p. 23 and "S.R.D.," I., "Petri Olai Annales," p. 175, give the same date. Hall: "Cistercienserordens historia in Sverige," p. 110, note 1, gives reasons for thinking it was 1143. See also Janauschek: "Origines Cisterciensium," No. 181, p. 73.

[556] "S.R.D.," IV., "Narratiuncula," p. 458. "Alvastrum autem primam omnium Abbatiarum tam in Svecia, quam in Dacia, Norvegia, ac Alemania."

tion and later on he was buried there,[557] and so were all the kings of his family.[558]

The same day that the monastery of Alvastra was founded, Gislo, Bishop of Linköping, is said to have founded the one at Nydala, for the support of which he set aside a certain part of his income[559]; and so successful were these establishments that before long they were able to send out bodies of colonists to found further convents. In this way Alvastra became the mother house of those at Varnhem[560] and Juleta,[561] and Nydala of that of Gutvalla or Gutnalia in Gottland.[562]

Of the new establishments Varnhem soon acquired special importance, though it had a troubled early history. Queen Kristina, wife of King Erik IX., claimed the estate, and persecuted the monks so bitterly[563] that the Abbot, Henry, resolved to lay the matter before the general chapter of the Order, and with its approval go to the Pope to obtain an interdict. Passing through Denmark, however, he was persuaded by King Valdemar to settle there, and founded on April 1st, 1158, the monastery of Hvitskol in Jutland, becoming its first abbot.[564] Twenty of the brethren from

[557] "S.R.S.," I., i., "Minsta Rimchrönikan," ll. 571, 572.
  "I Alwastra Closter man mik lade
    Som jak sjelver stichtat hade."
[558] "S.R.S.," I., i., pp. 11–13; "U.Ä.B.," pp. 35, 40, 43, 45.
[559] "S.R.D.," I., "Petri Olai Annales," p. 175. "MCXLIIII. . . . Nova vallis et Alvastra Abbatie fundantur uno die." "Capellæ et Monasteria Diocesis Lincopensis, S.R.S.," III., ii., p. 297. "Oc aa samma daag epter middagen funderede biscop Gisle Nydala closter aff biscopsbordsens renta. . . ." See also Janauschek, No. 182, p. 74.
[560] "S.R.D.," I., "Petri Olai Annales," p. 176. "1150. Conventus venit in Varnhem." See also "S.R.S.," I., i., pp. 23, 51; Janauschek, No. 307, p. 120.
[561] "S.R.D.," I., "Petri Olai Annales," p. 177. "MCLX. Conventus venit in Saba." This convent was originally founded at Viby, and was moved to Saby in Juleta, probably about 1184. See Hildebrand: "S.M.," III., p. 963; Janauschek, No. 364, p. 144. In "S.R.S.," I., i., p. 23, the date of the foundation is given as 1159.
[562] "S.R.D.," I., "Petri Olai Annales," p. 177. "1163. Conventus mittitur in Gutualiam." See also "S.R.S.," I., i., p. 51; Janauschek, No. 387, p. 152.
[563] "S.R.D.," IV., "Narratiuncula," p. 460. "Omnibus modis Abbatem et ejus Conventum molestabat."
[564] "S.R.D.," I., "Petri Olai Annales," p. 177. "MCLVIII. (vel. 1159) Vite-scola fundatur." For the full history of the foundation see "S.R.D.," IV., No. 120, "Narratiuncula de Fundatione Monasterii Vitæ Scholæ in Cimbria." The author of the narrative is unknown.

Sweden joined him, but when Queen Kristina altered her behaviour the greater part of them returned to Varnhem, which at the request of King Erik was reorganized by Abbot Gerhard of Alvastra, and soon the community was again in a flourishing condition.[565] Just as the kings of the Sverker line chose Alvastra as their last resting-place, so those of the Erik line favoured Varnhem, though St. Erik himself was not buried there but at Uppsala.[566]

In addition to these monasteries the Order established a number of nunneries in Sweden. That at Vreta in Öster-götland was founded in 1162 by Karl Sverkersson, whose sister Ingegerd became its first abbess[567]; others founded about the same time or somewhat later were those at Sko,[568] Marieberg,[569] Riseberga,[570] Gudhem,[571] Askaby,[572] Bya-rum,[573] and Solberga.[574] But although the inmates of these

[565] Hall : "Cistercienserordens historia," p. 154.

[566] "S.R.S.," I., i., pp. 11–13 ; "U.Ä.B.," pp. 38, 41, 45.

[567] "S.R.D.," I., "Petri Olai Annales," p. 177. "1162. Fundatum est Monasterium Wreta a Carolo Rege, filio Sverckeri Primi." See also "Capellæ et Monasteria Diocesis Lincopensis, S.R.S.," III., ii., p. 296 ; Olaus Petri : "Chrönika, S.R.S.," I., ii., p. 242 ; Hildebrand : "S.M.," III., p. 960.

[568] This seems to have been originally a Dominican monastery, but after being deserted by the monks it became a Cistercian nunnery. Rhyzelius : "Mon. Sv.," p. 63. "År 1225, när huset stådt öde i try år, uplåt Herr Knut Longe thet åt Nunnor af Cisterciensi ordine. . . ." The house was originally established at Byarum.

[569] The date of its foundation is unknown, but was probably at the beginning of the 13th century. See Reuterdahl : "S.K.H.," II., i., p. 194 ; Hildebrand : "S.M.," III., p. 969.

[570] Founded in the time of Knut Eriksson by Jarl Birger. Sv. Dip., Nos. 823, 824 ; Hildebrand : "S.M.," III., p. 965 ; Westman, p. 180.

[571] According to one account this nunnery was founded (not, of course, as a Cistercian one) by Gunhild, daughter of Anund Jakob ; Örnhjälm : "H.E.," II., xi., p. 233. More probably it was founded by Karl Sverkersson about the same time as that of Vreta. It is named for the first time in a papal bull of 1174–6 ; Hildebrand : "S.M.," III., p. 963. Westman, p. 180, thinks it was in existence in the reign of Erik IX.

[572] The date of its foundation is unknown. It received a bull from Pope Lucius III., confirming it in the possession of certain property. See Celse : "Bullarium," p. 44 ; Hildebrand : "S.M.," III., p. 965.

[573] Rhyzelius : "Mon. Sv.," p. 137, thinks this was one of the oldest nunneries. King Erik Knutsson confirmed it in possession of its property, and so did John Sverkersson. It was probably early in the reign of Erik Eriksson when it was moved to Sko.

[574] See Reuterdahl : "S.K.H.," II., i., p. 201 ; Hildebrand : "S.M.," III., p. 970. There is a letter of William of Sabina confirming the order of Bishop Lars of Linköping that the nuns should have the gifts made at the altar of St. Olav in Akergarn. Sv. Dip., No. 362. Dated May 25, 1248. Visby.

establishments followed the Cistercian rule they were not at first permitted to belong to the Order, but counted as Benedictine houses, and were placed under the bishop of the diocese in which they were situated. It was not till 1212 that a general chapter decided that they might be included in the Cistercian Order, and be placed under the jurisdiction of a neighbouring abbot. [575]

Through the various privileges given to the Order it became almost entirely independent of all other spiritual authority than that of the Pope. Lucius III. freed it from paying tithe on all lands which the monks cultivated with their own hands or at their own costs. [576] Innocent III. entrusted the Inquisition to twelve Cistercian abbots; confirmed all the privileges granted to the Order by previous Popes; forbade bishops or any other persons to summon Cistercians to synods or courts of justice, or to come to the convents; gave permission for Divine service to be still held by the monks if the land were placed under an interdict; and put them all under the protection of the law so that no violence of any kind should be committed on their lands. [577] These privileges were confirmed by Honorius III., [578] while Innocent IV. not only gave them further financial privileges, [579] but freed them from excommunication by the bishops, [580] and from being amenable to their courts, [581] and also from visitation or correction from any other person than the Pope himself [582]; and he

---

[575] Westman, p. 180.

[576] Sv. Dip., No. 93; Celse: "Bullarium," p. 44; P.L. 201, Lucius III., E. and P., No. 69; Jaffé, No. 14715. Dated Dec. 21, 1182, Velletri. He confirmed this by a second bull. Sv. Dip., No. 95; Jaffé, No. 15391. Dated March 21, 1185, Verona.

[577] See Hall: "Cistercienserordens historia," pp. 29–31.

[578] Sv. Dip., No. 241; Celse: "Bullarium," p. 61; Potthast, No. 7495. Dated Nov. 6, 1225. Rieti.

[579] Sv. Dip., No. 371; Celse: "Bullarium," p. 73; Potthast, No. 13808. Dated Sept. 22, 1249. Lyons.

[580] Sv. Dip., No. 372; Celse: "Bullarium," p. 73; Potthast, No. 13910. Dated Jan. 28, 1250. Lyons.

[581] Sv. Dip., No. 373; Celse: "Bullarium," p. 73; Potthast, No. 13909. Dated Jan. 28, 1250. Lyons.

[582] Sv. Dip., No. 375; Potthast, No. 13911. Dated Jan. 28, 1250. Lyons.

addressed a letter to the prelates of the Church informing them of the freedom he had granted to the Order. [583]

But in addition to the privileges given to the Order in general we may note that on a number of occasions letters of protection were given by the Popes to one or other of the Cistercian establishments in Sweden, more particularly to the nunneries. Thus Riseberga had no less than three given to it before 1250—those of Innocent III., [584] Gregory IX., [585] and the Papal legate, William of Sabina [586]; while Sko received one from Innocent IV., [587] Gudhem one from Alexander III., [588] and Juleta monastery one from William of Sabina. [589]

In return for the many privileges given to the Order the Popes naturally expected to find its members ready to do all in their power to increase Papal authority, and to carry out to the best of their ability any commissions entrusted to them. Throughout the Middle Ages we get many examples of such commissions entrusted to Swedish abbots, and we may note one or two of the earlier of these.

Albert, Canon of Bremen, had been consecrated Bishop of Livonia in 1199, and thinking that the military occupation of the country was necessary for the success of mission work there, he had founded the Order of the Sword Knights in

[583] Sv. Dip., No. 374; Potthast, No. 13912. Dated Jan. 28, 1250. Lyons. The letter is addressed "archiepiscopis et episcopis, ac dilectis filiis abbatibus, prioribus, decanis, archidiaconis, archipresbiteris, prepositis, officialibus, et aliis ecclesiarum prelatis."

[584] Sv. Dip., No. 157; Celse: "Bullarium," p. 54; P.L. 216, Reg. Innocent III., Supp. No. 227; Potthast, No. 5105. Dated May 7, 1216. Rome.

[585] Sv. Dip., No. 293; Celse: "Bullarium," p. 66; Potthast, No. 10078. Dated Jan. 12, 1236. Viterbo.

[586] Sv. Dip., No. 357; Celse: "Bullarium," p. 70. Dated Feb. 2, 1248. Risaberg (Celse, Feb. 1).

[587] Sv. Dip., No. 315; Celse: "Bullarium," p. 68; Potthast, No. 11711. Dated July 9, 1245. Lyons (Celse, July 8, 1244; Sv. Dip., July 9, 1244).

[588] Sv. Dip., No. 72; Celse: "Bullarium," p. 43; Örnhjälm: "H.E.," IV., vii., p. 562; P.L. 200, Alexander III., E. and P., No. 1230; Jaffé, No. 12672. Dated Jan. 19, 1174–6. Anagni.

[589] Sv. Dip., No. 355; Celse: "Bullarium," p. 70. Dated Feb. 1, 1248. Risaberg.

Conversion of Livonia

1202.[590] The conquest and christianization of the country now went on rapidly, and in 1210 Albert received the right to consecrate bishops for the mission region, while in 1213 his bishopric was placed directly under Papal control. Innocent III., however, seems to have been distrustful of Albert's ambition, and assigned some recently-conquered districts to the Sword Knights alone. Disputes arose between the Knights and Albert, and the former appealed to the Pope, who ordered the Abbot of Gutnalia, together with two provosts of Lund diocese,[591] to investigate the complaints of oppression made against the bishop,[592] and pass judgment accordingly. A few years later the Bishop of Livonia, Semigallen and Leal informed Honorius III. that the opposition of the heathen had broken down and the field was white to harvest. Thereupon the Pope wrote to the Archbishops of Lund and Uppsala, and the Bishop of Skara, that they should choose a number of clergy, for preference from the Cistercian Order, whom he, when they had been sent to Rome, could despatch as missionaries for the conversion of the heathen.[593] Again, in 1229, the Abbot of Gutnalia was ordered by Gregory IX. to help the Bishop of Linköping and the Provost of Visby to preserve from molestation the bishop, clergy and people of Finland, whom the Pope had taken under his protection[594]; to hinder all trade from their districts with the Russians, so long as the latter continued to harry the Finns, who had embraced the Catholic faith[595]; and to forbid the

---

[590] "M.G.H. SS. XXIII. Heinrici Chronicon Lyvoniæ," p. 246; Liv. U.B., No. 14.

[591] Sv. Dip., No. 152; Sv. Tr., No. 63; Liv. U.B., No. 31; P.L. 216, Reg. Innocent III., Book XVI., No. 122; Potthast, No. 4824. Dated Oct. 11, 1213. Segni.

[592] "Quia vero venerabilis frater noster, Rigensis episcopus, eos, sicut accepimus, in multis opprimere consuevit, volumus, ut, cum vobis constiterit, memoratum episcopum malitiose vexare fratres eosdem, eum ipsis in expensis legitimis condemnetis."

[593] Sv. Dip., No. 208; Celse: "Bullarium," p. 59; Reg. Honorius III., No. 3209; Potthast, No. 6599. Dated March 25, 1221. Lateran.

[594] Sv. Dip., No. 245; Sv. Tr., No. 74; Celse: "Bullarium," p. 62; Hjärne: "Medeltidens Statsskick," p. 294; Åbo D.S., No. 2; Potthast, No. 8321. Dated Jan. 23, 1229. Perugia.

[595] Sv. Dip., No. 250; Sv. Tr., No. 75; Åbo D.S., No. 4; Potthast, No. 8327. Dated Jan. 27, 1229. Perugia.

La traffic in arms to the heathen

Gottland merchants, whose trading instincts seem to have been stronger than their Christianity, to supply the heathen with munitions of war for use in their attacks on the Christian Finns. [596]

Commissions such as these naturally increased the prestige of the Order in Sweden; while the success of the monks as agriculturists could hardly fail to win them respect from the class that counted for most in the country, and their hospitality to travellers and care of the sick must have helped to gain the general goodwill of all. The bishops, too, seem to have acted with great generosity towards them, and much favour was shown them by the kings. Although no Swedish monarch followed the example of Sigebert of East Anglia, or anticipated the action of the Emperor Charles V., by resigning his crown and retiring to a monastery, almost all of those of the Erik and Sverker families were, as we have seen, buried either at Alvastra or Varnhem.

For seventy years or thereabouts convent life in Sweden seems to have had the Cistercians as its sole representatives, with the exception that the Knights Hospitallers had a house at Eskilstuna, [597] for though the Cluniacs and Premonstratensians had houses in the neighbouring Danish province of Skåne, [598] there is no record of their attempting to form any establishment in Sweden; but when the early part of the thirteenth century witnessed the rise of the Dominican and Franciscan friars, it was not long before both Orders made

---

[596] Sv. Dip., No. 253; Sv. Tr., No. 76; Åbo D.S., No. 7; Potthast, No. 8340. Dated Feb. 16, 1229. Perugia. Gregory speaks severely of the conduct of the merchants. "Ex parte venerabilis fratris nostri, Finlandensis episcopi, fuit propositum coram nobis, quod cum in dyocesi sua sit novella Christi plantacio, sic animos quorundam de Gudlandie partibus ceca cupiditas occupavit, ut qui gloriantur in nomine christiano paganis intendentibus ad exterminium plantacionis ejusdem in armis, equis, navigiis, victualibus et aliis mercimoniis subvenire presumunt. In quo pares aut eciam superiores in malicia fiunt illis, dum eis ad impungnandos christianos necessaria subministrant."

[597] Hildebrand: "S.M.," III., p. 57.

[598] Hildebrand: "S.M.," III., pp. 944–53. The Præmonstratensians had four monasteries—Öved, Tomarp, Vä and Bäckaskog; the Cluniacs two nunneries—Bosjö and Börringe. Reuterdahl: "S.K.H.," II., i., p. 204, thinks that Præmonstratensian monks may sometimes have worked in Sweden although they had no house there.

their appearance in the country, and quickly established a number of houses in the different dioceses; and though Sweden would not seem to have afforded a particularly suitable sphere of labour to either Order they shared between them at the time of the Reformation half of the religious houses in the country. [599] Then we have the Swedish saint Birgitta founding the Order that is usually called by her name, which had its mother house at Vadstena, [600] while in due course the Carthusians, Carmelites and Antonines were also represented, though in each case, at the time of the Reformation, apparently only by a single establishment. [601]

Monastic life in Sweden was brought to an end by the Reformation, though only very gradually and much less harshly than in England. It thus had an existence of only about four hundred and fifty years, but during that time its influence on the life of the people was profound. We have already outlined very briefly the various ways in which this influence was exercised; here we need only remind ourselves once more that the introduction of monasticism was largely due to the fellow-countrymen of those missionaries whose efforts had been so fruitful in achieving the evangelization of the country and the establishment of its Church.

---

[599] The principal Dominican convent was that of Sigtuna, founded there by the instrumentality of Archbishop Jarler in 1237. Other houses of this Order were those at Skeninge, Kalmar, Skara, Strängnäs, Västerås and Åbo. Noted houses belonging to the Franciscans were those at Stockholm, Enköping, Skara and Arboga.

[600] The Order of the Most Holy Saviour, founded by St. Birgitta for both monks and nuns, had its statutes confirmed by Pope Urban V. in 1370. It had only the mother house of Vadstena in Sweden, but spread to other lands, including England, where Henry V.—whose sister, Philippa, had married Erik of Pomerania, the contemporary ruler of Sweden—founded the famous monastery of Syon, near Isleworth, which lasted till the time of the Reformation. For the early history of Vadstena, see Höjer: "Studier i Vadstena Klosters och Birgittinordens Historia"; also the "Diarium Wazstenense," printed in "S.R.S.," I., i., pp. 99–229.

[601] The Carthusians had their only house at Mariefred on Gripsholm; it was the last convent to be founded in Sweden and the first to be dissolved at the Reformation. The single Carmelite monastery was at Örebro, and at its school Laurentius and Olaus Petri, who became the leading Reformers of Sweden, had their early education. The convent of the Antonines was that of Ramundaboda, on the borders of Närke and Västergötland.

CHAPTER VIII

THE MISSION OF NICHOLAS BREAKSPEAR

THE first thought that would naturally occur to an English churchman in connection with Pope Adrian IV. is that he was the only one of his fellow-countrymen who ever occupied the Papal chair; to the student of medieval European history his name is, of course, familiar as one of the protagonists in the struggle for supremacy between the Empire and the Papacy; but to a Swede or Norwegian he is chiefly of interest on account of his legatine mission, as Cardinal of Albano, to their respective countries a few years before he was chosen to succeed Anastasius IV. as Pope.

In both Sweden and Norway he exercised a profound influence on the development of the National Church, and with regard to that of the former land we may say that the process of its Romanization really commenced with his visit. To understand properly, however, the full significance of the part he played in the development of the Swedish Church we must go back to the beginning of the century and trace briefly the ecclesiastical and political history of the country up to the time of his arrival in it. One important event has been described in the previous chapter—the establishment of monasticism; it now remains to see what other developments had helped to prepare the way for the legate's mission.

After King Inge had recovered possession of the rule of Sweden, [602] about the year 1082, he seems to have had a long and peaceful reign, during which Christianity continued to make steady progress in his realms. He was still ruling when, in the first decade of the twelfth century, an event happened in the neighbouring kingdom of Denmark that was to affect the Church of Sweden very considerably up to the time of the Reformation. This was the establishment of the arch-

---

[602] Hervarar Saga, c. xx.

bishopric of Lund, which took place in 1103 or 1104.[603] Erik Ejegod, the Danish king, had paid a visit to Italy in 1098, and had met Pope Urban II. at Bari in Apulia, where he had gone to attend a council. Erik had made a double request of him—that his brother Knud should be canonized and that an archbishopric might be established at Lund, so that Denmark should no longer form part of the province of Hamburg-Bremen.[604]

The second of these requests was no doubt a pleasing one, for Urban favoured fully the policy of his predecessors of centralizing all ecclesiastical power in the Papacy, and it was a necessary part of this policy to prevent the great archiepiscopal sees from acquiring such influence as to make them almost semi-independent patriarchates. In England, York was about to acquire its independence at the expense of Canterbury,[605] while with regard to Sweden and the other northern lands the Popes had shown the importance they attached to the prevention of any one see obtaining such power as to become dangerous by emphasizing again and again, in the confirmatory bulls given to the Archbishops of Hamburg, that in regard to their jurisdictional powers over the northern bishops, neither Cologne, nor any other see, had any right of interference.[606]

[603] The actual date is uncertain as the bull authorizing the foundation of the new archbishopric has not been preserved. We have, however, the congratulatory letter of Anselm of Canterbury to Asser, the newly-made archbishop, and the accounts given in Saxo (XII.) and the Knytlinga-saga (c. 80) of the raising of Lund to be a metropolitan see. Asser seems to have received the pallium in 1104, but the bull was probably sent out the previous year.

[604] See Jörgensen, p. 810; Steenstrup: "D.R.H.," I., pp. 498-9. Erik was successful in procuring the canonization of his brother. "S.R.D.," I., No. 14, "Petri Olai Chronica Regum Danarum," p. 119. He died later while on a pilgrimage to the Holy Land, which he was the first European king to visit.

[605] For details of the proceedings by which Thurstan of York got himself consecrated by Pope Calixtus II., on Oct. 19, 1119, without professing obedience to Canterbury, see Stephens: "History of the English Church," II., pp. 136-9.

[606] E.g. The bull of Nicholas I. addressed to Anskar, May 31, 864. "Nullus vero archiepiscopus Coloniensis ullam sibi deinceps in eadem diocesi vindicet potestatem"; that of John XV. to Libentius, Nov. 8, 989. "Et insuper decrevimus et sanctimus, nullum archiepiscoporum, vel Coloniensem vel alium quemlibet, in vestro diocesi ullam sibi vendicare potestatem"; and those of Leo IX. and Victor II. to Adalbert, Jan. 6, 1053, and Oct. 29, 1055.

When Hamburg was a mere fishing village, its cathedral little more than a wooden hut, and the holder of the see so poor that he had to depend for his livelihood on his skill as a maker of nets and sails, the Pope had certainly nothing to fear in the way of rivalry from him. But as time went on, and Christianity continued to spread in northern Germany and Sweden, while Denmark and Norway with their colonies became wholly—even if only to a large extent superficially— christianized, the occupants of the Hamburg-Bremen see came to possess a jurisdiction that in the hands of an ambitious prelate could cause great trouble to the Papacy. The forma- tion of an archbishopric of Lund, with its occupant having jurisdiction over not only the Danish sees, but also over those of Norway and Sweden until those lands should be ready to have their own metropolitans, would certainly weaken the dangerous power of Hamburg; while by pleasing the King of Denmark it would presumably attach him more closely to the side of the Pope in the case of further strife with the Emperor.

But Urban died in the year following the Council of Bari, and it was not until the time of his successor, Paschal II., that, probably in 1103, the bull was issued that made Lund a metropolitan see, [607] with certain rights over the Churches of Norway and Sweden. As the bull has been lost [608] we do not know how far those rights were intended to be permanent or merely temporary, but the latter seems to be more probable in view of the fact that when, later in the century, both Throndhjem (Nidaros) and Uppsala were made arch-

[607] See Sv. Tr., No. 29; Celse: "Bullarium," p. 24. Previté-Orton: "Outlines of Medieval History," p. 425, gives 1105 as the date, but Asser is said to have received the pallium in 1104. See Note 603.

[608] Possibly it was burnt when in 1294 King Erik Menved and his brother Kristofer destroyed the documents belonging to Lund Cathedral. See Neumann: "De Fatis Primatus Lundensis," p. 59, note f. The congratulatory letter of Anselm of Canterbury written in 1106 to the new archbishop, Asser, has been preserved. Sv. Dip., No. 27; Hamb. U.B., No. 130; Bergman: "Latinska Källskrifter," p. 31. Anselm says, "Gratias agimus Deo, qui in regno Danorum vestram religiositatem ad archiepiscopatum sublimavit. Confidimus enim quia, gratia Dei cooper- ante, ea quæ corrigenda sunt corrigetis, et quæ ædificanda ædificabitis, et quæ nutrienda nutrietis. Audivimus namque a præfato Cardinali (i.e. Alberic) multa bona de vobis."

bishoprics[609] no protest seems to have been made by the Archbishop of Lund.

Naturally the diminution of their metropolitical authority was viewed with dislike by the Archbishops of Hamburg, and when Adalbero succeeded to that see he refused to submit without protest to the new state of affairs and laid his complaints before the Pope.[610] This seems to have caused a reconsideration of the matter at Rome, for we find first Calixtus issuing a bull in 1123 which confirms the old rights of the Church of Hamburg over the northern nations[611]; then Honorius sending Cardinal Gregorius de Crescentio to enquire into the dispute between the two sees[612]; and finally Innocent II. making particular efforts to satisfy the claims of Adalbero, for he not only issued a bull in 1133, in which he confirmed to the archbishop the privileges granted by Gregory IV., Sergius II., Leo IV., Benedict III., Nicholas I., and Adrian II.,[613] but wrote at the same time to Archbishop Asser,[614] to the King of Sweden,[615] and to all the Swedish

---

[609] Throndhjem in 1152, Uppsala in 1164.

[610] This appears from the bull of Innocent II. of May 27, 1133. See Note 613. He refers to Adalbero's complaint " Sæpe utique venerabilis frater Adalbero, Hammaburgensis archiepiscopus, in presencia predecessorum nostrorum felicis memoriæ Calixti et Honorii ac nostra questus es, Ascerum Lundensem et alios episcopos Daciæ tibi debitam, sicut metropolitano suo, quæmadmodum in antiquis privilegiis Gregorii, Sergii, Leonis, Benedicti, Nicolai, Ardiani, Romanorum pontificum, continetur, obedienciam denegare."

[611] The bull has been lost. See Sv. Tr., No. 31; Hamb. U.B., No. 135.

[612] Hamb. U.B., No. 140. Dated May 23, no year given. Honorius also wrote to the King of Denmark. Hamb. U.B., No. 141. Dated Dec. 29, 1129. Lateran.

[613] Sv. Dip., No. 29; Sv. Tr., No. 33; Celse: "Bullarium," p. 32; Hamb. U.B., No. 144; P.L. 179, Innocent II., E. and P., No. 137; Jaffé, No. 7622. Dated May 27, 1133. Rome. "Ad formam itaque privilegiorum Gregorii, Sergii, Leonis, Nicolai, Benedicti, et Adriani, episcopatus Daciæ, Swediæ, Norweigiæ, Farriæ, Gronlondiæ, Halsingaldiæ, Islandiæ, Scridevindiæ et Slavorum, carissimi filii nostri Lotharii regis precibus inclinati, tibi et per te Hammenburgensi ecclesiæ, suæ videlicet metropoli presentis scripti pagina confirmamus."

[614] Sv. Dip., No. 30; Sv. Tr., No. 34; Celse: "Bullarium," p. 32; Hamb. U.B., No. 147; P.L. 179, Innocent II., E. and P., No. 140; Jaffé, No. 7625. Dated May 27, 1133. Rome.

[615] Sv. Dip., No. 31; Hamb. U.B., No. 146; P.L. 179, Innocent II., E. and P., No. 139; Jaffé, No. 7624. Dated May 27, 1133. Rome.

bishops. [616] To the first named he wrote severely, specified
the complaint lodged by Adalbero, and peremptorily ordered
Asser to obey him as his metropolitan [617]; the King of
Sweden he urged to see that both he and the bishops of the
country again rendered due obedience to the Archbishop of
Hamburg; and to the King and bishops of Denmark he wrote
to the same effect. [618]

If we wonder at the sternness of the Pope's letter to
Archbishop Asser, and his eagerness to recall the King and
bishops of Sweden into " the way of uprightness," as offering
an apparent contradiction to the Papal policy of a short time
before, we must remember in partial explanation of the
seeming inconsistency that not only had the struggle between
Empire and Papacy lapsed for a time, but that the present
Emperor, Lothair II., had proved himself a good friend to
Innocent II.   Perhaps, too, this was an instance, of which
others were to occur later, of strict orders given by the Pope
being followed by weak action on his part.   Certainly there
seems to have been no real enforcement of the Papal decisions,
and Lund retained practical independence of the Hamburg-
Bremen see.

King Inge died in the year 1111, and was succeeded by his
brother Hallsten's son, Philip, [619] but whether he ruled alone
till his death and was succeeded by his brother, Inge II., or
whether they were joint rulers, is not quite clear, though the
latter is more probable. [620]   Philip would seem to have died

---

[616] Sv. Dip., No. 32 ; Celse : " Bullarium," p. 32 ; Örnhjälm : " H.E.,"
IV., i., p. 389; Hamb. U.B., No. 148; P.L., 179, Innocent II., E. and
P., No. 141 ; Jaffé, No. 7626. Dated May 27, 1133. Rome.

[617] " . . . fraternitati tuæ per præsentia scripta serio mandamus, ut ad
ejus subjectionem et reverentiam redeas, et ei tanquam metropolitano
tuo in omnibus pareas." He styles Asser only " episcopus."

[618] Celse :   " Bullarium,"   p. 32 ;   Hamb.   U.B.,   No. 145 ;   Jaffé,
No. 7623. Dated May 27, 1133. Rome.

[619] " S.R.S.," I., i., p. 10 ;   " U.Ä.B.," p. 33.   " Attundi war Philipus
konongaer, Hallstens sun.   Ok nöt at faðurs ok faðurbroðurs sins, at
þer foro wael maed Sweriki."

[620] Langfedgatal, "S.R.S.," I., i., p. 6, gives " Inge oc Philippus Hall-
stein synir," as coming after Inge I. and Hallsten, and so does the Series
Triplex Regum Septentrionis, in " S.R.D.," I., p. 13.   The list in the
West Gothic Law makes Philip eighth and Inge ninth in the order from
Olof Skötkonung. See " U.Ä.B.," pp. 33, 34.

in 1118, but the date of Inge's death is uncertain. We are simply told that he died of poison in Östergötland, [621] after which event there followed another period of great confusion. There was still much rivalry between Swedes and Goths; the struggle between Christianity and heathenism was still going on, and if on the whole Götaland was now Christian, that was far from being the case with Sweden. For a time we have the chief power in the hands of a certain Rangvald, but according to the chronicle he was put to a shameful death when on his Eriksgata, [622] on account of the disrepect shown by him to the men of Västergötland, who had assembled for a " thing " to be held at Karleby near Skara. [623] Then there ensued a period when a lagman ruled in Västergötland, [624] while Magnus Nielssön, a Danish prince, seems to have been king for a short time over at least a part of the land, [625] and eventually we have again a single ruler of the whole country in the person of Sverker, an East Gothic chief, [626] who was possibly the grandson of the Blot-Sven who had ruled for a time in place of Inge I. during the heathen reaction of which mention has been made.

In the time of Sverker the long struggle between Christianity and heathenism was finally decided in favour of the former. Heathenism, it is true, still lingered for some time in the more remote districts; we find, for instance, some years

---

[621] "S.R.S.," I., i., p. 10; "U.Ä.B.," p. 34. "Hanum war firigiort maeð ondom dryk i Östraegötlandi ok fek af þy banae."

[622] "U.Ä.B.," pp. 34, 35. The Eriksgata was a tour of the different provinces of his realm undertaken by a Swedish king after he had been elected at the Mora Stones, near Uppsala. The derivation of the word is uncertain. Kjellen: "Om Eriksgatan," p. 24, says that no Eriksgata was undertaken before 1172, but this seems very improbable. Schück: "S.F.H.," I., p. 285, speaks of Rangvald riding the Eriksgata according to custom, though the Chronicle does not definitely say he was doing so. On p. 315 Schück gives a map showing the route of the Eriksgata. In his "Studier i nordisk religions historia," p. 271, he assigns the origin of the Eriksgata to the old Freyr procession.

[623] "S.R.S.," I., i., p. 10; "U.Ä.B.," p. 34; Ericus Olai: "Chronica, S.R.S.," II., i., p. 42.

[624] "S.R.S.," I., i., p. 10; "U.Ä.B.," p. 34; "Styrði þa goðaer laghmaðaer Waestraegötlandi. . . ."

[625] Saxo, XIV., c. 628. His mother, Margareta Fredkulla, was a daughter of Inge I.

[626] "S.R.S.," I., i., pp. 6, 11; "U.Ä.B.," p. 35.

later, St. Erik busily engaged in trying to stamp it out among the Upper Swedes, and even among those who had accepted Christianity, certain of the old customs died hard.   But Sverker's reign witnessed the using of material from the idol temple at Uppsala [627] to help in the construction of the cathedral there, [628] and we may well take the date of this event—1138—as marking the real close of the conflict and the final triumph of Christianity.

For over three hundred years the struggle between the followers of the White Christ and those of Odin and Thor had been going on.   Slowly but surely, though with many a temporary check, the Cross had triumphed—probably the more surely because slowly.   When Christianity was forced upon an unwilling people at the point of the sword, a merely superficial conversion was all that could be looked for. [629] But on the whole there had been little force used in Sweden— even Inge's attempt to compel his subjects to become Christians exhibits little of the violence shown by Olav Trygevessön in Norway, and the one case where a Swedish district was compelled to change its faith was due to the crusading zeal of another Norwegian king, Sigurd Jorsala-

---

[627] Some historians are of the opinion that the Uppsala Temple was destroyed by Inge I. after the defeat and death of Blot-Sven, while it has also been suggested that Inge destroyed it before the revolt against him occurred, and that it was for that reason that the sacrifice at which St. Eskil met his death was held at Strängnäs.   It seems more likely, however, that it remained till Sverker's time.

[628] In the notes of Karl, Bishop of Västerås, appended to the Hervarar Saga, we have the statement: "MCXXXIIX. Suerchr I. jecit fundamenta templi Chatedralis Upsalæ, et cum opere vetusto III Deorum paganico, ab Yggemundo igne purificato et sanctificato conjunxit."

[629] Cp. Gjerset: "Hist. of Iceland," p. 70. "The leaven of the Christian faith had to work for centuries before the pagan mind of Iceland yielded fully to its spiritualizing and ennobling influence."   To show how little in some cases the nominal acceptance of Christianity affected the conduct of those who had embraced it, he gives as an example the life of Hallfred Ottarsson after his baptism (pp. 56–7).   How prevalent serious crime still was in Iceland in the time of Pope Innocent III. we may see from his letter to the Bishops of Holar and Skalholt of July 30, 1198. Dip. Norv., VI., No. 5 ; P.L. 21, Reg. Innocent III., Book I., No. 305 ; Potthast, No. 336.   See also on the subject Mawer: "The Vikings," p. 90 ; Worsaae: "Danes and Norwegians in England," p. 37.

farer, who in 1123 forced the inhabitants of Småland to "take Christianity." [630]

This, however, is not to say that it was only the appeal of its teachings, contrasting so greatly as they did with those of the ancient faith, or the influence of the heroic lives of its missionaries, that gradually caused the adoption of Christianity in Sweden. Other influences no doubt contributed to this result—the example of Christian kings must have counted for something, even if it were for far less than was the case in most lands; the close tie between chieftain and household, when the former accepted the new faith, perhaps counted for much more; the solemn ritual of the Christian services no doubt impressed the minds of many of the simple dwellers in the North; nor must we overlook the possible effect on those engaged in trading voyages of finding themselves looked down upon as heathen by those with whom their commerce was carried on. [631]

On the other hand, with regard to the reasons for the slowness of the conversion of Sweden, though we may say with Olaus Magni, the last Archbishop of Uppsala to receive the pallium from Rome, that it was due to the inscrutable providence of God who has placed times and seasons in His own power, [632] yet God works by means of human agents, and we may notice a number of contributory causes to the tardy acceptance of Christianity by the northern land.

If we compare the mission of Anskar with that of Augustine in England more than two hundred years earlier, we can hardly help noticing how surprisingly meagre its results seem when contrasted with those obtained by that of the Italian monk. Within a few years of the time of Augustine's landing at Ebbsfleet, not only had Ethelbert of Kent himself become

[630] Ágrip, LVI., i.; "Heimskringla: Saga of Sigurd the Jerusalem-farer," c. 28.

[631] Schück: "S.F.H.," I., p. 275, seems to think that if the relations of the missionaries can be trusted the power of working miracles was the chief cause of the conversion of the heathen.

[632] "Historia de Gentibus Septentrionalibus," p. 153. "... in primis causam præstare videtur inscrutabilis Dei providentia, quæ horas et monumenta (quando hoc opus piissimum fieri possit) in sua posuerat potestate."

a convert, but practically the whole of his subjects had
followed his example; his kingdom had become an organized
part of the Western Church, with see cities at Canterbury and
Rochester[633]; and a mission had been established at London,
in the neighbouring kingdom of the East Saxons.[634] At the time
of Anskar's death, however, over thirty years after he had
first visited Sweden, there seems to have been still but a single
Christian congregation—that of Birka—existing only on
sufferance, and liable at any time to be overwhelmed by a
heathen rising.

Or we may make a wider comparison between the two
lands. It was less than a hundred years from the time of
Augustine's reception by the Kentish king to that when
Bishop Wilfred, exiled from Northumbria, won for Christianity the last heathen kingdom in England.[635] It was more
than three times as long before Christianity had finally
triumphed in Sweden. Why should it have progressed so
much more slowly there than in England, when on the whole
the heathen religions which it supplanted in the two lands
were so much alike?

There was, of course, the vastness of the country, and the
fewness of the missionaries[636]; then there was the change in
manner of life demanded by even a nominal acceptance of
Christianity, such as the giving up of Viking raids on monasteries and churches, and such customs as those of blood-
revenge, the exposure of newly-born infants,[637] and the
marrying of several wives; there was too, no doubt, a certain
amount of affection for the old religion, which had been a
bond of unity between the different tribes; and the hallowing

[633] Bede: "Eccles. Hist.," I., cc. 25f., II., c. 3; "A.-S. Chron.," sub
annis 597,604; William of Malmesbury, I., cc. 1, 6.
[634] Bede: "Eccles. Hist.," II., c. 3; William of Malmesbury, I., c. 6.
[635] Bede: "Eccles. Hist.," IV., c. 13.
[636] Olaus Petri: "Chrönika, S.R.S.," I., ii., p. 231, remarks, "Sverige
är så vidt att thet icke står till omvändandes med fåå personer i en kort
tijd."
[637] In Iceland when it was decided at the Althing held in 999 or 1000
that the island should become a Christian state, certain heathen customs,
as the eating of horse-flesh and the exposure of infants, were allowed to
remain. Gjerset: "History of Iceland," pp. 63, 64.

of Sunday and the observance of Church fasts and festivals must have been to many very burdensome. Some, however, of these difficulties had also obtained in England, and if due allowance is made for the share of the Keltic missionaries in the conversion of the latter country, and for the special difficulties attached to missionary work in Sweden through the vastness of the country and the difficulties of communication between the different regions, it would seem that the difference in the attitude of the Papacy to the missionary work in the two lands was perhaps the chief reason for the differences in the results obtained through it.

While the mission of St. Augustine was sent directly from Rome, and behind it had all the influence, authority and resources of the Papacy, as well as the deep personal interest of Pope Gregory, in the case of St. Anskar it was the Emperor who was directly responsible for sending him, and for another two hundred and fifty years Papal interest in the Swedish mission seems to have been confined to the confirmation given to the successive archbishops of the Hamburg-Bremen see of their rights over the Swedish Church. With Gregory VII., as we have seen, a new era can be said to have commenced, but it was a commencement and little more. No noteworthy results apparently sprang from it; no important changes in the Swedish Church took place as the consequence of the intervention of the great Papal reformer; the christianization of the country continued to progress, but it was not until seventy years after the reception of the Gregorian epistles that Pope Eugenius III. gave the commission to Nicholas Breakspear, Cardinal of Albano, that began the process of drawing the Swedish Church into close touch with and dependence on the occupants of the Papal chair, who, though they hitherto had almost ignored the existence of Sweden, were from then onward to show a deep and sympathetic interest in its affairs —a greater interest, indeed, than might have been expected, when its poverty and isolation from the main current of European affairs are taken into account.

There had, however, been changes that made it much easier for Nicholas Breakspear, when he came, to carry out his mission with partial success, even if he failed to achieve its main object—that of forming Sweden into a separate ecclesiastical province. The organization of the Church had naturally been greatly improved by the establishment of the various sees, each with its orderly succession of bishops, some of whom were beginning to take a share in ecclesiastical affairs in general in the North in addition to carrying out their strictly diocesan duties. Thus at a synod held by Archbishop Eskil at Lund in 1139, at which the Papal legate, Theodignus, was present, and which was attended by Sigurd of Bergen and Orm of the Faroes, as well as by five Danish bishops, Sweden was represented by Bishop Gislo of Linköping[638]; while six years later both he and Ödgrim of Skara were present at the consecration of Lund Cathedral.[639] A Papal document of the year 1120[640] mentions six sees in Sweden—Skara, Linköping, Eskilstuna, Strängnäs, Sigtuna and Västerås—but of these, as we have already noticed, Eskilstuna was soon absorbed into Strängnäs, and Sigtuna transferred to Uppsala, so that at the time of the legate's arrival there seem to have been five sees—Uppsala, Linköping, Skara, Strängnäs and Västerås.

[638] " S.R.D.," VII., " Catalogus Pontificum Roskildensium," p. 157.
[639] " S.R.D.," III., " Necrologium Lundense," pp. 455, 456. Ödgrim, according to the old chronicle, was the eleventh Bishop of Skara. "S.R.S.," III., ii., p. 113; "U.Ä.B.," p. 54. The Chronicle speaks highly of him. " Han war goðaer maðaer ok sniaellaer."
[640] Tunberg: " En romersk källa om Norden vid 1100 talets början," quoted in Lindqvist: " Den helige Eskils biskopsdöme," p. 165. The document appears to be a list of the provinces of the Church compiled for the use of the Papal Curia. After it has mentioned the sees in Spain and Poland those in the North are enumerated under the heading " Provincia Danorum " :—
Provincia Danorum : Metropolis civitas Lunda.
Nomina civitatum in Norgueca : Civitas Lunda (Added later), Roskeada, Othensia, Hethabia, Ripa, Arosa, Vibiarga, Birgila.
Nomina civitatum in Suethia : Alpsa, Biargina, Nithirosa, Scara, Liunga, Kaupinga, Tuna, Strigiñ, Sigituna, Arosa.
It will be noticed that the compiler's geography was very faulty, for he places a number of Danish bishoprics in Norway, while the Norwegian sees—Oslo, Bergen and Throndhjem—are assigned to Sweden. He also implies that Liunga and Kaupinga are the names of two separate sees. It is just possible that Liunga = Linköping, and Kaupinga = Köping, on the island of Öland ; but it is far more probable that they really only represent the see of Linköping.

It has been pointed out that the jurisdiction over the Churches of Norway and Sweden, which was granted to the Archbishop of Lund, was probably intended to be only temporary; but even if this were not the case Pope Eugenius III. came to the conclusion that it was time that Sweden and Norway became separate provinces, and so resolved on their immediate creation. With this end in view he determined to send a legate to make the necessary arrangements, and his choice fell on Nicholas Breakspear, [641] an Englishman whom he had made Cardinal of Albano in 1146. The choice was a wise one, for Nicholas was in several ways particularly suited for the mission entrusted to him. For one thing, he was fully in sympathy with the Gregorian ideals, which still held sway at the Papal court; then, being an Englishman, he would not have the same language difficulty as a Frenchman or an Italian, for at that time there was a closer resemblance between the English and the Scandinavian languages than there is now, though this fact must not be over-emphasized. [642] He was also a man of considerable experience, renowned for his high character, learning and eloquence, and had for some time been abbot of the monastery of St. Rufus, near Valence. [643]

[641] " B. Eugenius eam (i.e. the English race) ad quæcunque vellet applicari, dixit esse idoneam, et præferendam aliis, nisi levitas impediret." John of Salisbury: " Polycratius," vi., 19. Quoted by Mann: " Nicholas Breakspear," p. 11, note 1.

[642] Breyer: " Die Legationen des Kardinalbischofs Nikolaus von Albano in Skandinavien," p. 7, says " Da ferner die angelsächsische Sprache mit der altnordischen nahe verwandt war, diese sogar damals in einigen Gegenden des heutigen Englands in Gebrauche war, so wäre es nicht unmöglich, dass Nikolaus auch dieser Sprache mächtig war." Compare, however, Mackie: " Pope Adrian IV.," p. 16, " Doubtless the Pontiff considered that a legate of northern extraction would be more acceptable than an Italian to the hardy Northmen; but . . . the resemblance between the Norse and English languages was far from being as close as has been supposed." In earlier times the resemblance had no doubt been closer than it was in 1152, and in the Saga of Gunnlaug Ormstungu, c. 7, we have the statement: "þá reð fyri Englandi Aðalraðr konungr Játgeirsson ok var goðr höfdingi. Hann sat þenna vetr i Lundunaborg. Ein var þá tunga á Englandi sem í Noregi ok í Danmörku; enn þá skiftust tungur í Englandi, er Vilhjálmr bastarði vann England."

[643] See " D.N.B.," I., pp. 143, 146. In the " Rerum Italicarum Scriptores III." there are three short lives of him, all by fourteenth century writers, who all refer to his mission to Norway. The Cardinal

It was in 1152 that Nicholas came by sea to Norway, which at that time was under the joint rule of three brothers— Sigurd, Inge and Eystein—and there established a metropolitan see at Nidaros or Throndhjem, which was to have authority over Iceland, Greenland, the Faroes, Orkneys, Hebrides and Isle of Man, as well as Norway, whose four sees—Throndhjem, Oslo, Bergen and Stavanger—were increased to five by the creation of one at Hamar. [644] As the see of Throndhjem was vacant at the time through the death of Bishop Reidar, [645] Jon Birgirssön was translated from Bergen and invested with the pallium by the legate. Nicholas seems also to have secured the promise of the payment of

---

of Aragon says of it (p. 441), " Processu vero modici temporis cognita ipsius honestate, ac prudentia, de latere suo eum ad partes Norvegiæ Legatum Sedis Apostolicæ destinavit, quatenus verbum vitæ in ipsa Provincia prædicaret, et ad faciendum Omnipotenti Deo animarum lucrum studeret. Ipse vero tamquam minister Christi, et fidelis, ac prudens dispensator mysteriorum Dei, gentem illam barbaram et rudem in lege Christiana diligenter instruxit, et Ecclesiasticis eruditionibus informavit." It will be noticed that no reference is made to the Cardinal's work in Sweden and the same is the case in the other two lives—those of Bernardus Guidonis and Pandulph.

In the "Vita" in Mansi, XXI., h.-p. 785, his character is summed up as follows, " Vir valde benignus, mitis ac patiens, in Græca & Latina lingua peritus, sermone facundus, eloquentia politus, in cantu ecclesiastico præcipuus, prædicator egregius, ad irascendum tardus, ad dignoscendum velox, hilaris dator, eleemosynis largus, & in omni morum compositione præclarus."

[644] The action of Nicholas was confirmed by a bull of Pope Anastasius IV. Dip. Norv., VIII., No. 1; Dip. Arna-Magnæanum II., No. 2; P.L. 188, Anastasius IV., E. and P., No. 84; Regesta Norvegica, No. 58; Jaffé, No. 9941. Dated Nov. 30, 1154. Lateran. "Et ne de cetero provincie Norvegie metropolitani possit cura deesse. commissam gubernacioni tue urbem Thruensem ejusdem provincie perpetuam metropolim ordinavit. et ei Asloensem. Hammarcopiensem. Bergenensem. Stawangriensem. insulas Orcades. insulas (Fareie) Suthraie. insulas Islandensium et Grenelandie episcopatus. tanquam sue metropoli perpetuis temporibus constituit subjacere. et earum episcopatus sicut metropolitanis suis tibi tuisque successoribus obedire." Cp. the bull of Innocent III. sent to the Archbishop of Throndhjem, Feb. 13, 1206. Rome. Örnhjälm: "H.E.," IV., iii., p. 439; Dip. Norv. VIII., No. 7; Hamb. U.B., No. 202; Regesta Norvegica, No. 196; Potthast, No. 2686. There were two sees in Iceland—Skalholt and Holar.

[645] Bishop Reidar had been chosen by the Pope to be the first archbishop and had been invested with the pallium, but had died on his way home. In view of the approaching visit of Nicholas no successor had been appointed by the joint rulers.

Peter's Pence, [646] and though he was unable to bring about
the introduction of clerical celibacy, [647] he much improved the
discipline of the Norwegian Church by insisting on the
canonical election of bishops by the cathedral chapters, and
the creation of archdiaconates so that the canon law might be
better administered, while he secured for the bishops the right
to appoint the parish clergy. [648]

From Norway Nicholas came to Sweden and a synod of
great importance was held at Linköping, probably the same
year. [649] Unfortunately the accounts of it are very scanty,
and we know little more than that his intention of creating
a metropolitan see for Sweden was frustrated in some way—
possibly by the machinations of Archbishop Eskil of Lund, [650]
more probably by the rivalry between the Swedes and
Goths, [651] which made it impossible to decide whether the

[646] No definite mention is made of the introduction of the payment of
Peter's Pence into Norway in connection with the visit of Nicholas.
Bang ("Udsigt," p. 152), Keyser (I., p. 225), Willson ("Hist. of Church
and State in Norway," p. 142) and Brilioth ("Den påflige beskattningen
af Sverige," p. 27) all think it was then introduced, but Jörgensen
(p. 540) and Taranger (p. 290) consider that it was introduced from
England at an earlier date. In the latter country the yearly payment
promised to the Pope by Offa of Mercia, in gratitude for his action in
making Lichfield an archbishopric, may be considered the first step of
those that led up to the final payment by every household in the land. See
Hunt: "History of the English Church," I., pp. 239, 240; Overton:
"The Church in England," I., pp. 113, 114.

[647] It seems probable that he made an attempt to do so, but found such
strong opposition to his proposals that he deemed it prudent to withdraw them, and that it was this action on his part that led the
Norwegian clergy later on to say that he had given permission for them
to marry.

[648] Keyser, I., pp. 222–8.

[649] The old chronologies give 1148. "S.R.S.," I., i., p. 23.
"MCXLVIII. Habitum est concilium lyncopie a nicolao Albanensi qui
fuit post papa Adrianus." See also pp. 48, 61. Örnhjälm: "H.E.,"
IV., iii., p. 439, gives 1151, and Messenius: Sc.Ill., II., p. 2, gives 1152,
which is almost certainly correct.

[650] This is the view of Breyer: "Die Legation des Kardinalbischofs
Nikolaus von Albano in Skandinavien." He argues that because the
great confusion that prevailed in Norway, with the rule shared between
three kings, did not prevent the erection of an archbishopric there,
therefore the failure to erect one in Sweden must be assigned to some
other cause than disunion. But in Norway there was only one nation,
while in Sweden there were two.

[651] Saxo, XIV., c. 697. "Quod in Svetia quoque legationis potestate
peragere cupiens, Sveonibus et Gothis de urbe et persona tanto muneri
idonea concordare nequeuntibus, certamini decus negavit, rudemque

honour should be conferred on Uppsala in Svealand, Linköping in Östergötland, or Skara in Västergötland,[652]—that King Sverker was prevailed upon to promise to pay Peter's Pence,[653] and that certain rules were laid down regarding the freedom of the Church, marriage, and the wearing of arms, as we learn from a letter of Pope Anastasius IV. sent to King Sverker and the Swedish nobles after the return of Nicholas to Rome.[654]

Nicholas seems to have made no attempt to force celibacy on the Swedish clergy. Possibly, as Bishop Wordsworth suggests,[655] some bargain was made in regard to this and the payment of Peter's Pence. Certainly we find later Archbishop Andreas of Lund informing Pope Innocent III. that the

adhuc religionis barbariem summo sacrorum honore dignatus non est." Westman: "Den svenska kyrkans utveckling," p. 43, thinks that the ill-feeling between the Swedes and Goths has been much exaggerated, and that the chief rivalry was between the various pretenders to the throne. He also suggests (p. 59) that Erik IX. was probably already king in Svealand, that there was a civil war, and that the clergy from his realm were absent from the synod. Cp. Kjellen: "Om Eriksgatan," pp. 5, 23, 24; Schück: "S.F.H.," I., p. 281.

[652] Messenius: Sc. Ill., II., p. 2. "Hi siquidem Lincopiæ vel Scaræ, illi tantam Upsaliæ dignitatem potiori jure, deferendam contenderunt nec convenerunt." Almedingen: "The English Pope," p. 218, suggests that the legate may have seen that the only solution of the difficulty was to have two metropolitans.

[653] According to an old legend the payment of Peter's Pence was introduced by Olov Skötkonung. Olaus Petri: "Chrönika, S.R.S.," I., ii., p. 234. "Och är en allmennelig mening att thenna Konung Olof skulle förthenskull vordet kallat Skottkonung, att han pålade thet Romskott som här i landet hafver plägat utgå hvilket till Rom sändas skulle, Påfvenom till undsättning emot the Saracener Christenhetenes fiender, thet honom (utan tvifvel) hafver varit ingifvit af the Engelska predikare." See also Örnhjälm: "H.E.," III., viii., pp. 220–2, and Porthan: "Opera Selecta IV., Observationes circa historiam Denarii Petrini in Svecia," p. 337, note 10. "Quum jam a. 1140 Papa Paschalis II. Archiepiscopum Lundensem admonuerit de more census b. Petri pendendi, per aliquod tempus in Dania intermisso; aegre credas, nihil fuisse in Svecia de eo exprimendo, ante a. 1152 tentatum?"

[654] Unfortunately the Pope gives no details of these rules, but merely says, ". . . monemus vos et exhortamur in Domino quatenus per eundem fratrem nostrum ymbre sacri eloquii irrigati fructum vitæ facere studeatis, et cogitantes apud vos qualiter cum fueritis aliquando tenebræ, nunc sitis lux in Domino, quæ sursum sunt sapiatis, non quæ super terram, et per verum Noe ac ministros ipsius ab inundatione diluvii in archam ecclesiæ congregati, præcepta Dominica et præfati fratris nostri statuta de libertate Ecclesiarum, matrimonio, armis non portandis et aliis ad salutem populi spectantibus firmiter observetis."

[655] "N.C.S.," pp. 108, 109.

Swedish clergy asserted that they had received Papal permission to marry, though they apparently did not produce any documentary evidence in support of their claim,[656] which seems to show that the bargain—if bargain there were—must have been a verbal one. After the return of the legate to Rome, Pope Anastasius IV., who had succeeded Eugenius III., addressed a letter to Sverker and the principal men of the country,[657] urging them to see that the rules which Nicholas had given them were kept, and to remain true to the holy Roman Church, the mother of all the faithful, and, as a proof that they are continuing in the good way they have begun, to pay Peter's Pence to the bishops. He wrote also to the bishops,[658] expressing his thankfulness at the spread of Christianity in Sweden, and urging them to keep the statutes given them by the legate, and to get the people to do so also. He also gives them permission to give absolution in less serious cases of violence done to the clergy,[659] and orders them to collect Peter's Pence in their respective dioceses and forward it to Rome.[660]

If we consider the letter of Gregory VII. to King Inge as the first serious attempt of the Papacy to bring the Church of Sweden into immediate relationship with itself, the Synod of Linköping was certainly the second. Gregory's letter was little more than an enquiry; the suggestions in his second, to Inge and Hallsten, do not seem to have been carried out; but the promise made by the synod to pay Peter's Pence meant an acknowledgment of Papal authority far beyond any pre-

---

[656] See Note 512.

[657] Sv. Dip., No. 38; Sv. Tr., No. 38; Celse: "Bullarium," p. 33; Örnhjälm: "H.E.," IV., ii., p. 452; Hjärne: "Medeltidens Statsskick," p. 278; P.L. 188, Anastasius IV., E. and P., No. 87; Jaffé, No. 9938. Dated Nov. 28, 1153–4. Lateran. For a full discussion of the date of this letter and of the one to the bishops see Samuelsson: "Datering af påfvebrefven om Nicolaus' af Albano Legation."

[658] Sv. Dip., No. 820; Sv. Tr., No. 39; Celse: "Bullarium," p. 34; P.L. 188, Anastasius IV., E. and P., No. 86; Jaffé, No. 9937. Dated Nov. 28, no year. Lateran.

[659] In more serious cases—murder or mutilation—right of absolution was reserved for the Pope himself.

[660] " . . . ut censum, quem regnum et populus b. Petro annuatim statuerat solvendum, quisque de suo episcopatu annis singulis colligere et sedi apostolicæ transmittere fideliter studeat."

viously accorded by the Swedish Church. We may well say that it inaugurates a new era—that of the Romanized Church—though much remained to be done before that Romanization would be complete, and remember that it was an Englishman who was the agent in inaugurating it.

With regard to the payment of the tax we learn from the compilation made by Albinus,[661] and incorporated in the " Liber Censuum " made in 1192, by Cencio Savelli,[662] the camerarius of Pope Celestinus III., that not only was the " penny " paid by each household in the country, but that the Bishops of Linköping and Västerås each made a special payment,[663] though no reason is given for it[664] As to the

---

[661] This is included in Fabre: "Le Libre Censuum de l'Église Romaine," II., pp. 85–137. In it there are three references to Sweden. On p. 101 we have
" In regno Suetie
Metropolitanus Ubsalensis hos episcopos suffraganeos habet sub se
          Arusiensem
          Straganensem
          Lingacopensem
          Scarensem
          Sunt igitur numero V."
On p. 121 we have the entry of the payments.
" Singule domus I denarium monete ipsius terre.   Episcopus Arusiensis II marcas pro unoquoque anno."
And then, after a notice about Hungary,
                    " In Suevia.
     Episcopus Lingacopensis XI marcas pro unoquoque anno ad
          pondus Colonie."
[662] Cencio Savelli afterwards became Pope, taking the name of Honorius III.
[663] Fabre: "Liber Censuum," p. 229.   The actual entry in the compilation of Cencio Savelli reads,
                    " Suethia
     In archiepiscopatu Ubsalensi
     In episcopatu Arusiensi
          Episcopus ipse II marcas singulis annis
     In episcopatu Straganensi
     In episcopatu Lincopensi
          Episcopus ipse XI marcas et dimidiam
          singulis annis ad pondus Coloniense
     In episcopatu Scarensi
          Notandum autem quod singule domus
          Suetie singulos dant denarios monete ipsius terre."
It will be noted that the payment assigned to the Bishop of Linköping here differs slightly from that given in the compilation of Albinus. No mention is made of Växjö, although in 1192 it again had a bishop of its own.
[664] It may have had something to do, in the case of the Bishop of Västerås, with the fact that he seems to have acted at this time as the agent of the Pope for the collection of the tax in Sweden. See Brilioth: " Den påfliga beskattningen af Sverige, pp. 29–34.

Peter's Pence

regularity with which the payments were made during the first hundred years after its introduction the few references to it that have come down to us are somewhat conflicting. We have, for instance, Innocent III. sending his thanks to the inhabitants of Uppsala diocese, for the promptitude with which they paid the tax,[665] while not many years later, we find Honorius III. ordering its payment by the faithful in Sweden, and saying that the Bishop of Västerås stated that it had not been paid for five years.[666] Gregory IX., too, wrote to three " præpositi " in Uppsala diocese to urge them to see that the inhabitants of Hälsingland paid the tax to the Papal court, and also instructed them to recompense the Archbishop of Uppsala, who had apparently paid on their behalf.[667]

The failure of the Swedish clergy to agree upon the city to be made an archiepiscopal see had serious consequences for their Church, for it lost them complete provincial independence when later on the province of Uppsala was formed. Nicholas, on his way back to Rome, left the pallium with Eskil, Archbishop of Lund, so that when the Swedes and Goths had settled their differences he could bestow it on the occupant of the new archbishopric.[668] He seems to have wished to make up to Eskil for the loss he had suffered in having Norway removed from his jurisdiction by giving him the honour of the primacy of Sweden, while he also possibly thought that the conduct of the Swedes and Goths at the synod made them unworthy of complete provincial independence. The consequence was that when, a few years later, Uppsala became a metropolitan see, its holder had to recognize

---

[665] " Baronibus, militibus et aliis per Upsalensem diocesim constitutis." Sv. Dip., No. 158; P.L. 216, Reg. Innocent III., Supplementum, No. 230; Potthast, No. 5115. Dated May 31, 1216. Perugia.

[666] Sv. Dip., No. 203; Celse: "Bullarium," p. 58; Reg. Honorius III., No. 2943; Potthast, No. 6467. Dated Jan. 3, 1221. Lateran.

[667] Sv. Dip., No. 268; Celse: "Bullarium," p. 65; Potthast, No. 9033. Dated Nov. 2, 1232. Anagni.

[668] Saxo XIV., cc. 697, 698, " Qui (i.e. Nicholas) veniens apud ipsum futurum Svetici sacerdotii insigne deposuit dandum ei, in quem concors Sveonum Gothorumque suffragium convenisset. Statuit quoque, ut quicumque maximi Sveonum pontifices creandi essent, pallio a curia dato per Lundensem insignirentur antistitem eamque sedem perpetuo venerarentur obsequio."

the primacy of Lund—a primacy that, in spite of its irksome-
ness, was not formally withdrawn till the fifteenth century.

It is most probable that at the time of the Synod of
Linköping, Sverker was no longer king of the whole country,
but that the Swedes, dissatisfied with his rule, had already
chosen Erik Jedvardsson, a nobleman related to the family of
Stenkil, as their king. [669] Erik is usually reckoned to have
reigned ten years, [670] and as he was killed in 1160 this would
make him already king for two years at the time of the Synod
of Linköping. Then the question arises as to whether he was
present at it, and if so, did he equally with Sverker promise
the payment of Peter's Pence. Though it has been asserted
that it was Nicholas Breakspear who urged on Erik the expedition which he undertook about the year 1157 against the
heathen Finns, [671] this seems very improbable. [672] On the
other hand, Bishop Henry of Uppsala, who accompanied
Erik on that expedition, is supposed to have been consecrated
by the legate during his stay in Sweden. [673] The old chronicles

[669] Erik was apparently the grandson of Blot-Sven. Chronologia,
"S.R.S.," I., i., p. 83. "Mater ejus fuit Cecilia filia Swenonis Regis
quæ fuit soror Ulps Ducis Galla et Chols." Erik's wife Kristina was
according to one account grand-daughter of Inge I., whose daughter
Katarina married the Danish prince Björn Jernside; according to
another she was the daughter of Inge II. See "S.R.S.," I., i., p. 4.

[670] All the old chronologies seem to agree in assigning this length to his
reign. E.g. Chronologia, "S.R.S.," I., i., p. 23. "MCLX. Passus est
beatus ericus rex swecie in Upsalia XV kal. Junii. Qui regnavit annis
X. . . ."; Petrus Olai: "Annales, S.R.D.," I., p. 177. Stjerna: "Erik
den helige," p. 8, puts the outside limits of his reign as 1156–61.
The legendary life of Erik, printed in "S.R.S.," I., i., pp. 272–7,
seems to be of little value. For instance, although Sverker was certainly
ruling part of the country at the time of his accession, and continued to
do so for several years, it says "Hic, regno vacante, propter innatam
sibi clementiam et vitæ bonitatem conspicuam dilectus, a principibus
terræ et omni populo in Regem unanimiter eligitur, ac in regni solio apud
Upsaliam honorifice sublimatur." Ericus Olai: "Chronica, S.R.S.,"
II., i., p. 45, repeats this statement.

[671] Koskinen: "Finlands Historia," I., p. 29. Johannes Magni:
"Gothorum Sveonumque Historia," XIX., c. 3, says that it was Bishop
Henry of Uppsala who persuaded Erik to make the expedition. Cp.
Rhyzelius: "Epis.," I., p. 27.

[672] Bååth: "Den kanoniska rättens historia," p. 8. "Nikolaus trädde
sannolikt ej i någon förbindelse med sveakonungen ty den förre skulle
hafva hållit ett möte blott in Linköping, alltså i själfva medelpunkten
för östgötafolket, som först korat Sverker till konung och förblifvit
honom troget."

[673] Rhyzelius: "Epis.," I., p. 27.

are too scanty for any positive assertion about Erik's relationship to the synod to be made, but we may note that Pope Anastasius, in the letter previously mentioned, addressed himself solely to Sverker and the Swedish chiefs, [674] and it is hardly likely that Erik is included among the latter.

On the death of Sverker, [675] however, which seems to have happened about 1156, he became sole king, though his title was disputed, so far as the Goths were concerned, by Karl, son of Sverker, who some time before Erik's death seems to have acquired the rule of Östergötland. [676]

Erik had a busy time furthering the spread of Christianity among his Uppland subjects. [677] His expedition to Finland we shall describe later; he only ruled for about two years after his return from it, and then in May, 1160, [678] he was attacked suddenly at Uppsala by the Danish prince, Magnus Henrikssön, who claimed the throne through his mother, a granddaughter of King Inge I., and seems to have gained many adherents, especially in Västergötland. Erik, who was attending the church of the Holy Trinity, remained till the end of the service—a proceeding that reminds us of the conduct of Ethelred I. at the battle of Ashdown, [679]—and then sallying forth was overwhelmed and killed in spite of his heroic defence. [680]

In after years, Erik, though never formally canonized, apparently because of the influence of the rival Sverker family at Rome, became the patron saint of Sweden. He does not

[674] " Carissimis in Christo filiis S. regi et universis proceribus Swechie."
[675] " S.R.S.," I., i., p. 11 ; "U.Ä.B.," p. 35. " Hans hestaeswen myrði han julaeotto, sum han skuldi til kyrkiu farae. Ok han aer jorðaeðaer i Alwastrum." See also Ericus Olai : " Chronica, S.R.S.," II., i., p. 43, where, however, his death is wrongly assigned to the year 1151.
[676] Olaus Petri : " Chrönika, S.R.S.," I., ii., p. 241.
[677] " Vita S. Erici, S.R.S.," II., i., p. 272.
[678] Erik is said to have been killed on Ascension Day, May 18, 1160. But that year Ascension Day fell on May 5th, so that there is an error somewhere. Strinnholm : " S.F.H.," IV., p. 110, note 274, suggests that Ascension Day may be named to give more honour to the sainted king.
[679] Asser : " Life of Alfred," cc. 37–9 ; William of Malmesbury, II., c. 3.
[680] " Vita S. Erici, S.R.S.," II., i., p. 276.

seem to have cultivated any close relations with the Papacy, and it was possibly due to the conservative ecclesiastical policy adopted by him and other members of his family that Sweden was, on the whole, the least thoroughly Romanized of the three northern kingdoms in the Middle Ages. [681]

Magnus reaped little benefit from the death of Erik. Karl Sverkersson, who, as already mentioned, had been ruling for some time in Östergötland, attacked and killed him at Örebro in 1161. [682] Erik's son, Knut, fled to Norway, and Karl Sverkersson became king of the whole country, and seems to have styled himself—being the first Swedish king to do so—" King of the Swedes and Goths." [683]

Karl proved himself to be a good friend of the Church, and under him much was done to bring Sweden into closer relationship with the Roman see. It seems strange that Nicholas Breakspear, after all that he had done as legate in the North, should, after becoming Pope as Adrian IV., have given so little attention to Swedish affairs, especially as he seems still to have taken a great interest in the North, [684] while he had certainly made a most favourable impression on the people of Norway, and possibly too on those of Sweden as well. It is true that practically the whole of his pontificate was taken up with struggles, first with the people of Rome, and then with the Emperor, Frederick Barbarossa [685]; but he found time to grant Henry II. of England the bull authorizing

---

[681] Westman in "Den svenska kyrkans utveckling" emphasizes very strongly, perhaps somewhat too much so, the conservative ecclesiastical standpoint of the kings of the Erik line. Cp. Stjerna: "Erik den helige," p. 8.

[682] "S.R.S.," I., i., p. 12; "U.Ä.B.," p. 40. "Han tok af daghum Magnus konung . . . i Öraebro." This was possibly not Örebro in Närke, but Örsundsbro in Uppland, though the former is more probable. See "S.R.S.," I., i., p. 12, note n.

[683] Kjellberg: "Den äldsta konungatiteln," pp. 5–7. See also Tunberg: "Äldre Medeltiden," p. 56.

[684] Saga of the Sons of Harald, c. 23. "According to the report of the men who went to Rome, he had never any business, however important, to settle with other people, but he would break it off to speak with Northmen who desired to see him."

[685] See "Camb. Med. Hist.," V., pp. 424–6, 429, 430.

the conquest of Ireland, [686] and there was much that might have been done in regard to Swedish affairs. The assertion of Vastovius that Bishop Henry of Finland was formally canonized by him on January 19th, 1158, [687] seems to be of very doubtful validity, and the same may be said of the statement that he made the church at Räntämäki the seat of the Bishop of Finland. [688] He did, however, confirm the primatial rights of the archbishops of Lund over Sweden, though the bull has been lost. [689]

[686] The authenticity of this bull, however, has been much called in question, among others by Cardinal Gasquet and Professor Thatcher of Chicago. See Mann: "Nicholas Breakspear," p. 3; and for the bull, Hjärne: "Medeltidens Statsskick," p. 213; Mansi: "Concilia," XXI., h.-p. 788; P.L. 188, Adrian IV., E. and P., No. 76; Jaffé, No. 10056. Rome. Undated.

[687] "Vitis Aquilonia," p. 65. See also Celse: "Bullarium," p. 35. He is also said to have canonized Sigfrid. "Vitis Aquilonia," p. 32.

The bishop is certainly referred to as St. Henry in certain papal bulls. Porthan: "Juusten-Chronicon," p. 110, note 10, quotes from that of Boniface VIII., dated May 10, 1296. Rome. "Cupientes igitur ut Ecclesia Aboensis, in honorem b. Marie Virginis et Sancti Henrici Episcopi et Martiris fundata. . . ."; also that of Innocent VI. (wrongly given in Porthan as Innocent IV.), dated Nov. 11, 1353. Avignon. "Cupientes igitur ut ecclesia Aboensis . . . frequentetur . . . omnibus vere penitentibus . . . qui in . . . (festivitate) Sancti Henrici Martiris. . . ." Both bulls are printed in Åbo Domkyrkas Svartbok, Nos. 18, 155.

[688] Another erroneous statement about him is that he moved the see from Räntämäki to Åbo. This certainly did not take place till later. We have the letter of Gregory IX., dated Jan. 23, 1229, Perugia, and addressed to the Bishop of Linköping, the Cistercian Abbot of Gottland and the Provost of Visby, with regard to the removal of the Finnish see to a more suitable place. Åbo Domkyrkas Svartbok, No. 1; Sv. Dip., No. 246; Celse: "Bullarium," p. 62; Potthast, No. 8322. Whether, however, this refers to the removal from Nousis to Räntämäki, or from Räntämäki to Åbo is not clear. See also Messenius: "Chronicon Episcoporum," p. 19; Örnhjälm: "H.E.," IV., iv., p. 464.

[689] See Sv. Tr., No. 40.

CHAPTER IX

THE ESTABLISHMENT OF THE ARCHBISHOPRIC OF UPPSALA

THOUGH Nicholas Breakspear had been unable to establish a separate province of the Western Church in Sweden—whether owing to the inability of the Swedes and Goths to agree as to which see should be raised to metropolitical rank, or from some other reason—and does not seem to have made any further attempt to carry through the project after his elevation to the Papal chair, yet the pontificate of his successor, Alexander III., witnessed the fulfilment of the plan that he had been unable to consummate : Sweden became a separate province of the Western Church, Uppsala became the seat of an arch-bishopric, and the first person to fill the newly-created metro-political see was an Englishman. Once more, then, we have the indebtedness of the Swedish Church to the English emphasized.

Like his predecessor, Alexander played a leading part in the fierce struggle between the Empire and the Papacy, which now assumed an even greater intensity. An anti-Pope, Victor IV., was elected by the Emperor's friends in the College of Cardinals [690] and before long Alexander was driven from Rome. After staying for a time first at Anagni and then at Terracini, he eventually took up his residence at the old archiepiscopal city of Sens in France, and here there came to him the English monk, Stephen, from the Swedish mon-astery of Alvastra, [691] for the Swedish Church, although at first hindered from making a decision on account of the unsettled state of the country, had eventually taken the side

---

[690] "Camb. Med. Hist.," V., pp. 430, 431.
[691] "H.S.H.," VI., p. 4. "Anno Domini millesimo sexagesimo tertio consecratus est magnificus Dominus pater Stephanus de primis monachis Alvastri monasterii natione Anglus in Archiepiscopum Upsaliensem primum anno Karoli regis quinto filii Sverkeri regis primi fundatoris monasterii Alvastri." Cp. "S.R.S.," I., i., p. 51 ; III., ii., p. 99 ; Petrus Olai : "Annales, S.R.D.," I., p. 177.

of Alexander in the struggle.[692]   Stephen had brought a request from King Karl, the jarl Ulv, and the bishops,[693] that having been chosen as the first Archbishop of Uppsala, he might receive Papal confirmation of his office.   It is possible that the legate, Stephen of Orvieto, whom Alexander had sent to Norway in 1163, had also visited Sweden, and had helped to influence the Swedish Church to give its support to the exiled Pope; it is possible, too, that the fact that Stephen belonged to the Cistercian Order had great weight with Alexander; at any rate, he seems to have complied willingly with the request of the Swedish king, and thus in 1164[694] Sweden got its first archbishop.   The actual rite was performed by Eskil of Lund, who, like the Pope, was in exile;[695] but although Alexander did not himself perform the ceremony, it took place in his presence and he showed his goodwill towards the newly-consecrated prelate by presenting him with a Gospel Book and some relics of the Cross.[696]

Before returning to Sweden, Stephen is said to have procured from the Pope the canonization of St. Helena of

---

[692] Jennings: "Medieval Church and the Papacy," p. 24, says that Sweden took the side of Victor but gives no authority for the statement. The mere fact of the mission of Stephen seems to prove the contrary.

[693] " . . . precibus et interventu karissimi filii nostri, Caroli illustris regis Sveorum et Gothorum, Episcoporum quoque et Ulfii, Ducis Regni illius. . . ."

[694] Sometimes the previous year is given as the date.   Chronologia, "S.R.S.," I., i., p. 23.   "MCLXIII. Consecratus est Stephanus Archiepiscopus Upsalensis anno karoli regis quinto."   Cp. p. 51, also Petrus Olai: "Annales, S.R.D.," I., p. 177; "H.S.H.," VI., p. 4.   It is given as 1164 in "S.R.S.," I., i., pp. 40, 48, 61, 83, and this year is undoubtedly the correct one.   See Gams: "Series Episcoporum," p. 340; Westman: "Den svenska kyrkans utveckling," p. 133; and for the ritual used Söderblom: "Stefans invigning," pp. 3–22.

[695] Eskil had taken the side of Alexander III. against the anti-Pope Victor IV., and in consequence had been obliged to flee from Denmark, as King Valdemar, largely it would seem for political reasons, had espoused the cause of Victor.   On leaving the country, he paid a visit to the Holy Sepulchre and then came to stay with Alexander at Sens.   Later he became reconciled with Valdemar, after the latter had acknowledged Alexander, and in 1168 he returned to Denmark. See further, Steenstrup: "D.R.H.," I., pp. 606–10; Westman, pp. 122–24.

[696] "Chronicon de Episcopis et Archiepiscopis Ecclesiæ Upsalensis, S.R.S.," III., ii., p. 99.   " . . . huic archiepiscopo contulit dominus papa librum ewangeliorum dictum carla knap et duas cruces ligneas parvas auro tectas in quibus conditum fuit lignum domini."

Skövde,[697] a lady who had lived in Västergötland in early Christian times.[698] She had been largely instrumental in building the church at Skövde, and, after becoming a widow, had devoted her time largely to works of mercy and was also said to possess the gift of prophecy. Her daughter's husband having been killed by his servants on account of his cruelty to his wife, Helena was thought by the relatives of the murdered man to have been the instigator of the crime. In consequence of this she went on a pilgrimage to Jerusalem and to various shrines, but her enemies refused to be reconciled, and on her return found opportunity to slay her when she was on her way to the consecration of the church at Götene. After her death many miracles were said to have happened, certain of them at her burial, others through invocation of her help, and consequently Stephen was able to procure her canonization. Whether the writer of the legend[699] is in error or not in regard to this, it is certain that St. Helena was a much-reverenced saint in Sweden in pre-Reformation times, especially in Västergötland. Her festival was observed in the dioceses of Uppsala, Linköping, Strängnäs and Västerås on July 31st, and in Skara on July 30th, with the Octave August 6th,[700] although according to the legend her death occurred on August 1st.[701]

Later in the year Alexander despatched two bulls to Sweden. The first, addressed to Stephen himself,[702] is

[697] "Legenda S. Helenæ Schedviensis, S.R.S.," III., ii., pp. 137, 138. "Set quia deus sanctam suam signis tam evidentibus mirificare dignatus est, procurante felicis recordacionis domino Stephano archiepiscopo Upsalensi, dominus Alexander tercius ipsam sanctorum cathalogo censuit ascribendam." Cp. "H.S.H.," VI., p. 5; Petrus Olai: "Annales, S.R.D.," I., p. 177.

[698] Although the legend seems to imply this, it is more probable that she lived in the early part of the twelfth century. The first known person in Sweden to bear the name of Helena was the wife of Inge I.

[699] This is supposed to have been Brynjulf, Bishop of Skara from 1278 till his death in 1317. He was the compiler of her office in the Skara Breviary, in which the legend appears.

[700] "Kalendarium Svecicum," pp. 309, 310.

[701] "Legenda S. Helenæ Schedviensis," p. 137. "Occubuit autem kalendis Augusti. . . ."

[702] Sv. Dip., No. 49; Sv. Tr., No. 43; Celse: "Bullarium," p. 38; Örnhjälm: "H.E.," IV., v., p. 482; Hjärne: "Medeltidens Statsskick," p. 280; P.L. 200, Alexander III., E. and P., No. 260; Jaffé, No. 11047. Dated Aug. 5, 1164. Sens. (Örnhjälm and Celse give 1163.) There is a Swedish translation of the bull in Spegel: "Skriftelige Bewis," No. 5.

interesting as setting forth clearly the claims of the Pope to
govern the Church. Alexander says that although all the
disciples of the Lord had the same power to loose and to bind,
and the same commission to preach the Gospel, yet a certain
difference was found among them, and Peter received through
the Lord's words, " Lovest thou me? Feed my sheep," a
special prerogative in regard to the care of the flock. He
became Prince of the Apostles and was given a special command to strengthen the brethren, so that posterity should
understand that though many are appointed to the rule of
the Church, there is only one who has the highest place of
dignity, and that everything is regulated through his ruling
and guiding power. Consequently in the Church there is a
whole series of dignitaries and authorities with varying
ministries, but over them all there presides the Roman Bishop
(Romanus Pontifex), as Noah in the Ark, judging and enacting
in regard to all matters, and strengthening the children of the
Church throughout the world in accordance with the words,
" When thou art converted, strengthen thy brethren." In
consideration of this, and at the request of his very dear son,
Karl, King of the Swedes and Goths, and of the bishops, and
the jarl Ulv, Stephen is given the pallium as archbishop and
metropolitan of the province of Sweden, with Uppsala as his
see city, and Skara, Linköping, Strängnäs and Västerås [703] as
suffragan sees, but at the same time he is to remember that he
and his successors are to pay due reverence to the Archbishop
of Lund as their primate. [704] He also gives a list of

[703] Wordsworth : " N.C.S.," p. 112, remarks, " What the position of
Åbo in Finland was intended to be is not clear." There was no Bishop
of Åbo as yet, and if Henry's successor, Rudolf, was now labouring in
Finland, he was only a missionary bishop.

[704] " . . . precibus et interventu karissimi filii nostri, Caroli, illustris
regis Sveorum et Gothorum, Episcoporum quoque et Ulfii Ducis Regni
illius, pallium, Pontificalis scilicet officii plenitudinem duximus indulgen-
dum. Et ne de cætero Provinciæ Sveciæ Metropolitani possit cura deesse,
commissam gubernationi Tuæ Upsaliam urbem ejusdem Provinciæ perpetuam Metropolim ordinavimus, et Scarensem, Lincopensem, Streg-
enensem et Arusiensem Episcopatus ei, tamquam suæ Metropoli perpetuis
temporibus constituimus subjacere, et eorundem locorum Episcopos, tam
præsentes quam futuros, sicut Metropolitanis suis, tam tibi quam tuis
successoribus obedire. Statuimus autem, ut sicut tu de concessione et
mandato nostro consecrationis munus a Venerabili fratre nostro Lundensi

the occasions when the pallium is to be worn. [705]

The letter to the bishops impresses on them the duty of rendering lawful obedience to their new metropolitan, and also urges them to exercise due care in their ordinations, so that unfit persons shall not be admitted to the ranks of the clergy. [706]

It says much for the statesmanship and forbearance of Karl Sverkersson that he permitted Uppsala to be chosen as the metropolitan see, for as a Goth he might naturally have been expected to press the claims of either Linköping or Skara. Perhaps he had in mind the long period during which Uppsala had been the centre of the religious life of the country; perhaps he recalled the unifying effect which the old heathen worship had exercised on the various tribes, and hoped for a like result from the present arrangement; possibly his object was merely to acquire the goodwill of his subjects in Svealand, and prevent their thoughts from straying to the neighbouring land of Norway and summoning Knut Eriksson from thence to claim his inheritance—but, whatever his reasons were, there is no doubt about the wisdom of his action.

Anglo-Saxon Britain had furnished a good example of the part that the Church might play in helping to bring about the unification of a land with divided rule, for the assertion that "the Dane was the real, though involuntary, maker of a

Archiepiscopo suscepisti, ita et successores tui ab eo, et a successoribus suis, consecrationem debeant absque ulla contradictione recipere, et tamquam proprio Primati obedientiam et reverentiam exhibere."

[705] " Porro concesso tibi pallio, Pontificalis scilicet officii plenitudine infra ecclesiam tuam ad sacra tantum missarum solemnia per universam provinciam tuam his solummodo diebus uti fraternitas tua debebit, qui inferius leguntur inscripti : Nativitate Domini, Epiphania, cæna Domini, Resurrectione, Ascensione, Pentecostes, in solennitatibus beatae Dei genitricis, semper Virginis Mariæ, natalitio beatorum Apostolorum Petri et Pauli, in inventione et exaltatione S. Crucis, Natalitio S. Johannis Baptistæ, in festo Johannis Evangelistæ, commemoratione omnium sanctorum, in consecrationibus Ecclesiarum vel Episcoporum, benedictionibus Abbatum, ordinationibus Presbyterorum, in die dedicationis Ecclesiæ Tuæ, ac festo S. Laurentii, et anniversario tuæ consecrationis die."

[706] Sv. Dip., No. 50 ; Sv. Tr., No. 44 ; Celse : "Bullarium," p. 40 ; Örnhjälm : "H.E.," IV., v., p. 484 ; P.L. 200, Alexander III., E. and P., No. 261 ; Jaffé, No. 11048. Dated Aug. 5, 1164. Sens. (Örnhjälm, Celse, 1163.)

united England," is at best but a half-truth,[707] making, as it does, no allowance either for the remarkable ability that characterized as a whole the kings of the line of Cerdic from Egbert onwards, or for the unifying influence of the Church. The existence of a single ecclesiastical province while there were still several kingdoms undoubtedly helped to weld Jutes, Angles and Saxons into one nation, while the experiment of Offa in persuading Pope Adrian I. to erect Lichfield into an archbishopric was soon realized to be a mistake,[708] and the later independence of York had its unsatisfactory side; and there can be little doubt that in Sweden the formation of the province of Uppsala assisted materially to bring the Swedes and Goths into a closer relationship, and so make the unity of the kingdom a much greater reality than it had previously been.

Not all the credit for bringing about this much-desired consummation is due to Karl Sverkersson. He must share it with the Pope, who appears to have been determined that the Swedes and Goths must settle their differences as to the city to be chosen as the metropolitan see, as well as become united under one sovereign, before their country could become a separate province of the Church. It seems, however, a decided exaggeration to say that it is less Karl Sverkersson than Alexander III. that Sweden has to thank that it became a state[709]; both acted in a statesmanlike way, and there is no need to attempt to apportion exactly the amount of credit due to each respectively.

[707] Cp. for a different view Hodgkin: "History of England from the Earliest Times to the Norman Conquest," p. 263; and for the help rendered by the Church in the unification of the State, Bright: "Early English Church History," p. 284.

[708] For the archbishopric of Lichfield see William of Malmesbury, I., c. 4. Cp. Hunt: "History of the English Church," I., pp. 236–7, 239–40, 244–5, 251. Note his remark, "Offa's policy of providing Mercia with a separate ecclesiastical government would, if successful, have hindered the attainment of national unity, and its defeat by Aethelheard is therefore an event of the highest importance in the making of the nation," p. 251. Cp. the letters of King Kenulf and Pope Leo as given in William of Malmesbury, I., c. 4.

[709] Bååth: "Den kanoniska rättens historia i Sverige," p. 18, "Det är mindre Karl Sverkersson, än Alexander III., som Sverige har att tacka för, att det blef en stat."

There is, however, one question that arises in connection with the creation of Uppsala as a metropolitan see, and that is why it was placed under the primacy of Lund. When Nicholas Breakspear came to Scandinavia with legatine powers for the establishment of the two fresh northern provinces, was it the Pope's intention that the Swedish province should be, like that of Norway, completely independent of Lund, or were the conditions of its creation left to the discretion of Nicholas? As we have seen, the latter dropped for the time the project of making Sweden a separate province because of the inability of the Swedes and Goths to agree upon a see city, but he is also said to have written to Archbishop Eskil, before coming to Denmark on his way to Rome, to say that the honour he had lost—jurisdiction over the Church in Norway—would be more than compensated for by a greater one, namely, the primacy over Sweden. [710] We know, too, that when he visited Eskil he left with him the pallium, ready for its bestowal when the Swedes and Goths should have settled their differences; and furthermore, [711] when he himself became Pope as Adrian IV., he confirmed the Archbishop of Lund in his primacy, and also made him Papal legate for the North. [712]

Possibly, then, in creating the archbishopric of Uppsala, Alexander considered himself bound by the action of his predecessors, but it seems also possible that the state of affairs in the ecclesiastical world—and more particularly in the Danish part of it—may have affected his decision. The year 1159 had witnessed the great Papal schism, when Alexander III.,

[710] Saxo XIV., c. 697. Neumann: "De Fatis Primatus Lundensis," p. 69, says with regard to the reasons for Lund's primacy, "Rationes primatum Lundæ condendi, ut illi asserunt scriptores, istæ fuere: Pontifex Romanus, ut Sveciam jam antiquitus inde libertate elatam in perpetuum sibi subjiceret, odiisque mutuis grassantibus septentrionales terras sua sub ditione facilius retineret, Lundæ primatum condidit, quo bellis dissidiisque causa nunquam deesset."

[711] Saxo XIV., c. 698.

[712] The bull has been lost, but it is referred to in one of Innocent III. "Constituit (Adrianus) quod Lundensis archiepiscopus, qui pro tempore fuerit, super regnum illud primatum semper obtineat, et ordine, quo subsequitur, debeat ei præesse." Sv. Dip., No. 110; Sv. Tr., No. 54; Celse: "Bullarium," p. 48; P.L. 214, Reg. Innocent III., Book I., No. 419; Potthast, No. 435. Dated Nov. 23, 1198. Lateran.

who represented the Gregorian ideals, and Victor IV., who represented the party of the Emperor, were both elected to fill the Papal chair.

Valdemar of Denmark sent his chancellor to the Council of Pavia to promise his adherence to Victor, probably being influenced to do this by his friendship with Henry the Lion, who was the cousin of the Emperor Frederick I. All the Danish bishops acknowledged Victor with the exception of Archbishop Eskil, who presently found himself obliged to go into exile, and eventually came to stay with Alexander III. at Sens, where he was when Stephen of Alvastra arrived with his request to be made archbishop.

England, France, Sicily, Hungary and Spain were supporting Alexander in the struggle, and he was, of course, glad that Sweden too had taken his side, while as Stephen was a Cistercian monk, he could be relied on to uphold the cause of Alexander to the best of his ability. At the same time the faithfulness of Eskil deserved consideration, and he might object to Uppsala being made an archbishopric. He does not, however, seem to have done so, and hence it appears not improbable that a bargain may have been struck—Uppsala should be made an archbishopric, which would retain the goodwill of Sweden; Eskil and his successors should keep their primacy over the Swedish Church, which would satisfy the Danish archbishop.

Alexander may also have thought that the backward state of Swedish culture as compared with that of Denmark made it inadvisable to give the Swedes complete provincial independence; he may even have hoped that the new arrangement would bring about kindlier relations between the two countries, which had so often been at war with each other; but whatever the reasons for his action, the fact remained— Uppsala was subordinated to Lund, and its archbishops must look to the latter church as their " Mother and Mistress."

Stephen himself does not seem to have offered any objection to the retained primacy of the Danish metropolitan, but many of his successors found it irksome and tried to get the Pope to release them from it. At first, however, the Pope upheld the rights of Lund. Thus Innocent III., in 1198, wrote to the newly-elected archbishop, Olov, that the pallium was to be given to him through the Archbishop of Lund, [713] and a few weeks later confirmed to Archbishop Absalon and his successors the right given to them by Adrian IV. to be primates of Sweden, and in consequence to consecrate the archbishops of Uppsala, [714] a confirmation which he renewed when in 1201 Absalon was succeeded as archbishop by Andreas. [715] He also authorized Andreas to collect the whole of Peter's Pence in Sweden, [716] and sent a bull giving him wide authority to regulate Swedish ecclesiastical affairs on the Pope's behalf. [717] Honorius III. gave Andreas a confirmatory renewal of his privileges, [718] having previously made him legate for both Denmark and Sweden. [719] When Bishop Bengt of Skara visited Rome a few years later he attempted in vain to get the primatial rights of Lund abrogated, and Gregory IX., the successor of Honorius, followed the usual course when sending the pallium for Archbishop Jarler to Lund, [720] though the actual consecration and bestowal of the pallium seems to have been entrusted to Bishop Laurentius of Linköping. [721] Jarler's successor, Laurentius, was consecrated and given the pallium by Jakob Erlandi in Lund [722]; but Archbishop Folke, who was present at the Council of Lyons,

[713] Sv. Dip., No. 106; Celse: "Bullarium," p. 47; P.L. 214, Reg. Innocent III., Book I., No. 374; Potthast, No. 378; Dated Sept. 26, 1198. Perugia.

[714] Sv. Dip., No. 110; Sv. Tr., No. 54; Celse: "Bullarium," p. 48; P.L., 214, Reg. Innocent III., Book I., No. 419; Potthast, No. 435. Dated Nov. 23, 1198. Lateran.

[715] Sv. Dip., No. 117; Sv. Tr., No. 57; Potthast, No. 1505. Dated Nov. 23, 1201. Anagni.

[716] Celse: "Bullarium," p. 49; P.L. 215, Reg. Innocent III., Book VII., No. 155; Potthast, No. 2320. Dated Nov. 6, 1204. Rome.

[717] Celse: "Bullarium," p. 50. P.L. 215, Reg. Innocent III., Book VII., No. 157; Potthast, No. 2326. Dated Nov. 19, 1204. Rome.

[718] Sv. Dip., No. 172; Sv. Tr., No. 65; Celse: "Bullarium," p. 60; Reg. Honorius III., No. 882; Potthast, No. 5621. Dated Nov. 16, 1217. Lateran.

[719] Sv. Dip., No. 169; Celse: "Bullarium," p. 55; Reg. Honorius III., No. 305; Potthast, No. 5445. Dated Feb. 1, 1217. Lateran.

[720] Sv. Dip., No. 292; Reg. Gregory IX., No. 2887. Dated Dec. 17, 1235. Viterbo.

[721] Rhyzelius: "Epis.," I., p. 33.

[722] Rhyzelius: "Epis.," I., p. 34.

managed to obtain from Pope Gregory X. the right to be consecrated and invested with the pallium by Israel, Bishop of Västerås, though the Pope expressly stated in his letter of authorization to Israel that the permission was given without prejudice to the rights of the Church of Lund.[723]   Other archbishops followed the example of Folke, and got themselves consecrated without the act being performed by the Archbishop of Lund, but the primacy of the latter was not formally abrogated till Nicholas Ragvaldi, Bishop of Växjö, obtained from the Council of Basle the independence of the see of Uppsala,[724] and even then the Archbishops of Lund did not abandon their use of the title of Primate of Sweden.

Although we have no contemporary chronicle to relate to us the course of events in Sweden during the time that Stephen occupied the archiepiscopal see, we can learn a good deal about the state of affairs there from the letters of Alexander III., and can see that the archbishop had no easy task in carrying on the work begun by Nicholas Breakspear of trying to secure for the Church the privileges that the Gregorian ideals demanded, and enforcing on the lower clergy the discipline required by those same ideals.   He had indeed a good friend in King Karl, but for the most part the nobles, *bonder* and lower clergy seem to have wished to maintain unaltered the prevailing state of affairs, and thus to have made it very difficult for the archbishop to bring about the required reforms.

The first great blow to the reforming party came in 1167, when Knut Eriksson came suddenly from his place of exile in Norway, defeated and slew Karl at Visingsö,[725] and seized the crown, while Karl's little son, Sverker, was hurried off for

---

[723] Celse: "Bullarium," p. 87. Dated Aug. 18, 1274. Lyons. "Istis de Lundensis ecclesiæ prærogativis, cui Upsalensis jure primatiæ subesse dicitur, nihil derogantibus."

[724] Johannes Magni: "Gothorum Sveonumque Historia," XIX., c. 7. "Si tamen aliqua talis præeminentia Lundensi Archiepiscopo permissa fuit, ea in concilio Basiliensi per Nicolaum Raualdi Archiepiscopum Upsalensem abrogata fuit, et extincta." Cp. his "Hist. Met., S.R.S.," III., ii., pp. 65, 66; also Mann: "Nicholas Breakspear," p. 14.

[725] "Chronologia, S.R.S.," I., i., p. 23. "MCLXVII. Karolus rex interficitur in Visingxö et rex swærkerus fugit." See also "S.R.S.," I., i., pp. 51, 62, 83; "H.S.H.," VI., p. 4.

safety to Denmark. Knut, however, had much more fighting
to do before he could gain undisputed possession of the
throne, for the late king's brothers, Kol and Burislav, [726]
offered a strong opposition to his rule, and for six years the
country was in the throes of civil war. Archbishop Stephen
apparently threw in his lot with the Sverker party, a very
natural thing for him to do, and in consequence found it
necessary to leave the country for a time. As it seems most
likely that Knut's power was strongest in Sweden proper we
can understand that Stephen, whose diocese lay within its
bounds, must have been in an awkward position as favouring
the claims of the rival king or kings, and it is not improbable
that he was called to account for this before a civil tribunal—
for a letter of the Pope seems to hint at some such happening
—and may even have been sentenced to exile. Whether this
was so, or not, he left the country for a time.

He first went to Denmark, and then undertook a mission to
Pope Alexander III. on behalf of King Valdemar. The latter
was anxious to procure the canonization of his father, Knud
Lavard, [727] and also to secure the addition of the island of
Rügen—the heathen Slavonian inhabitants of which had
recently been conquered by the Danes and their famous idol
temple at Arkona destroyed [728]—to the diocese of Bishop
Absalon of Roskilde. Entrusted with this commission, Stephen
—accompanied by the Abbot Briennus of Kalvö, a certain

[726] We know very little about either of these kings. Strinnholm sug-
gests (" S.F.H.," IV., p. 135, note 347) that they were only half-brothers.
Possibly Kol ruled first in that part of the land which adhered to the
house of Sverker, and Burislav took his place after he was killed in battle.
The latter is referred to in a Danish source—" Waldemari II. liber Census
Daniæ, S.R.D.," VII., p. 529. " Hee sunt possessiones regis Waldemari
I. in Swethia. . . . illas possessiones quas bulizlaws hereditavit mortuo
patre suo Swærcone antiquo. et mortuo dicto bulizlauo easdem posses-
siones hereditavit soror ejus Sophia regina dan. mater regis waldemari
II. Et sciendum quod omnes predictas possessiones dedimus duci Kanuto
preter hereditatem bulizlaui."

[727] Knud Lavard, a nephew of St. Knud, was Duke of Schleswig in the
first half of the twelfth century. He was done to death in 1133 by one
of his kinsmen, and so came to be regarded as a martyr. He was afterwards commemorated on January 7th. See " S.R.D.," III., " Necrologium Lundense," p. 435, where, however, he is styled " gloriosus
Slavorum Rex," and the year of his death is given as 1131.

[728] Saxo XIV., c. 170a.

O

Master John, who was the special representative of King Valdemar, and Walter, one of Absalon's clergy—made his way to Italy and was successful in securing the desired concessions for the Danish monarch.[729] But apart from carrying out his special mission Stephen apparently took the opportunity that it afforded him of acquainting the Pope with the state of affairs in Sweden, and the difficulty he had found in introducing the Gregorian reforms there, with the result that Alexander despatched a letter to Sweden addressed to the inhabitants of the diocese of Uppsala.[730]

He had received information, he said, that the bishops were being brought before the civil courts on various charges. Such actions must cease, for sheep must not judge the shepherd. The archbishop must be judged only by the Pope, and neither he nor any other prelate must be brought before civil tribunals. We may note, however, that complete clerical exemption from civil courts is not yet claimed, but only that of prelates, while it is interesting to recall that it was also to Alexander III. that Thomas Becket appealed during his struggle with Henry II. in regard to this same question.[731]

On his return from Italy, Stephen was present at Ringsted in 1170 when the translation of the body of the recently-canonized saint took place with great ceremony, and Knud, the young son of Valdemar, was crowned as the future king.[732] He also played a prominent part in the

---

[729] P.L. 200, Alexander III., E. and P., Nos. 632, 633; Jaffé, Nos. 11645, 11646. Dated Nov. 4 and 8, 1169. Benevento. The first is addressed to Absalon, the second to Eskil and the chief ecclesiastics of Denmark.

[730] Sv. Dip., No. 62; Sv. Tr., No. 45; Celse: "Bullarium," p. 42; Örnhjälm: "H.E.," IV., v., p. 533; Hjärne: "Medeltidens Statsskick," p. 284; P.L. 200, Alexander III., E. and P., No. 634; Jaffé, No. 11648. Dated Nov. 8, 1169. Benevento.

[731] See Mann: "P.M.A.," X., pp. 170ff., Brooke: "The English Church and the Papacy," c. 13.

[732] "S.R.D.," I., No. 20, pp. 277–8. "CIƆCLXIX. Mense Septembri Oratores Regii et Stephanus Pontifex Upsalensis Roma in Daniam redeunt cum literis Alexandri III. Papæ, quibus ille Archiepiscopo, Episcopis aliisque sacratis viris scribit Beneventi VI., Id Novemb. ut Canutum, Obotritorum Regem, Waldemari patrem, Apotheosi celebrata, in Deorum numerum recipiant propter miracula et fonticuli Scatebram ipso cædis die exortam, diem ipsius natalem VII. Kal. Julii sacrum et celebrem omnibus ceremoniis habeant, ipsum precibus, votis nuncupandis,

negotiations for peace between Denmark and Norway, acting on behalf of the jarl Erling, the father of Magnus, King of Norway[733]; and that these negotiations were eventually successful was in a large measure due to his efforts. He afterwards returned to Sweden where civil war was still raging.

In England the civil war in Stephen's reign had enabled the Church to increase its influence and acquire greater privileges, but this certainly does not seem to have been the case in regard to the anarchy prevailing in Sweden, and in the autumn of 1171 we find Pope Alexander III. sending a whole series of letters of Sweden, the contents of which may be regarded as offering material for a reform programme to be carried out by the hierarchy there, while there is little doubt that the abuses mentioned in them as needing to be remedied had been much heightened owing to the disturbed state of the country.

The first is directed to the archbishop and his suffragans.[734] In it the Pope points out the evils brought about by the abuse of power by laymen.[735] They assign churches to whatever priests they wish, irrespective of episcopal approval; they are

uti tutelarem et genium loci, colant, venerentur." "S.R.D.," I., No. 16, Petrus Olai: "Annales." "MCLXX. Sanctus Kanutus Dux et martyr translatus est in crastino Johannis Baptiste. Et Rex Kanutus filius Waldemari coronatus est in Regem. Presentibus Eschillo Lundensi et Stephano Upsalensi Archiepiscopis." Cp. "S.R.D.," II., No. 59, p. 380. In "S.R.D.," I., No. 27, p. 389, the date is wrongly given as 1168, as also in the first quotation above.

[733] "Thomæ Gheysmeri Compendium Historiæ Danicæ, S.R.D.," II., p. 381. "Quibus peractis (i.e. the translation of Knud Lavard and the coronation of Knud) Helgo, Episcopus Asloensis, et Stephanus Upsalensis, ab Erlingo, . . . missi, pacem Norwegie petunt." Cp. Saxo XIV., c. 852.

[734] Sv. Dip., No. 54; Sv. Tr., No. 47; Celse: "Bullarium," p. 40; Örnhjälm: "H.E." IV., v., p. 500; P.L. 200, Alexander III., E. and P., No. 979; Jaffé, No. 12117. Dated Sept. 10, 1171. Tusculanum. "Audivimus enim et audientes non potuimus non dolere, quod apud vos, tam in Svetia videlicet quam in Gothia, ex nimia et perversa non libertate, sed abusione potius et insolentia laicorum, consuetudo pessima et detestabilis inolevit: ex qua etiam multa illicita provenerunt, et mala non solum enormia verum etiam intolerabilia pullularunt."

[735] It would seem that a similar state of affairs prevailed also in Norway, for somewhat later we have a letter from Celestine III., in answer to the complaint of the chapter at Throndhjem, forbidding laymen to exercise any spiritual jurisdiction. Dip. Norv., I., No. 1; P.L. 206, Celestine III., E. and P., No. 253; Jaffé, No. 17343. Dated March 17, 1196. Lateran.

letters
Alex III
to Sweden

guilty of simony; benefices are given to foreigners without their producing proper evidence of ordination, and priests obtain positions by bribery; clergy are brought before civil courts, and trial by ordeal is inflicted on the bishops; and throughout the kingdom clergy are maltreated, and even killed, without their assailants being punished.

To remedy this state of affairs reforms must be made; simony must be stopped; foreign clergy must produce a certificate from their bishop before being allowed to minister in any diocese; clerics must not be brought before civil courts; trial by ordeal or by duel must no longer be made; payment of tithes must be enforced, if necessary by anathema; and excommunication pronounced for violence used towards the clergy is only allowed to be removed by the Pope himself or in accordance with his order.

The letter shows us that all clergy—and not merely prelates—were now to be granted exemption from trial by civil courts; but, as is shown by later Papal letters, much difficulty was experienced in securing this privilege for them, not so much it would seem from the opposition of the kings, but because the general feeling of the country was opposed to it. In the bull of Anastasius IV., it will be remembered, the Pope's right of granting absolution in cases of violence to the clergy was delegated to the bishops in less severe cases. This privilege was now withdrawn, but it is worthy of note that no reference is made in the letter to the method of appointment of bishops or to the enforcement of clerical celibacy.

The second letter is also addressed to the Archbishop and his suffragans, [736] and shows how the Pope was endeavouring to bring the Swedish people still more closely into direct contact with the Papacy and make them still more subject to its authority. It treats first of certain crimes against morality, including child murder. Those guilty of such crimes—unless prevented by age, sickness or poverty—must be sent to Rome to be judged. Those who accidentally suffocated a sleeping

[736] Sv. Dip., No. 56; Celse: "Bullarium," p. 41; Örnhjälm: "H.E.," IV., v., p. 507; P.L. 200, Alexander III., E. and P., No. 975; Jaffé, No. 12113. Dated Sept. 11, 1171, Tusculanum (Jaffé, Sept. 9).

child must do penance for three years if it were baptized; for
five, if it were unbaptized; while a priest guilty of such a
crime must never again exercise his office. Then follow
instructions as to the administration of the sacraments. Mass
is not to be celebrated with dry lees of wine, or breadcrumbs
dipped in wine, as that is not in accordance with the institution of the service; secret marriages are not to take place,
and the prohibited degrees are to be observed, while separa-
tion must only take place canonically with the bishop's
approval.

Alexander also began the practice of taking certain dioceses
under special Papal protections; a practice which must have
helped to a considerable extent to bring the Swedish Church
into closer union with and greater dependence on the Roman
see. Naturally in such cases the Pope would look for greater
activity on the part of the bishops thus favoured in giving
effect to his decrees in their respective dioceses, while they
would also be encouraged by their privileged position to refer
to him various difficulties that they might otherwise have
endeavoured to solve for themselves.

The first of such protective letters was that to William,
Bishop of Strängnäs, [737] which took his Church under Papal
protection, and confirmed him in the possession of his see, and
especially in the district of Närke, which had formerly been an
independent diocese under the Bishop of Eskilstuna. [738]

---

[737] From his name it would seem that Bishop William was a foreigner,
possibly an Englishman. According to Rhyzelius he ruled his diocese for
48 years. "Epis.," I., p. 209.

[738] Sv. Dip., No. 58; Celse: "Bullarium," p. 41; Örnhjälm: "H.E.,"
IV., v., p. 538; P.L. 200, Alexander III., E. and P., No. 973; Jaffé,
No. 12111. Dated Sept. 7, 1171–2. Tusculanam. "Fratres et Co-
episcopos nostros, et eos præcipue qui in medio pravæ nationis sunt positi,
et in remotis mundi partibus constituti, arctiori nos convenit caritate
diligere, et ut in commisso sibi amplius talento proficere valeant, et ad
cultum justitiæ et domus Dei decorem fortius accingi, eis Apostolicæ
Sedis gratiam et favorem impertiri. Attendentes igitur tuæ devotionis
constantiam, et fidei puritatem, qua beato Petro et nobis immobili
firmitate adhærere conspiceris, te sicut Venerabilem fratrem nostrum
diligere et honorare, et tuis rationabilibus votis et desideriis debita cupi-
mus benignitate favere. Inde est quod Ecclesiam tuam sub beati Petri ac
nostra protectione recipientes, ea quæ impræsentiarum pacifice ac legi-
time possidet, et specialiter Neeric, sicut a Rege et Metropolitano tuo, et
a Venerabili fratre nostro Eskilo Lundensi Archiepiscopo, Apostolicæ

To Kol, the new Bishop of Linköping, who had been elected by the clergy and people of the diocese, in conjunction with Archbishop Eskil, the king, and the jarl, in place of Stenar,[739] who, possibly for political reasons, had laid down his office and retired to a monastery, Alexander points out that such resignation without his consent is unlawful.[740] However, in consideration of the need of the Church of Linköping, he will tolerate it and confirm Kol's election.[741] This letter he followed up by one addressed to the clergy and laity of Linköping diocese,[742] exhorting them to show Kol due respect and obedience, while some years later, at Kol's request, he took his diocese with its possessions under his protection in the same way as he had previously taken that of Strängnäs.[743] He also gave a similar letter to the nuns at Gudhem, confirming them in the property given to them by King Knut and others.[744]

It is hardly likely that these letters had much immediate effect as the struggle for the throne was still proceeding. For some time it would seem as if the Sverker party held their own

---

Sedis Legato, tibi confirmata est, et scripti sui munimine roborata, tibi, et per te eidem Ecclesiæ auctoritate Apostolica confirmamus, et præsentis scripti patrocinio communimus, statuentes, ut nulli omnino hominum liceat, hanc paginam nostræ confirmationis infringere, vel ei aliquatenus contraire."

[739] Stenar's name does not appear in the " Chronicon Rhythmicus Episcoporum Lincopensium " (" S.R.S.," III., ii., p. 104), where that of Kol follows Gislo. He afterwards left the monastery and became Bishop of Växjö. See " Chronicon Episcoporum Wexionensium, S.R.S.," III., ii., p. 129 ; Rhyzelius : " Epis.," I., pp. 102, 296.

[740] " Verum licet illi non licuit absque auctoritate Romani Pontificis Episcopali Dignitati abrenunciare." This rule with regard to resignation had been made by Alexander himself.

[741] Sv. Dip., No. 57 ; Celse: "Bullarium," p. 37 ; Örnhjälm : " H.E.," IV., v., p. 535 ; Hjärne : "Medeltidens Statsskick," p. 285 ; P.L. 200, Alexander III., E. and P., No. 974 ; Jaffé, No. 12112. Dated Sept. 8, 1171–2. Tusculanum.

[742] Sv. Dip., No. 61 ; Celse: "Bullarium," p. 37 ; Örnhjälm : " H.E.," IV., v., p. 536 ; P.L. 200, Alexander III., E. and P., No. 984 ; Jaffé, No. 12122. Dated Sept. 17, 1171–2. Tusculanum.

[743] Sv. Dip., No. 74 ; Celse : "Bullarium," p. 43 ; Örnhjälm, "H.E.," IV., vii., p. 563 ; P.L. 200, Alexander III., E. and P., No. 1338 ; Jaffé, No. 13033. Dated March 17, 1177. Lateran.

[744] Sv. Dip., No. 72 ; Celse : "Bullarium," p. 43 ; Örnhjälm : " H.E.," IV., vii., p. 562 ; P.L. 200, Alexander III., E. and P., No. 1230 ; Jaffé, No. 12672. Dated Jan. 19, 1174–6. Anagni.

in Västergötland and the Erik party in Svealand, while the fighting took place mainly in Östergötland, which lay between them. [745] There King Kol fell in battle at Bjälbo, [746] and somewhat later Burislav was also killed in a second battle at the same place. [747] This latter battle may have been fought in 1173, for in that year Knut seems to have thoroughly crushed his opponents, after which he ruled the country in peace for twenty-three years, a remarkable achievement in those troublous times. [748]

Before the conclusion of the war Stephen had possibly become reconciled with Knut, while the latter had evidently realized that it would be well to obtain the recognition and support of the Pope, and with this end in view had sent a certain Richard as messenger to the Papal court. The result was that Alexander decided to recognize Knut's claim to the throne and to do his best to win the Swedish King's sympathy for a reform programme, though he evidently thought that he must proceed somewhat cautiously in this respect and not demand too great a change in the conservative ecclesiastical policy which Knut might be supposed to have inherited from his father. The letter of Alexander [749] is addressed not only to Knut, King of the Swedes and Goths, but to the jarl, the

---

[745] It was in Östergötland in earlier times that the final struggle between Swedes and Goths took place, resulting in the conquest of the latter.

[746] Catalogus Regum Sveciæ, "S.R.S.," I., i., p. 18. "Fæntande knuther eriksson. then sama tyma tha war Kwl oc sagdis wara konungher han fiöll i biælbo." Remains have been found at Bjälbo indicating that a battle was fought there.

[747] Messenius: "Sc. Ill.," II., p. 8, states that Burislav fell at Bjälbo, but on what authority is not known.

[748] "S.R.S.," I., i., p. 12; "U.Ä.B.," p. 41. "Faemtandi war Knutaer konongaer. Han van Sweriki maed swaerdi ok tok af daghum Karl Konong ok Kol konong ok Byrislef konong ok atti marghaer orostaer widh Sweriki ok fek i allum sighaer. . . . Ok þre wintaer ok tyughu war han konongaer. . . ." It is to be noted that in Knut's time Swedish money was again coined after a lapse of over a hundred years.

[749] Sv. Dip., No. 41; Sv. Tr., No. 49; Celse: "Bullarium," p. 38; Örnhjälm: "H.E.," IV., v., p. 496; P.L. 200, Alexander III., E. and P., No. 1447; Jaffé, No. 13546. Dated July 6, 1172. Tusculanum. Sv. Dip., Celse and Örnhjälm make the bull addressed to Karl Sverkersson. The Pope only addresses the king by the initial "K," but Alexander did not stay at Tusculanum during the reign of Karl. There is, of course, the possibility that it was addressed to the rival king, Kol, brother of Burislav.

bishops and all the clergy and people of Götaland. Why only Götaland is mentioned, and why the archbishop's name is omitted, it is difficult to say. It has been suggested that the Sverker party was in power in Svealand, while Västergötland was now entirely under Knut's rule; and Kol, the Bishop of Linköping, had been won over to his side. [750] It seems more probable, however, that from the beginning of the struggle Svealand had acknowledged Knut, himself a Swede, and that Kol and Burislav had exercised authority in Götaland; that Knut had now conquered Västergötland, and gained a number of adherents in Östergötland, which, however, was still partly in the hands of the Sverker party. The Pope had already written to the archbishop and his suffragans, but at a time when he was still unwilling to acknowledge Knut; now that he had decided to do so it was necessary to emphasize the fact to the people of Götaland, so that this part of the country, equally with Svealand, might acknowledge Knut as its king.

With regard to the contents of the letter, Alexander, after an introduction in which he states fully the claims of the Roman Church to complete authority to instruct, [751] proceeds to give directions in regard to various matters. Husbands are to have one wife only, and warnings are given against unlawful unions, though nothing is said about the prohibited degrees; due honour is to be given to bishops, priests and monks, and to persecute them is to persecute Christ Himself; property given to churches or monasteries for the good of the soul of the donor must not be taken from them; tithes must be regularly paid; and those who leave property to the Church must not make it their sole heir if they have children. In concluding the letter he modifies the severity of the fast before Michaelmas, but before doing this says that he has

[750] Westman: "Den svenska kyrkans utveckling," pp. 161, 162.

[751] "Eterna et incommutabilis divini consilii providencia sacrosanctam Romanam ecclesiam, omnium ecclesiarum omniumque fidelium caput, matrem et magistram esse constituit et super catholice et christiane fidei petram protinus nascentis erexit, dicente Domino ad Petrum; tu es Petrus et super hanc petram edificabo ecclesiam meam et porte inferi non prevalebunt adversus eam, et tibi dabo claves regni celorum."

heard with horror that some are found who imitate the heathen by honouring a man who was killed while in a state of intoxication, for the Church hardly permits such a one to be even prayed for.[752] If this refers to the honour paid to St. Erik, the Pope probably got this account of his death from some member of the Sverker party who was anxious to vilify the founder of the rival dynasty. Even then it seems strange that he should write to Knut about his father in such terms, for he could well have left the archbishop to deal with the matter. Possibly, as has been suggested, it is not Erik, but Harald Gille of Norway who is referred to,[753] though it must be remembered that the fact that Erik was never formally canonized seems to have been due to the influence of the Sverker party at Rome. In any case, however, we may notice the claim on the part of the Pope to the right to permit or forbid the veneration of a new saint.

To what extent the letter of Alexander was successful in accomplishing the aims of its sender cannot be said, but it evidently did not avail to secure from the king sufficient respect for the hierarchy, for we find the Pope writing to point out to him and Jarl Birger that the greater power they had received through the gift of God, the greater zeal they should show to do His will, which certainly included honouring the archbishop and other bishops of the kingdom.[754] The

[752] " Denique quiddam audivimus, quod magno nobis fuit horrori, quod quidam inter vos sunt, qui dyabolica fraude decepti, hominem quendam in potacione et ebrietate occisum quasi sanctum, more infidelium, venerantur, cum vix eciam pro talibus in suis ebrietatibus interemptis orare permittat ecclesia."

[753] Beckman: " U.Ä.B.," pp. 42, 43. He points out that though Harald was murdered while in a state of intoxication he was looked upon shortly after in Norway as a saint, and suggests that there may have been some attempt made to get his sanctity recognized in Sweden.

[754] Sv. Dip., No. 852; Celse: "Bullarium," p. 77; Potthast, No. 17447. Dated Jan. 9, no year. Anagni. Though given by all three authorities as a letter of Alexander IV., it seems certain that it should be assigned to Alexander III. for it is addressed to "K. illustri regi Suetis et dilecto filio nobili viro B. comiti." The "K" does not fit in with the fact that Valdemar was king during the whole of the pontificate of Alexander IV.; on the other hand if K is Knut Eriksson, and B = Jarl Birger Brosa, the letter can be assigned to either of the years 1174, 1176, 1178, in all of which Alexander III. was at Anagni on Jan. 9. For further discussion of the matter see Brulin: "Några feldaterade påfvebref," pp. 3–6.

clergy also were apparently remiss in this respect, for they are told that when the archbishop came on a visitation or other errand he should be respectfully received and his orders obeyed.[755] The Pope also reproves them for drunkenness and other grave faults, by which they set a bad example to their people, and gives the further admonition that they are not to appear before a civil court under risk of suspension or deposition, an injunction that apparently implies that the previous instructions on this matter had not been carried out.

Perhaps this second letter accomplished what the first failed to do; perhaps as time went on Knut and Stephen came to understand one another better, for as far as we know there was no further trouble between them, and they had at least one ecclesiastical interest in common—the encouragement of conventual life in Sweden. A series of letters has been preserved, the contents of which show the keen interest displayed by Knut in the welfare of the Cistercian monastery of Juleta, which had been established at Viby in the reign of his predecessor, probably in 1160.[756] In the first of these letters he assured the monks of Viby of his protection, and confirmed them in the possession of the property left to them by pious benefactors[757]; then he made with them the exchange of land that enabled them to transfer the monastery from Viby to Saby in Juleta[758]; and then on the new convent he bestowed certain estates and fishing rights, at the same time anathematizing any person who should attempt to deprive the monks of their rights and privileges, for it was, he said, a duty pertaining to his office as king to protect those who had abandoned the world to consecrate their lives to the service of God, and who by their prayers called down blessings on the king and kingdom from the King of kings.[759] Nor was

---

[755] Sv. Dip., No. 853; Celse: "Bullarium," p. 80; Potthast, No. 17448. Dated Jan. . . . no year. Anagni. This letter is also wrongly assigned to Alexander IV.

[756] See Note 561.

[757] Sv. Dip., No. 63.

[758] Sv. Dip., No. 64.

[759] Sv. Dip., Nos. 63, 64, 65, 67. "Cum omnium utilitati regia deceat providere prudentia maxime religiosorum quietem avidissima debet protectione munire, qui sibi et mundo mortui, solique Deo viventes, Regi regnoque Regem Regum assiduis orationibus propiciare student."

Juleta the sole conventual object of his care, for he also confirmed the monks of Nydala in certain fishing rights, [760] while the nunneries of Gudhem and Byarum [761] were both indebted to his benefactions.

The archbishop, as himself a Cistercian, must have been gratified by the goodwill displayed by the king towards the Order, especially as he would realize that the influence of its members would be exercised in favour of the stricter ecclesiastical ideas which he wished to prevail in the National Church, but which were so difficult to enforce. The Cistercian was still the only Order with monastic establishments in Sweden—though the nunneries connected with it had at first to be reckoned as Benedictine, and were placed under the supervision of the bishop of the diocese in which they were situated,—but before the close of Stephen's rule the Johannites founded a house at Eskilstuna with his consent and that of the king and Bishop William of Strängnäs. [762] The archbishop also joined with the latter in 1176 to consecrate the new stone church at Botkyrka, which had been erected to take the place of the old wooden building built in the honour of the martyr St. Botvid. [763]

These are the last facts we have recorded about Stephen, whose death occurred in 1185. [764] His occupancy of the archiepiscopal see had been both long and eventful, but on the whole he must have felt a sense of disappointment in regard to what he had been able to accomplish. He had started his tenure of office with good hopes of imposing on the Swedish Church to a considerable extent the Gregorian standards of discipline and organization, and untoward circumstances had

---

[760] Sv. Dip., Nos. 70, 71.

[761] According to one account Gudhem was founded by Gunhild, daughter of Anund Jakob. Örnhjälm: "H.E.," II., xi., p. 233. More probably it was founded by Karl Sverkersson about 1162. Rhyzelius: "Mon. Sv.," p. 137, thinks that Byarum was one of the oldest nunneries, but it is not known when it was founded.

[762] Sv. Dip., No. 839 .

[763] "Vita S. Botvidi, S.R.S.," II., i., p. 382.

[764] "S.R.S.," I., i., p. 24. "MCLXXXV. Obiit Stephanus Archiepiscopus Upsalensis XV. kal. Augusti et sepultus est in templo monachorum in alvastrum." Cp. pp. 48, 84. Other dates given in the old chronologies are 1180 ("S.R.S.," I., i., p. 62), and 1181 (p. 52).

largely nullified his efforts. Even the very moderate later demands of Pope Alexander incurred opposition and were but partially complied with, as we can see from the letters of later popes.[765] But whatever disappointment he may have felt when lying on his death-bed and reviewing the course of events during his tenure of his high office, in one thing he could justly take comfort. He had shared successfully in the bringing about of the establishment of the archbishopric; the changes in the royal succession had not demanded the reversal of the bull that had made Sweden a separate province of the Western Church and Uppsala a metropolitical see. Not only from a religious, but also from a political point of view this had been a tremendous achievement. Even if he had not brought about the reforms in the Swedish Church that he had hoped to do, he—Stephen, the Englishman—had laid a foundation on which his successors could build; it was for them to complete the work that he had begun.

[765] E.g. that of Innocent III., dated Jan. 12, 1206, Rome. Sv. Dip., No. 127; Celse: "Bullarium," p. 50; Hjärne: "Medeltidens Stats-skick," p. 287; Potthast, No. 2650. "Non absque cordis amaritudine intelleximus, quod quidam laici de regno Svethie, in viros ecclesiasticos dampnabilem insolentiam exercentes, cum ipsi eorum subire judicium et secundum voluntatem ipsorum ecclesias recipere et dimittere contra-dicunt, illi domos eorum incendunt et tam in personis quam in rebus eos molestant graviter et affligunt. Cum igitur vexatores ecclesiastice libertatis non tam spirituali quam materiali gladio sunt arcendi, sereni-tatem regiam rogamus, monemus et in Domino exhortamur, quatinus presumptores hujusmodi, ut a tali presumptione desistant, tradita tibi potestate compellas."

Cp. the letter of Honorius III. to King John. Sv. Dip., No. 186; Celse: "Bullarium," p. 57; Reg. Honorius III., No. 2753; Potthast, No. 6379. Dated Nov. 3, 1220. Lateran.

There were evidently similar difficulties in Norway, for Celestine III. issued a bull prohibiting the laity from exercising ecclesiastical jurisdic-tion in the diocese of Throndhjem. Dip. Norv., I., No. 1; Dip. Arna-Magnæanum II., No. 7; P.L. 206, Celestine III., E. and P., No. 253; Jaffé, No. 17343. Dated March 17, 1196. Lateran.

CHAPTER X

THE ENGLISH MISSIONARIES IN FINLAND

It is impossible to say when the Swedes first came to Finland, but in the old chronicles we get a reference to the conquests of Erik Segersäll, the father of Olov Skötkonung, there,[766] while a number of place-names—Onsby, Torsö, Friggeberg, Torsbacka, etc.—bear witness to pre-Christian Swedish settlements in the country. Finnish history, however, may be said to commence with the Crusade of Erik IX. of Sweden, which took place about the year 1157.[767] Whether, as has been asserted,[768] Erik was urged to make this expedition by the Cardinal of Albano, when as Papal legate he visited Sweden in 1152, and whether the latter, after he became Pope as Adrian IV., renewed his solicitations seems extremely doubtful. The letter of Anastasius IV. to Sweden, with regard to the arrangements made by the Cardinal, only recognizes Sverker as king, and there are no preserved records of any Papal communications with Erik.

It seems, however, too much to argue from this, as Stjerna does, that the expedition never took place.[769] He is on firmer ground when he says that the internal state of affairs in Sweden was unfavourable for foreign adventures; that it would have been unwise to leave the kingdom open to attack from the two claimants to the throne—Magnus Henriksson, the Dane, and Karl Sverkersson, the Östgötlander—while Erik was away; and that there was probably still strife between Christians and heathen in his own kingdom, which would be

[766] "Minsta Rimchrönikan," ll. 282–5 ; Ericus Olai : "Chronica, S.R.S.," II., i., p. 24 ; Olaus Petri : "Chrönika, S.R.S.," I., ii., p. 232.
[767] "S.R.D.," I., "Petri Olai Annales," p. 176. "1154. Sanctus Ericus Rex Svecie et Sanctus Henricus Archiepiscopus Upsaliensis converterunt Finlandiam ad Christum." This appears to be the only date given in any of the old chronicles, but there are reasons for thinking the crusade must have taken place a few years later. In 1154 Sverker was still ruling in Götaland, so that Erik was not yet king of all Sweden.
[768] Koskinen : "Finlands Historia," I., p. 29.
[769] Stjerna : "Erik den helige," p. 13. Cp. also Schmid : "Sveriges Kristnande," p. 98.

likely to prevent any such expedition from being undertaken.[770] His contention that Erik was only a lukewarm Christian at the beginning of his reign can be ignored, for it seems to depend almost entirely on the harsh treatment at first meted out to the monks of Varnhem by Queen Kristina, and this was apparently due to reasons other than religious ones.[771] But whatever reasons may have militated against the undertaking of the expedition its reality cannot well be doubted, for apart from the relations of the chronicles there is indirect confirmation of Erik's success in two Papal bulls. In the first of these, addressed by Alexander III. to Archbishop Stephen, his suffragans, and Jarl Guttorm,[772] the Pope speaks of the Finns as having accepted Christianity, though they made bad converts, while in the second Innocent III. confirms to King Erik Knutsson the land won by his ancestors from the heathen,[773] which it is not unreasonable to take as referring to the conquests of St. Erik.

Although, as we have seen, it is improbable that Nicholas Breakspear in person urged upon King Erik the desirability of undertaking a crusade to Finland, he may yet indirectly have been to a certain extent responsible for it, for he is said to have consecrated his fellow-countryman Henry as Bishop of Uppsala,[774] and the latter has been credited with making the

Henry

[770] Stjerna : " Erik den helige," p. 13.

[771] Hall : " Cistercienserordens Historia i Sverige," p. 154.

[772] Sv. Dip., No. 59 ; Sv. Tr., No. 46 ; Celse : " Bullarium," p. 41 ; Örnhjälm : " H.E.," IV., v., p. 491 ; P.L. 200, Alexander III., E. and P., No. 976 ; Jaffé, No. 12114. Dated Sept. 9, 1171–2. Tusculanum.

[773] Sv. Tr., No. 64 ; Hjärne : " Medeltidens Statsskick," p. 293 ; F.M.U., No. 52. Dated April 4, 1216. Lateran. " . . . terram, quam clare memorie predecessores tui a paganorum extorserunt. . . ."

[774] Rhyzelius : " Epis.," I., p. 27. It is interesting to compare what Johannes Magni says of him, with regard to his leaving England to come to Sweden, with what the author of his life says about his leaving Uppsala for Finland.

Johannes Magni : " Hist. Met., S.R.S.," III., ii., p. 15. " In Anglia felix episcopus bonis omnibus abundabat ; in Suetia alieno beneficio illi vivendum erat. In Anglia jucundi amici, docta ingenia, morum civilitas : in Suetia atroces Christi inimici, nullaque eo tempore erudita, aut pia ingenia, sed conversatio omnibus periculis cumulata."

" Vita et Miraculi S. Henrici, S.R.S.," II., i., p. 333. " O quantus fidei fervor, quantus ardor divini amoris altare aureum cordis devotissimi Pontificis accenderat, qui postpositis opulentiis rerum, et amicorum solatiis, et Upsalensis præsulatus sede sublimi, pro pauperum et paucarum ovium salvatione, multis se mortis periculis exponebat."

representations that induced the king to embark on his expedition. [775] Possibly, however, the old legend is right in stating that when Eric took his kingly oath at the Mora stones he promised three things—to build churches and improve the services held in them; to rule his people justly; and to fight both for his faith and against the enemies of his kingdom [776]—and that it was in order to keep the last of the promises that he undertook the crusade against the heathen Finns, who for some time had been harrying the coasts of Sweden. [777]   But whether the expedition was due in any way to him or not, Henry, about whose previous career we have only the scantiest knowledge, accompanied the king, and so came to earn the title of the Apostle of Finland.

The Crusaders probably made a landing not far from where the town of Åbo now stands, but Erik did not at once attack the Finns for he offered them first the choice of accepting Christianity as an alternative to doing battle with him.   As they refused to embrace the new faith he attacked them, won a complete victory, and "manfully avenged the Christian blood which they for so long and so often had shed."   But the spirit in which the Swedish king engaged in the crusade is shown by his action after the fight.   One of his men, to his great astonishment, found the king weeping bitterly, and on his expressing surprise that he was not rather rejoicing over the victory he had gained was told by him, "I am glad and render thanks to God that He has given us the victory, but I sorrow over the destruction of so many souls who could have obtained eternal life if they had accepted the Christian faith." [778]

Erik did not stay long in Finland after his victory, and how far he penetrated into the country we do not know.   A number

[775] Johannes Magni: "Gothorum Sveonumque Historia," XIX., c. 3. Fryxell: "Berättelser," II., p. 24; Strinnholm: "S.F.H.," IV., p. 105.
[776] "H.S.H.," VI., "Konung Erik den Heliges Legend," pp. 6, 7; "Vita S. Erici, S.R.S.," II., i., p. 272.
[777] "Vita S. Henrici, S.R.S.," II., i., p. 382.   Most historians agree as to the trouble caused by the Finns to their Swedish neighbours, but Lagerbring ("S.R.H.," II., vii., 3) is of a different opinion.
[778] "H.S.H.," VI., K.E. Leg., p. 9.

of Finns after their defeat accepted Christianity, and when Erik returned to Sweden he left behind him Bishop Henry to have the care of the converts and to work for the spread of Christianity in the land.[779]   With apostolic zeal, though occasionally hardly with apostolic wisdom, Henry set about his task.   Very probably he journeyed round accompanied by an interpreter, and visited in particular those places where markets were held, and where consequently he would be able to address his message to a considerable number of hearers. Thus he "worked wisely and faithfully to build up and strengthen the Finnish Church," and his journeyings seem to have taken him as far north as the river Kumo, while later tradition associated the well of Kuppi, not far from Åbo, with his administration of the sacrament of baptism,[780] and its waters were credited with healing properties.   The Ormberg, near Nousis, was also associated with his memory, for it is said that on his meeting with a snake he caused it to vanish into the hill, leaving, however, its likeness on the outside, so that in future it bore the appropriate name of Ormberg (Snake Mountain).[781]

It was not for long, however, that Henry was able to carry on his missionary work, for he had probably only spent about six months in the country when he was murdered on Kjulo marsh by a bonde named Lalli.   According to one account this was in revenge for a penance laid on him by the bishop because of a crime that he had committed.[782]   Another version of his death says that on his journey he called at the house of Lalli, together with his servant, and asked that they might be supplied with food and drink, offering at the same time ample payment.   Lalli himself was absent, but the saint's request was roughly refused by his wife, whereupon Henry instructed his servant to take what was needed, in spite

---

[779] "Vita S. Erici Regis, S.R.S.," II., i., p. 274.

[780] Rein: "Biskop Thomas," p. 4, note 1, is of opinion that Henry would not have been likely to use the well for this purpose when the river Aura and the sea were so near.

[781] "En Kårt Beskrifvelse om Sancto Henrico Englando, S.R.S.," II., i., p. 336.

[782] "Vita S. Henrici," p. 333.

of her refusal, and to leave a payment of much more than its
value. This was done and the travellers proceeded on their
way. On Lalli's return the matter was misrepresented to him
by his wife, and the bonde, full of anger, set off in pursuit of
Henry, and overtaking him on the ice of Kjulo marsh, cruelly
killed him.[783] He then took the cap from the saint's head and
returned home rejoicing at his deed, but when, after reaching
his farmstead and being welcomed by his wife, he attempted
to remove the cap, the hair and skin of his head came off
with it.[784]

The bishop seems to have had a premonition that his death
would take place on this journey and had left instructions
with his servants as to what they were to do when it happened.
His corpse was to be drawn by a pair of untamed oxen, and
where they stopped a cross was to be raised, while where they
lay down it was to be buried and a church built on the spot.
Such, according to the legend, was the origin of the church at
Nousis, and there the relics of the saint remained until in 1300
they were translated to the cathedral at Åbo and placed in a
silver shrine.[785] They remained in the latter resting-place
until the year 1720, when they were carried off by the
Russians and all traces of them lost.[786]

The thumb of the saint had been cut off by the murderer
and was not recovered till some time later. According to the
picturesque account of its finding given in the legend, it was
about the time of the festival of St. John when an old blind
man and his son were crossing the marsh and the latter
noticed a raven pecking at something on a floating lump of
ice. On telling his father what he had seen, the latter made
him row to the spot. At their approach the raven flew away,
and the boy found on the piece of ice a thumb with a gold
ring on it at which the bird had been pecking. At his father's
request he gave him the thumb, with the result that he stroked

[783] " S.R.S.," II., i., p. 336.
[784] " Vita S. Henrici," p. 334.
[785] " S.R.S.," II., i., p. 331.   Cp. Porthan: " Juusten-Chronicon," I.,
p. 111, notes 11, 12.
[786] Porthan: " Juusten-Chronicon," I., p. 113.

his eyes with it, and at once had his sight restored to him.[787] The thumb and the ring afterwards figured on the Chapter seal of Åbo in the same way as the heads of Sigfrid's nephews on that of Växjö.

It is not only in connection with his death, however, that miracles are recorded in relation to St. Henry. Several instances of the healing of the sick are said to have resulted from invoking his aid, while in one case a dead girl was restored to life when her parents made supplication to the saint.[788] His cult spread throughout the land and even outside it,[789] and he became known not only as the Apostle of Finland, but also as its patron saint. Whether he was formally canonized by Pope Adrian IV. in 1158, as Vastovius expressly asserts,[790] is very doubtful, for he also states that the same Pope removed the seat of the Finnish see from Räntämäki to Åbo, and this almost certainly did not happen till much later. But whether formally canonized or not, the sanctity of Henry was eventually recognized at Rome, as is shown by bulls of Boniface VIII. and Innocent VI., in which the title of St. Henry the Martyr is given to him.[791] His feast was afterwards observed in Finland on January 20th, and that of his translation on June 18th, and both had the highest festal rank, that of " totum duplex," in the Åbo Calendar.[792]

---

[787] " S.R.S.," II., i., p. 337. Cp. " Vita S. Henrici." " Digitus Martyris gloriosi in hieme abscissus, in vere, cum ubique glacies tota liquefacta et resoluta esset, corvo super ipso crocitante, cum annulo ipsius est inventus in quadam particula glaciei."

[788] " Vita S. Henrici," pp. 334, 335.

[789] The name of St. Henry still appears in the calendars of the dioceses of Mohilev, Minsk and Telsiai. The feast is kept as a " duplex majus " in the Vicariate of Sweden.

[790] " Vitis Aquilonia," p. 65. See also Celse: " Bullarium," p. 35.

[791] Åbo D.S., No. 18. Dated May 10, 1296. Rome. " Cupientes igitur, ut ecclesia Aboensis, in honorem b. Marie Virginis et Sancti Henrici Episcopi et Martiris fundata. . . ." Åbo D.S., No. 155. Dated Nov. 11, 1353. Avignon. " Cupientes igitur, ut ecclesia Aboensis . . . frequentetur . . . omnibus vere penitentibus . . . qui in . . . (festivitate) Sancti Henrici Martiris. . . ."

[792] " Kalendarium Svecicum," pp. 301, 306; Lindberg: " Die Schwedischen Missalien des Mittelalters," pp. 240, 309–11; Malin: " Der Heiligenkalender Finnlands." The feast on Jan. 20 also occurs as a " totum duplex " in the Calendars of Kangasala, Vesilahti and Hollola, and that of June 18th with the same rank in the first two.

His cult was not confined to Finland, but was widespread in
Sweden, due most probably to his association with St. Erik,
the national saint and hero, but in the Swedish dioceses he was
commemorated on January 19th instead of the 20th,[793] and
the feast of his translation does not seem to have been
observed.   In the Norwegian Missal his feast occurs in the
Calendar with the rank of " simplex,[794] while it was assigned
the rank of " duplex " in Poland.[795]

The successors of Henry—Rudolf, who came from Västergötland,[796] and Folkvin, who had been a canon of Uppsala,[797]
—met with great difficulties in carrying on their missionary
work.   Little support could be got from Sweden owing to the
disturbed state of affairs there, while we learn from a bull of
Pope Alexander III.,[798] to which reference has already been
made and which is the first in which the Finns are mentioned,
that they made very unreliable converts, promising when
threatened by their enemies to hold the Christian faith and
asking for missionaries to be sent; and then, when the danger
had disappeared, renouncing their Christianity and persecuting the missionaries.[799]   To avoid such conduct on their
part in future the Pope suggested that they should be asked to
place in the hands of the representatives of the Church their
fortified places, if they had any, or in some other way to give
security for their good faith.   Then, too, the country seems to
have suffered much from attacks by Russians and others.
Apparently some Swedish Crusaders in Finland were the
aggressors, for in 1164 they made an expedition against
Ladoga, but were defeated by Prince Svjatoslav with a loss of

---

[793] " Kalendarium Svecicum," p. 301.
[794] Missale pro totius regni Norvegie.   " xiiii. kal. Feb. Hērici ēpi &
mr. simplex."
[795] Officia Propria P.S.   Here it is assigned to Jan. 19.
[796] " Chronicon Episcoporum Finlandensium, S.R.S.," III., ii., p. 132.
[797] Porthan : " Juusten-Chronicon," I., p. 119.
[798] See Note 772.
[799] " Phinni semper, imminente sibi exercitu inimicorum, fidem servare
christianam promittunt et prædicatores et eruditores christianæ legis
desideranter requirunt, et recedente exercitu fidem abnegant, prædicatores
contemnunt et graviter persequuntur."

forty-three out of their fifty-five "snäckor" or war ships. [800]
This expedition naturally caused reprisals on the part of the
Russians and their allies, and in 1178 the Karelians, who
inhabited what is now south-eastern Finland, made an attack
on Finland proper, and carried off and slew Bishop Rudolf. [801]
In 1186 the Novgorodians made a plundering expedition to
the lands of the Tavastians, who dwelt in the lake region of
central Finland, partly it would seem with the object of pre-
venting them from being brought under Swedish rule; and
it was probably at their instigation that the following year the
Karelians with a great fleet actually sailed into Lake Mälar,
destroyed the town of Sigtuna, slew Archbishop Johannes,
and carried off a large amount of booty. [802] The year 1191
witnessed a united attack of the Novgorodians and Karelians
on the Tavastians, [803] while Åbo is said to have been burnt by
the first-named in 1198, on which occasion it is possible that
Bishop Folkvin was killed, though another account makes him
save his life by flight and later on take up his work again. [804]

All these raids naturally hindered the work of the missionaries, and it was not until the time of Pope Innocent III. that
Christianity began to be firmly established. By some means
he had been made cognizant of the dire plight of the infant

---

[800] Novgorod Chronicle, A.D. 1164, A.M. 6672. Cp. Schybergson, I.,
p. 31. The fact that this expedition is not mentioned in any early
Swedish chronicle has caused its actuality to be questioned. If, however,
it was not organized in Sweden, as seems probable, the omission is easily
accounted for.

[801] Porthan: "Juusten-Chronicon," I., p. 117. "Dominus Rudolphus,
natione Vestgothus, captivatus a Curonibus, et ab eis deportatus, interficitur in Curonia, A.D. 1178." See also Leinberg: "Det odelade Finska
biskopsstiftets herdaminne," p. 2.

[802] "S.R.S.," I., i., pp. 24, 40, 48, 52, 84. The raid is sometimes
attributed to the Esthonians. Possibly both nations took part in it.
Alexander III. had addressed a letter to Sweden and the other Scandinavian lands, urging an expedition against the Esthonians and other
pagans of those parts, and promising the same indulgences to those who
took part in it as were given to those who visited the Holy Sepulchre, but
there seems to have been no immediate response to it. Sv. Dip., No. 55;
Sv. Tr., No. 48; Liv. U.B., No. 45; P.L., 200, Alexander III., E. and
P., No. 980; Jaffé, No. 12118. Dated Sept. 11, 1171–2. Tusculanum.

[803] Koskinen: "Finlands Historia," I., p. 31.

[804] Porthan: "Juusten-Chronicon," I., p. 119; Rhyzelius: "Epis.,"
I., p. 327; Leinberg, p. 3.

Church, and his letter to Andreas, Archbishop of Lund,[805] gives us a glimpse of the state of affairs there—what small progress the Church has made and the difficulties with which missionaries have to contend, owing to the severity of the climate and the obstinacy of the people, so that the one who accepts the office of bishop can well look forward to martyrdom.[806] A strong man is needed as bishop, and there is a missionary who has laboured for several years in the land, and who is well suited to fill the office, but for the fact that he was not born in lawful wedlock. In the circumstances the Pope gives Andreas a dispensation to consecrate him.

Innocent does not name this person, but he is sometimes identified with the Dominican monk Thomas, an Englishman by birth,[807] who eventually did a remarkable work as Bishop of Finland, though he did not win the predicted martyr's crown. If, however, it is someone else who is referred to, the consecration probably did not take place as no name appears in the list of bishops of Finland between those of Folkvin and Thomas.[808] Two years later Innocent wrote again to Andreas, making him Papal legate in Sweden and Denmark for the special work of forwarding the conversion of the heathen,[809] under which term, of course, were included those Finns who had not yet embraced Christianity.

There was very possibly also a particular reason why

[805] Sv. Dip., No. 136; Celse: "Bullarium," p. 52; F.M.U., No. 48; P.L. 216, Reg. Innocent III., Book XII., No. 102; Potthast, No. 3807. Dated Oct. 30, 1209. Lateran.

[806] "Nam cum propter novellam plantationem et ejusdem regionis hominum pertinaciam ac loci etiam intemperiem electus ibidem non ad honorem assumptus sed expositus martyrio reputetur, nullus fere ad illius regimen sedis aspirat nisi qui divini verbi zelo succensus pati exoptat pro Christi nomine cruciatus."

[807] Porthan: "Juusten-Chronicon," I., p. 126. "D. Thomas, natione Anglicus. . . ."

[808] Schybergson: "Finlands Historia," I., pp. 33, 34, thinks that the consecration was not carried out; and Reuterdahl: "S.K.H.," II., i., p. 18, considers it doubtful that the Pope is referring to Thomas. On the other hand, Neumann: "De Fatis Primatus Lundensis," p. 86, says "Thomas ab archiepiscopo Lundensi consecratur a:o 1209." See also Bergroth: "Den Finska Kyrkans Historia," p. 15; Helsingius: "Finlands Kyrkohistoria," pp. 74, 75.

[809] Sv. Dip., No. 143; P.L. 216, Reg. Innocent III., Book XV., No. 14; Potthast, No. 4416. Dated April 4, 1212. Lateran.

Innocent was anxious that aggressive missionary work should be carried on among the Finns, for if they were not now won by missionaries in communion with the Roman see there was the possibility that before long they might be christianized through the instrumentality of the schismatic Russians. Later events showed that this danger was a real one. In 1227 Prince Jaroslav caused a number of Karelians to be baptized, [810] and the same year he made an expedition against the Tavastians and took many prisoners. [811] A counter-attack by the Tavastians on Novgorod the following year ended in failure, [812] while, as we shall see later, the important expedition of the Finns and Swedes against the same city in 1240 failed equally.

To return, however, to Bishop Thomas, it seems probable that he was appointed to his office about the year 1220, for although some historians are of opinion that he is the person referred to in the letter of Innocent III., previously mentioned, the facts as we know them seem on the whole to point the other way. In one respect, indeed, Thomas resembled the unknown missionary of the Papal bull—in his suitability for the task of rescuing the infant Church of Finland from extinction and placing it in a position of security. It needed a man of burning zeal and dauntless courage to undertake the threefold mission of spreading the Gospel among the heathen population of the land; of organizing the converts gained into congregations and arranging for the erection of churches and the supply of priests to serve them; and of protecting the Christian community from attacks by unfriendly neighbours, whether schismatics or heathens. And if Thomas did not make a success in every way of his episcopate, he at least left the Finnish Church in a very different state from that in which he had found it when he entered upon his office. Christianity, indeed, had not triumphed completely; there had been at least one dangerous heathen reaction in a newly-evangelized region; heathenism was still strong enough to

[810] F.M.U., No. 68.
[811] *Ibid.*, No. 69.
[812] *Ibid.*, No. 70.

justify the crusade of Birger Jarl a few years later; but the position of the Church in Finland proper had changed from one of insecurity to one of comparative security; the foundation laid by Bishop Henry that had proved so inadequate under his successors had been carefully relaid; under God, Bishop Thomas had rendered the final triumph of Christianity not merely possible, but practically certain.

Thomas, however, in carrying out his great work was favoured in one respect; he had the goodwill and strong support of the Papacy. Not only did Innocent III. display a keen interest in the affairs of the infant Church, but his successors, Honorius III. and Gregory IX., followed his example, and it is their letters that give us the chief information of what was taking place in Finland, and of the difficulties which beset the bishop in the carrying out of his task.

Honorius III. showed much interest not only in the protection and upbuilding of Christianity in Finland itself, but also in the conversion of those Baltic lands where heathenism still held sway, and it is interesting to note that we have at this time the first known Finnish missionary, Peter Kaikivalta, who seems to have worked for a considerable period among the Esthonians. [813] Honorius apparently thought that the aggressiveness of the heathen neighbours of the Finns might be checked if the latter refused to supply them with food and other necessities, and accordingly wrote to Bishop Thomas ordering him to stop the trade in these things, [814] while he also instructed the Archbishop of Uppsala and the Bishop of Skara to send a number of clergy to Rome for employment as missionaries among the heathen. [815]

From Gregory IX. we have a whole series of bulls relating to Finnish affairs. First he issued one addressed to the Bishop of Linköping, the Cistercian Abbot in Gottland and the

[813] F.M.U., Nos. 51, 62, 67. All extracts from the " Henrici Chronicon Lyvoniæ."
[814] Sv. Dip., No. 206; Sv. Tr., No. 69; Celse: "Bullarium," p. 58; F.M.U., No. 64; Reg. Honorius III., No. 2977; Potthast, No. 6482. Dated Jan. 13, 1221. Lateran.
[815] Sv. Dip., No. 208; Celse: "Bullarium," p. 59; Reg. Honorius III., No. 3209; Potthast, No. 6599. Dated March 25, 1221. Lateran.

Provost of Visby, ordering them not to allow anyone to attack the bishop, clergy and people of Finland, as he had taken them under the protection of the Apostolic See[816]; and he quickly followed this up by another in which he instructed them to prevent the merchants of their districts from engaging in commerce with the Russians, who hated the Finns because they had embraced the Catholic faith and had wrought them much harm,[817] while he also sent similar instructions to the Bishops of Lübeck[818] and Riga and the Cistercian Abbot of Dünamünde.[819] But the business instincts of the Gottland merchants had evidently led them into even greater delinquencies than that of trading with the schismatic Russians; they had had extensive dealings with the pagan nations of the Baltic and had actually supplied them with munitions of war, and consequently Gregory ordered the three above-named dignitaries to see that no further trade took place in arms, horses, ships, provisions, or merchandise of any kind.[820] He also gave instructions for the preaching of a Crusade in Gottland and elsewhere against the heathen Prussians.[821]

[816] Sv. Dip., No. 245; Sv. Tr., No. 74; Celse: "Bullarium," p. 62; Hjärne: "Medeltidens Statsskick," p. 294; Åbo D.S., No. 2; Potthast, No. 8321. Dated Jan. 23, 1229. Perugia. "Cum venerabilem fratrem nostrum episcopum, clerum et populum Finlandensem sub proteccione receperimus apostolice sedis et nostra, discrecioni vestre per apostolica scripta mandamus, quatinus non permittatis eos contra proteccionis nostre tenorem temere molestari, molestatores eorum indebitos, monicione premissa, per censuram ecclesiasticam, appellacione postposita, compescendo. Quod si non omnes hiis exequendis potueritis interesse, tu, frater episcope, cum eorum altero ea nichilominus exequaris."

[817] Sv. Dip., No. 250; Sv. Tr., No. 75; Celse: "Bullarium," p. 62; Åbo D.S., No. 4; Potthast, No. 8327. Dated Jan. 27, 1229. Perugia. (Celse, Jan. 23.)

[818] Åbo D.S., No. 5. Dated Jan. 27, 1229. Perugia. The Abbot of St. Johannes is addressed jointly with the Bishop.

[819] Åbo D.S., No. 3; Potthast, No. 8320. Dated Jan. 23, 1229. Perugia.

[820] Sv. Dip., No. 253; Sv. Tr., No. 76; Åbo D.S., No. 7; Potthast, No. 8340. Dated Feb. 16, 1229. Perugia. In Sv. Dip. and Sv. Tr. two letters addressed to the Archbishop of Uppsala and the Bishop of Linköping, relating to similar matters, and dated Jan. 9, 1230, Lyons, are assigned to Gregory IX. These almost certainly belong to the time of Gregory X., and should be dated 1275, for Gregory IX. was not at Lyons in 1230. See Potthast, Nos. 20983, 20984, and Brulin: "Några feldaterade påfvebref i Svenskt Diplomatarium," pp. 8, 9.

[821] Sv. Tr., No. 80; Theiner: Vet. Mon. Pol., No. 41; Potthast, No. 8603. Dated Sept. 13, 1230.

Little seems to have been done in Sweden in response to the exhortations of the Pope, and in 1232 he ordered the Sword Knights in Livonia to assist Bishop Thomas to defend his people against the Russians[822]; then, turning again to the Archbishop of Uppsala,[823] he urged that he and his suffragans should preach a Crusade against the Tavastians, who, after having embraced the Christian faith, had relapsed into heathenism, and had subjected the Christians to a most cruel persecution of which Gregory gives some gruesome details.[824] All who took part in this Crusade were to have the same privileges as they would have gained by going to the Holy Land.

By some historians Bishop Thomas is credited with having formed the plan of making his diocese a kind of independent ecclesiastical state, under the protection of the Pope and the Blessed Virgin Mary, though with the Archbishops of Lund and Uppsala still retaining certain rights there.[825] If this was indeed the case it would help to account for the great interest which Pope Gregory IX. undoubtedly took in Finland; but the failure of a crusade which followed his bull of 1237 spoilt the chance of carrying through any such plan to a successful

---

[822] Sv. Dip., No. 276; Sv. Tr., No. 83; Åbo D.S., No. 9; Liv. U.B., No. 128; Potthast, No. 9047. Dated Nov. 24, 1232. Anagni.

[823] Sv. Dip., No. 298; Sv. Tr., No. 86; Celse: "Bullarium," p. 67; F.M.U., No. 82; Potthast, No. 10486. Dated Dec. 9, 1237. Lateran.

[824] "Nam sicut transmisse ad nos vestre littere continebant, illorum qui Tavesti dicuntur nacio, que olim multo labore ac studio vestro et predecessorum vestrorum ad fidem catholicam conversa extitit, nunc, procurantibus inimicis crucis prope positis, ad antiqui erroris reversa perfidiam cum quibusdam barbaris novellam ecclesie Dei plantacionem de Tavastia funditus, dyabolo adjuvante, subvertunt, parvulos, quibus in baptismo Christi lumen illuxit, violenter de hac luce subtractos interimunt, quosdam adultos, subtractis ab eis primo visceribus, demonibus immolant, et alios usque ad amissionem spiritus arbores circuire compellunt, sacerdotes vero quosdam exoculant, et, quibusdam eorum manibus et ceteris membris crudeliter mutilatis, reliquos in combustionem et cibum ignis paleis involutos exponunt; sicque ipsorum paganorum seviciis regnum Sweorum opprimitur quod de facile extremam fidei desolacionem incurret, nisi sibi Dei et apostolice sedis auxilio succurratur."

[825] See Koskinen: "Finlands Historia," I., p. 36; Helsingius: "Finlands Kyrkohistoria," pp. 79–82; Bergroth: "Den Finska Kyrkans Historia," pp. 15–17. Schybergson: "Finlands Historia," I., pp. 37–8, does not think that Thomas had this intention, though he acknowledges that Gregory IX. took a special interest in Finland.

issue. A strong army, composed of Swedes, Norwegians, Christian Finns and Tavastians, and possibly also a number of Sword Knights, marched against the Russian city of Novgorod. Had it been conquered the subjugation of the heathen Tavastians would have followed as a matter of course, and then the bishop might have been able to realize his ambition. But the decisive defeat of the crusading army by Prince Alexander on the banks of the Neva, July 15th, 1240, [826] effectually frustrated any such design as that attributed to the bishop, while he possibly only narrowly escaped with his life, as a report seems to have spread that he had been killed.

Five years later he requested Pope Innocent IV. to be allowed to resign his office, as he was filled with remorse because he had caused to be mutilated a certain man who died from the effect, and had also falsified certain Papal letters. The Pope appointed the Archbishop of Uppsala and the Dominican Prior in Denmark to receive his resignation, and also to see that he was suitably provided for, [827] and the old bishop passed his last years in a Dominican monastery in Gottland.

According to the chronicle of the Bishops of Finland Thomas was himself a member of the Dominican Order, [828] but whether he first became so on becoming an inmate of the monastery is unknown. It seems improbable that he should have taken such a step during his episcopate, while if he were indeed consecrated as early as 1209, and had already taken the vows, he must have been one of St. Dominic's earliest followers, as the Order did not receive formal Papal approval till 1215.

[826] F.M.U., No. 83 ; Novgorod Chronicle, sub anno 1240.
[827] Sv. Dip., No. 321 ; F.M.U., No. 88 ; Reg. Innocent IV., No. 1086 ; Potthast, No. 11557. Dated Feb. 21, 1245. Lyons. It is from the Pope's letter that we get the reasons for the resignation of Thomas. "Thomas Episcopus Fillandie nobis humiliter supplicavit, ut cum idem quendam fecerit mutilari, qui hujusmodi occasione mortem incurrit, ac quasdam litteras Apostolicas præsumpserit diabolico instinctu falsare propter non potest licite pastorale officium exercere, cessionem ejusdem recipere curaremus."
[828] "Chronicon Episcoporum Finlandensium, S.R.S.," III., ii., p. 132. "Anglicus de ordine fratrum predicatorum. . . ."

Though he had failed to accomplish his plan of creating in Finland a state somewhat similar to that of the Sword Knights, he had established the Church there on a firm basis, although the power of heathenism was still strong in some parts of the country. Under him the seat of the Finnish bishopric was very possibly moved, for Pope Gregory IX. authorized the Bishop of Linköping, the Cistercian Abbot of Gottland, and the Provost of Visby to choose a more convenient place than the present one for the see city and effect the necessary transference. [829] Whether this was from Nousis, where the first Christian church had been built and where St. Henry was buried, to Räntämäki, or from Räntämäki to Åbo, is not at all clear, for the Pope mentions no names, but the former seems more probable if the bull was acted upon, which is not at all certain. Thomas is credited with having begun the building of the cathedral at Åbo, but, on the other hand, his three successors—Bero, Ragvald and Kettil—were all buried at Räntämäki, [830] and the cathedral at Åbo does not seem to have been consecrated till the year 1300. [831] It is clear, however, that under Thomas the Church began to acquire a considerable amount of property, and in 1229 Gregory confirmed it in the possession of the groves and holy places that had formerly been used for the purpose of heathen worship, but had been voluntarily given by converts to the

[829] Sv. Dip., No. 246 ; Celse: "Bullarium," p. 62 ; Åbo D.S., No. 1 ; Potthast, No. 8322. Dated Jan. 23, 1229. Perugia. "Venerabilis frater noster Finlandensis episcopus nobis exposuit, quod in primitiva christianitatis plantacione in partibus illis cathedralis ecclesia sua fuit in loco minus ydoneo constituta ; unde petebat, ut (cum) nunc plura loca, crescente in eisdem partibus per Dei graciam fide katholica, magis ad hoc commoda esse noscantur, transferri episcopalem sedem ad locum competenciorem in sua dyocesi mandaremus. Quocirca discrecioni vestre per apostolica scripta mandamus, quatenus, inquisita super hoc diligencius veritate, si rem inveneritis ita esse, cum consilio ejusdem episcopi et clericorum suorum transferatis auctoritate nostra sedem eandem ad locum in eadem diocesi magis aptum."
[830] Porthan : "Juusten-Chronicon," I., pp. 140, 142, 147 ; "Chronicon Episcoporum Finlandensium, S.R.S.," III., ii., p. 133.
[831] "Chronicon Episcoporum Finlandensium, S.R.S.," III., ii., p. 133. "Magnus. Primus Finno ex Mertiala in Rusko natus hic ecclesiam cathedralem de Ränthemäki ad Åbo transtulit, Anno MCCC:o." . . .

bishop. [832] In connection with such gifts it must be remembered that Finnish heathen worship took place in the open air, and knew nothing of temples, so that there would be no occurrences in Finland similar to those which took place in Sweden when the great idol temple at Uppsala was destroyed, and its stones used to help to build the cathedral there.

It is unfortunate that there is no contemporary Swedish or Finnish chronicle to give an account of the activities of Thomas during his occupancy of the Finnish episcopate, and that we are almost entirely dependant on certain Papal bulls and the Russian chronicles for what we know of the work that he accomplished. His confession with regard to his mutilation of an opponent, and falsification of a Papal bull—a matter of which nothing is known in regard to which bull it was, or in what way it was tampered with—show that his actions on occasion stood in need of much excuse, though perhaps not more so than certain of those of the canonized saint, Olav of Norway. But he lived in troublous times, and whatever his faults the Church of Finland is deeply indebted to him, for it was he, with his fiery zeal and tremendous energy, who did more than any other man in the days of its deadly struggle with heathenism to save it from extinction and bring it to a firm and honourable position in the land.

It was not many years after the retirement of Bishop Thomas that the Papal legate, William of Sabina, visited Sweden and held the important Synod of Skeninge in 1248. One result of his visit was the completion of the christianization of Finland, for William urged on King Erik Eriksson the organizing of a Crusade against the heathen Tavastians. [833] The leadership of this was entrusted to Sweden's chief noble,

---

[832] Sv. Dip., No. 251 ; Celse: "Bullarium," p. 62 ; Åbo D.S., No. 6 ; Spegel: Skriftelige Bewis, No. 94 ; Potthast, No. 8329. Dated Jan. 31, 1229, Perugia (Spegel: 1228). "Annuere consuevit sedes apostolica piis votis et honestis petencium precibus favorem benivolum impertiri. Eapropter, venerabilis in Christo frater, tuis justis precibus inclinati lucos et delubra, deputata olim ritibus paganorum, que de novo per te conversi ad fidem ecclesie tue voluntate spontanea contulerunt, ipsi ecclesie auctoritate apostolica confirmamus et presentis scripti patrocinio communimus."

[833] Donner: "Kardinal Wilhelm von Sabina," p. 394.

Jarl Birger, who having landed, probably somewhere on the south coast of Nyland, forced Christianity on the people at the point of the sword.[834] Those who accepted it retained their lives and property; those who refused to do so were slain.[835] The fortress of Tavasthus in Kronoberg was built on the shores of Lake Wanajavesi to prevent any rising on the part of the recently-subjugated inhabitants of the district, and for long one of its walls witnessed to Birger's crusading zeal, which seems to have resembled that of Olav Trygvessön. The jarl was depicted as holding in one hand a rod, in the other a scourge; on one side of his feet stood a chalice, on the other there burnt a flaming fire.[836] But, however reprehensible his methods, he had broken the power of heathenism in Finland; and when the following year he returned to Sweden, the Dominican monks who had accompanied the crusading army were able to carry on the work he had begun.[837]

We may therefore reckon the time of his Crusade as marking the final triumph of Christianity in Finland, rather less than a hundred years after that of Erik IX. and Bishop Henry. Many factors, no doubt, contributed to make its struggle with heathenism a much shorter one than it had been in Sweden. The crusading efforts of Erik IX. and Birger Jarl, and the great interest shown by the Popes in the matter, must both have had much to do with this; but while giving due weight to these circumstances it does not seem unjust to say that the two names that stand out most prominently in the history of the christianization of Finland are those of the two English bishops—pioneer and consolidator respectively—Henry and Thomas.

---

[834] Ericus Olai: " Chronica, S.R.S.," II., i., pp. 52, 53.
[835] " Stora Rimchrönikan," ll. 305-10.
> " Hoo them ville til handa gaa,
> Ok Christen varda ok Doopen faa,
> Honom lato the godz ok Liff,
> Ok frijd at lifva uthan alt kijff.
> Hvilken Heden ey ville saa,
> Honom lato the Döden öfvergaa."
[836] Bergroth: " Den Finska Kyrkans Historia," p. 20.
[837] Leinberg: " De Finska Klostrens Historia," pp. 19, 20, 37f. The first convent was founded at Åbo.

INDEX

PRINTED IN GREAT BRITAIN
BY THE FAITH PRESS, LTD.
LEIGHTON BUZZARD

PUBLISHED FOR THE
CHURCH HISTORICAL SOCIETY

1. **ST. AUGUSTINE'S CONVERSION.**
An Outline of His Development to the Time of his Ordination.
By W. J. SPARROW-SIMPSON, D.D.   **10s. 6d.** net.

2. **A HISTORY OF THE ICONOCLASTIC CONTROVERSY.**
By EDWARD JAMES MARTIN, D.D.   With Maps.   **16s.** net.

3. **THE CARTHUSIAN ORDER IN ENGLAND.**
By E. MARGARET THOMPSON.   With a Frontispiece and Maps.   **21s.** net.

4. **THE NEW COMMANDMENT.**
An Inquiry into the Social Precept and Practice of the Ancient Church.
By C. S. PHILLIPS, M.A., D.D.   **6s.** net.

5. **STUDIES IN ENGLISH PURITANISM FROM THE RES-TORATION TO THE REVOLUTION, 1660-1688.**
BY C. E. WHITING, D.D., B.C.L.   With six Illustrations.   **21s.** net.

6. **SITTING FOR THE PSALMS.**
An Historical Study.
By the Rev. CLEMENT F. ROGERS, M.A.   **1s. 6d.** net.

7. **A HISTORY OF THE CHURCH IN BLACKBURNSHIRE.**
By JOHN EYRE WINSTANLEY WALLIS.   With Maps and Plans.   **7s. 6d.** net.

8. **EXORCISM AND THE HEALING OF THE SICK.**
By REGINALD MAXWELL WOOLLEY, D.D.   **3s. 6d.** net.

9. **THE RENEWED CHURCH OF THE UNITED BRETHREN, 1722-1930.**
By WILLIAM GEORGE ADDISON, B.D., Ph.D. (Lond.).   **12s. 6d.** net.

10. **THE KING'S BOOK, OR A NECESSARY DOCTRINE AND ERUDITION FOR ANY CHRISTIAN MAN, 1543.**
With an introduction by T. A. LACEY.   **6s.** net.

11. **THE REFORMATION AND THE IRISH EPISCOPATE.**
By the Very Rev. H. J. LAWLOR. **1s.** net.

12. **ANGLICAN ORDERS (ENGLISH).**
The Bull of His Holiness Leo XIII., September 15, 1896, and the answer of the Archbishops of England, March 29, 1897. **2s. 6d.** net.

13. **Also IN LATIN.**
Paper cover, **2s. 6d.** net.

14. **THE TREASURE OF SAO ROQUE.**
A sidelight on the Counter-Reformation. By W. TELFER. **8s. 6d** net.

15. **CANTERBURY ADMINISTRATION.**
The administrative machinery of the Archbishopric of Canterbury illustrated from original records. By IRENE JOSEPHINE CHURCHILL, D.Phil., Lady Margaret Hall, Oxford; F.R.Hist.S.; Assistant Lambeth Librarian. Vol. I.: The Archbishop in his Diocese and Province. Vol. II.: Documents Illustrative and Lists. **42s.** Not sold separately.

16. **SAINT WULSTAN, PRELATE AND PATRIOT.**
A Study of his Life and Times.
By JOHN W. LAMB, M.A. **8s. 6d.** net.

17. **BISHOP BARLOW'S CONSECRATION AND ARCHBISHOP PARKER'S REGISTER: WITH SOME NEW DOCUMENTS.**
By CLAUDE JENKINS, D.D. **1s. 6d.** net.

18. **THE PASSION AND MARTYRDOM OF THE HOLY ENGLISH CARTHUSIAN FATHERS.**
The Short Narration, by Dom Maurice Chauncy, Prior of the Charterhouse of Sheen Anglorum within the walls of Bruges, formerly Monk of the London Charterhouse, A.D. 1570.
Edited by the Rev. G. W. S. CURTIS. With several illustrations. **8s. 6d.** net.

19. **THE CHURCH IN FRANCE, VOL. II., 1848-1905.**
By C. S. PHILLIPS, D.D. **12s. 6d.** net.
Also Vol. I., **1789-1848. 8s. 6d.** net.

20. **THE LIFE AND LETTERS OF CHARLES INGLIS.**
His Ministry in America and Consecration as First Colonial Bishop, from 1759 to 1787.
By JOHN WOLFE LYDEKKER, M.A., Archivist to the Society for the Propagation of the Gospel. With 12 illustrations and a map. **12s. 6d.** net.

21. **THOMAS SHERLOCK, 1678-1761.**
By EDWARD CARPENTER, M.A., B.D., A.K.C. With a Frontispiece. **15s.** net.

22. **A STUDY OF BOSSUET.**
By W. J. SPARROW SIMPSON, D.D. **7s. 6d.** net.

23. CONVOCATION OF THE CLERGY.

A study of its antecedents and its rise with special emphasis upon its growth and activities in the thirteenth and fourteenth Centuries. By DOROTHY BRUCE WESKE, A.M., Th.D. **15s.** net.

24. THE TREATISE ON THE APOSTOLIC TRADITION OF ST. HIPPOLYTUS OF ROME, BISHOP AND MARTYR.

Edited by the Rev. GREGORY DIX. **12s. 6d.** net.

25. THE ANAPHORA OR GREAT EUCHARISTIC PRAYER.

An eirenical study in Liturgical History. By W. H. FRERE, C.R., D.D. **8s. 6d.** net.

26. THE ENGLISH MISSIONARIES IN SWEDEN AND FIN-LAND.

By C. J. A. OPPERMANN, M.A., Ph.D. **12s. 6d.** net.

27. THE SAINTS OF EGYPT.

By DE LACY O'LEARY, D.D. **12s. 6d.** net.

28. THE CANDLE OF THE LORD.

Studies in the Cambridge Platonists. By W. C. DE PAULEY, D.D **7s. 6d.** net.